DAY HIKING

Southcentral Alaska

DAY HIKING
Southcentral Alaska

anchorage area · kenai peninsula · mat-su valley

Lisa Maloney

MOUNTAINEERS
BOOKS

This book is for everyone who takes the time to watch the sun set,
listen to the birds sing, feel the breeze blow, and explore new
places in a respectful way—and for anyone who'd like to start.

MOUNTAINEERS BOOKS is dedicated to
the exploration, preservation, and enjoyment of outdoor
and wilderness areas.

1001 SW Klickitat Way, Suite 201, Seattle, WA 98134
800-553-4453, www.mountaineersbooks.org

Printed in China
Distributed in the United Kingdom by Cordee, www.cordee.co.uk
First edition, 2019

Mountaineers Books and its colophon are registered trademarks of The Mountaineers organization.

Copyeditor: Kerrie Maynes
Layout: Jennifer Shontz/Red Shoe Design
Cartographer: Pease Press Cartography
Cover photograph: *Turnagain Arm* (© andyKRAKOVSKI)
Frontispiece: *Matanuska Peak, aka Byers Peak, presides over the McRoberts Creek valley.*
All photos by author unless credited otherwise

The background maps for this book were produced using the online map viewer CalTopo.
For more information, visit caltopo.com.

Library of Congress Cataloging-in-Publication data is on file for this title

Mountaineers Books titles may be purchased for corporate, educational, or
other promotional sales, and our authors are available for a wide range of events.
For information on special discounts or booking an author, contact our customer
service at 800-553-4453 or mbooks@mountaineersbooks.org.

Printed on FSC®-certified materials
ISBN (paperback): 978-1-68051-066-9
ISBN (ebook): 978-1-68051-067-6

An independent nonprofit publisher since 1960

Contents

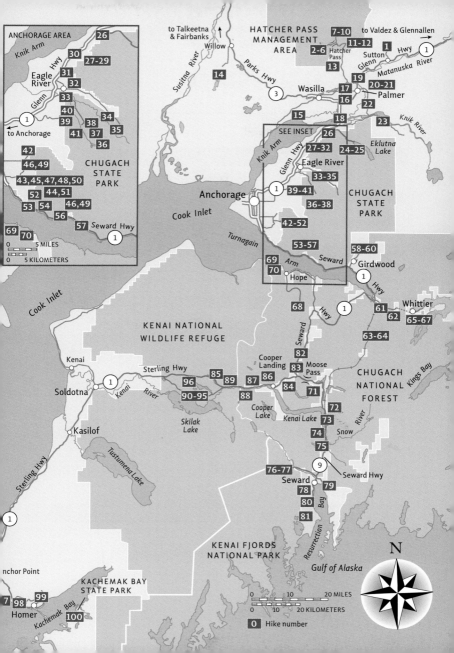

Hikes at a Glance

HIKE	DISTANCE IN MILES (ROUNDTRIP)	RATING	DIFFICULTY
NORTHERN MAT-SU VALLEY			
1. Eska Creek Falls	8.3	*****	3
2. Craigie Creek	9	****	3
3. April Bowl	2.7	****	3
4. Skyscraper Peak	2.2	***	3
5. Summit Lake	0.5 (loop)	****	2
6. Gold Cord Lake	1.6	****	3
7. Reed Lakes	8.8	*****	4
8. Snowbird Mine	4.7	***	4
9. Fairangel Lakes	2.6	*****	3
10. Lane Hut	4.2	***	2
11. Marmot Mountain	3.2	***	4
12. Gold Mint	16.6	*****	4
13. Government Peak	6.5	******	5
WASILLA AREA			
14. Red Shirt Lake	5.6	***	3
15. Scout Ridge and Cottonwood Creek	1.2 (loop)	***	2
16. Long Lake Loop	5.7 (loop)	***	2
17. Crevasse Moraine to Long Lake	3.7 (one-way)	***	2
18. Reflections Lake	1.2 (loop)	***	1
PALMER AREA			
19. Palmer–Moose Creek	6.9 (one-way)	***	3
20. Lazy Moose and Lazy Mountain	8	****	4
21. Matanuska Peak	10.6	*****	5
22. Bodenburg Butte	2.6	***	2
23. Pioneer Ridge and Pioneer Peak	9.6	*****	5
EKLUTNA AREA			
24. Eklutna Lakeside Trail and Eydlu Bena Loop	25.4	*****	3
25. Twin Peaks to Pepper Peak	8.6	*****	5
26. Thunderbird Falls	1.75	***	2

KID-FRIENDLY	DOG-FRIENDLY	VIEWS	WILDLIFE	LAKES	WATER-FALLS	WINTER HIKING	FISHING	GLACIERS
		•			•			
	•	•		•				
•	•	•		•				
•	•	•						
•	•	•		•				
•	•			•				
		•		•	•			
	•	•						
		•		•				
•	•	•			•			
	•	•						
	•	•			•			
		•						
•	•		•	•		•		
•		•		•		•		
•				•		•		
•				•		•		
•			•	•		•		
•		•				•		
		•						
		•						
•		•				•		•
		•						•
•	•	•		•		•		
		•		•				
•					•	•		

HIKE	DISTANCE IN MILES (ROUNDTRIP)	RATING	DIFFICULTY
EAGLE RIVER AND VICINITY			
27. Big Peters Creek	6.5 (loop)	**	2
28. Bear Mountain (Peters Creek version)	4	****	4
29. Mount Eklutna	6	***	4
30. Ptarmigan Valley	9	**	3
31. Baldy and Blacktail Rocks	2.5	****	3
32. Mile Hi Saddle and Mount Magnificent	6.4	****	4
33. Barbara Falls	6.2	***	2
34. Albert and Rodak Loops	3.2 (loop)	***	2
35. Dew Mound	6.1 (loop)	***	3
36. Eagle and Symphony Lakes	11.4	****	3
37. Hanging Valley	10	****	3
38. Harp Mountain	3.5	***	4
39. Rendezvous Ski Loop	3.6 (loop)	***	3
40. Mount Gordon Lyon	3.8	***	3
41. Rendezvous Ridge	7.9 (one-way)	*****	4
ANCHORAGE AREA			
42. Lost Cabin Valley and Basher Loop	4.1 (loop)	***	3
43. Flattop Mountain (front side)	3.4	***	3
44. Flattop Mountain (back side)	3.4	***	3
45. Powerline Pass	12.2	****	3
46. Middle Fork Loop	8.9 (loop)	***	2
47. Williwaw Lakes	14.4	****	3
48. Little O'Malley Peak and O'Malley Peak	6.6	****	4
49. Wolverine Peak	10.6	****	4
50. Hidden Lake	10.4	***	3
51. Rabbit Lake	10.2	***	2
52. McHugh Peak	6	****	4
SOUTH OF ANCHORAGE			
53. Turnagain Arm Trail	10.4 (one-way)	***	3
54. McHugh Lake	13.2	*****	3
55. Rainbow Knob	4	***	5
56. Falls Creek	7.4	****	5
57. Bird Ridge	5.2	****	5
58. North Face	5	***	4
59. Winner Creek	7	****	2
60. Raven Glacier	7.4	*****	4
61. Trail of Blue Ice	9.7	****	2

KID-FRIENDLY	DOG-FRIENDLY	VIEWS	WILDLIFE	LAKES	WATER-FALLS	WINTER HIKING	FISHING	GLACIERS
•	•		•			•		
	•	•						
	•	•	•					
•	•							
•	•	•						
	•	•						
•	•				•	•		
•			•	•		•		
•	•			•		•		
•		•		•			•	
•	•	•		•				
	•	•						
•	•	•						
•	•							
•	•	•						
•	•					•		
		•						
•	•	•						
•	•	•	•	•				
•	•		•			•		
•	•	•	•	•				
•		•	•	•				
	•	•	•	•				
•	•	•	•	•				
•	•	•		•			•	
•		•						
•	•	•	•					
	•	•		•				
		•						
	•	•		•				
	•	•						
•		•						•
•					•			
	•	•		•	•			•
•		•		•				•

HIKE	DISTANCE IN MILES (ROUNDTRIP)	RATING	DIFFICULTY
SOUTH OF ANCHORAGE (CONTINUED)			
62. Byron Glacier	2.3	★★★★	2
63. Spencer Overlook	7	★★★★★	2
64. Spencer Bench	11.8	★★★★★	4
WHITTIER AREA			
65. Horsetail Falls	2	★★★	2
66. Portage Pass	5.2	★★★★★	3
67. Emerald Cove	4.3	★★★	3
HOPE AREA			
68. Palmer Creek Lakes	2.6	★★★★★	3
69. Gull Rock	11.6	★★★★★	3
70. Hope Point	8.1	★★★★★	4
MOOSE PASS TO SEWARD			
71. Carter Lake	6.6	★★★★	3
72. Ptarmigan Creek and Lake	7.2	★★★★	3
73. Victor Creek	5	★★★★	3
74. Lost Lake	15.6 (one-way)	★★★★★	3
75. Meridian Lakes	3	★★	2
76. Exit Glacier	2.1 (loop)	★★★★	1
77. Harding Icefield	9.2	★★★★★	5
78. Mount Marathon	6	★★★★	5
79. Alice Ridge	3.5	★★★★★	4
80. Caines Head and North Beach	11.4	★★★★★	3
81. Fort McGilvray	4	★★★★	2
COOPER LANDING AREA			
82. Summit Creek	18	★★★★★	4
83. Devils Creek	17.2	★★★★	3
84. Crescent Creek	12.8	★★★★★	3
85. Skyline Trail	4.5	★★★★★	5
86. Slaughter Gulch	4.2	★★★★★	5
87. Juneau Creek Falls	7.5 (one-way)	★★★★	2
88. Russian River Falls and Russian Lakes	4.8	★★★★	2
89. Fuller Lakes	7.4	★★★	3
SKILAK LAKE AREA			
90. Skilak Hideout	2.2	★★★	3
91. Kenai River Trail	5.6	★★★	2
92. Hidden Creek	3.2 (loop)	★★★★	2

KID-FRIENDLY	DOG-FRIENDLY	VIEWS	WILDLIFE	LAKES	WATER-FALLS	WINTER HIKING	FISHING	GLACIERS
•		•						•
•		•		•				•
		•		•				•
•		•			•			
•		•		•	•			•
					•			
•	•	•		•	•			
•		•						
		•						
•	•			•			•	
•		•		•			•	•
•	•	•			•			
	•	•		•			•	
•	•	•		•			•	
•		•						•
		•	•					•
		•			•			
		•						
		•			•			
•		•						
	•	•	•	•				
		•		•	•		•	
•		•		•			•	
		•		•				
	•	•		•				
•	•	•			•			
		•	•	•	•		•	
	•	•	•	•			•	
•	•	•		•				
	•	•	•			•		
•		•		•		•	•	

HIKE	DISTANCE IN MILES (ROUNDTRIP)	RATING	DIFFICULTY
SKILAK LAKE AREA (CONTINUED)			
93. Skilak Lookout	4.5	****	3
94. Bear Mountain (Skilak version)	1.8	***	3
95. Vista Trail	3.4	****	3
96. Seven Lakes	5.5 (one-way)	***	2
HOMER AND KACHEMAK BAY			
97. Diamond Gulch	1.2	****	2
98. Homestead Trail	4.5 (loop)	***	2
99. Wynn Nature Center	2 (loop)	***	2
100. Grewingk Lake to Saddle Trail	4.5 (one-way)	****	2

KID-FRIENDLY	DOG-FRIENDLY	VIEWS	WILDLIFE	LAKES	WATER-FALLS	WINTER HIKING	FISHING	GLACIERS
•		•	•	•		•		
•		•		•				
•		•		•				
•	•			•		•	•	
•	•	•				•		
•						•		
•						•		
•		•		•				•

Parking and (rare) permit fees go toward trail maintenance and improvements, like this recently updated stretch along the very popular Harding Icefield Trail (Hike 77).

Introduction

It's hard not to fall back on superlatives when talking about hiking in Southcentral Alaska. Thanks to its southerly and central location (as the name suggests), Southcentral has a little bit of everything wonderful that you can find in this state. We have dramatic glaciers, coastal rainforests, tide-washed beaches, mighty glacier-fed rivers, and majestic mountains. We can't quite match the twenty-four-hour daylight of the true Arctic tundra, but we come pretty close around the summer solstice.

What sets Southcentral Alaska's grand stretches of wild beauty apart from the rest of the state is their accessibility. This part of the state is peppered with a collection of ATV tracks, game trails, old mining roads, deliberately crafted footpaths, and so-called social trails worn in by the passage of many feet.

Even if you're an experienced hiker, a few things make hiking in Southcentral Alaska (or anywhere else in Alaska) very different from hiking in other parts of the country. One of the most obvious is that many of our trails have little to no signage once you get past the trailhead. The second is that many of them have few, if any, switchbacks.

And finally, despite their relative nearness to established communities, these trails are also quite remote in many ways. You often won't have cell phone service, bad weather can come up quickly, wildlife encounters are very common, if you take a wrong turn you could walk for days without reaching another community, and the scale of the terrain means that rescue can take hours in coming—if it comes at all. So even on well-established trails, self-sufficiency remains the key to a safe, fun hike.

While the sum total of our assorted trails may not be as regulated or, dare I say it, as civilized as hiking in the Lower 48, it's the perfect mix of access options for day hikers. The hundred trails in this book are either maintained hiking/multiuse trails or unmaintained trails that are so well known and traveled, they've become part of the regional lexicon.

PERMITS AND REGULATIONS

Almost every day hike in this book takes place on public land, so you don't need a permit to hike. The sole exceptions are the area near Arctic Valley Ski Area (Hikes 39, 40, and 41) where the inattentive might stray onto military land, which you do need a permit to explore, and a privately owned homestead that's part of an alternate route for Hike 31. With that said, many of these hikes pass near private land, so please be respectful and don't stray onto posted private property.

In this part of the state there are no parking fees in the national forest, the wildlife refuges, or in Kenai Fjords National Park. You do have to pay to park in the state parks, though. Only very rarely will you find an attendant on hand to take your payment; the fee is usually payable in cash or check only via self-pay kiosks, so bring exact change and a pen. So far I have seen exactly one electronic kiosk that accepts credit cards—at the uber-popular Glen Alps Trailhead—but maybe there'll be more soon.

PORTAGE PASS
ELEVATION 800'

Don't put too much faith in Alaska weather forecasts; rain, brutal winds, snow, and cold (or hot) temperatures all come and go at the drop of a hat (Hike 66).

These fees are also covered by the Alaska State Parks Pass, which you can buy online or through some sporting goods stores. It's a great deal if you do a lot of hiking. Also, in a very few cases, some state trailheads and campgrounds are maintained by private contractors. In those cases, the access fees vary and are subject to change. And finally, a handful of borough- and privately owned trailheads come with their own fees, which are all noted in the text.

WEATHER

Because Alaska is so big and wild, even a short day hike can bring you intimately close to the land—and its weather. During the summer that might mean gusting gale-force winds, thick fog, downpours, slippery rocks or mud, and, although it's rare, freezing temperatures and snow. Despite the potential for cold weather year-round, our summers are getting warmer, which means that sunburn, heat stroke, and heat exhaustion are all potential issues on unusually warm days, especially since people don't tend to look out for them in Alaska.

Thunderstorms are still rare here, but more common than they used to be, introducing the potential hazards of hail (thankfully, it's usually small) and lightning strikes. Flash floods are rare but can happen when ice dams form on creeks and in glaciers or at lake outflows during the spring melt, backing up the water until it all releases in a rush.

AVALANCHE HAZARD

During winter and spring travel, avalanche hazard is a common concern on many Alaska trails. I've noted well-known areas of avalanche hazard in the book whenever possible, but just because I haven't mentioned it doesn't mean it's not there.

If you plan to hike during the winter, the very best investment you can make in your safety is avalanche education. The gold standard for learning the basics is a multiday field workshop, but you'll also find a variety of classroom courses, books, and online resources to help make you "avy savvy." Learning even the barest basics could save your life or that of a friend. That's a pretty amazing return on an hour or two spent in a classroom!

When it comes to books, *Snow Sense: A Guide to Evaluating Snow Avalanche Hazard*, by Jill Fredston and Doug Fesler (published by the Alaska Mountain Safety Center), is the best pocket reference you could ask for. Locally, REI and Alaska Avalanche School are both great places to start looking for workshops of all types. And no matter where you are in the nation, avalanche.org offers great educational information and links to resources in your area.

Here's one last thing to keep in mind as you hike: even if the trail itself is free of snow, there might still be enough snow on the slopes above you to avalanche and spread debris across the trail. That doesn't mean you need to run around in a panic all summer, looking for avalanches crashing down from the hills! Just understand that such risks *can* exist when there's snow hanging above you, and use that knowledge to make informed decisions.

Avalanche hazard might seem like a danger for snowmachiners and extreme skiers, but it can strike hikers too. Educate yourself about the warning signs of a possible avalanche (Hike 53).

WATER SAFETY

Quite a few of Alaska's day hikes involve water crossings of some sort. Because we're dealing with established trails, those crossings are usually relatively shallow and/or slow moving, or have boulders you can hop across to keep your feet dry. Still, even the mild-mannered Clark Kents of water crossings can be amped up to Superman-level intensity by cold temperatures and unusually high water levels, so always evaluate conditions on the spot, and keep an eye out for factors such as heavy rainfall, rising tides, or impending darkness that might make for a difficult crossing on the way back.

Glacier-fed lakes and rivers are always c-o-l-d in any season, but when temperatures get into the eighties, as now tends to happen at least a few times during the summer, that cold can start to feel pretty good! Still, be careful: cold-water immersion can quickly sap strength from even the strongest swimmer, even on the hottest day.

Another Type of Water Safety

Even if you're not doing any stream crossings, at some point you're going to need a drink. No matter how clear the water in Alaska looks, it can be inhabited by *Giardia*, *Cryptosporidium*, or, if you're unlucky enough to be downstream from someone with poor manners or hygiene, other parasites and diseases caused by human waste. Dog waste leaches into streams too. So always carry a trail-worthy water filter or water purification tablets.

DAYLIGHT HOURS

While some parts of the state enjoy true midnight sun during the summer, Southcentral Alaska is far enough south that the great glowing orb does dip below the horizon briefly on the summer solstice. But if you

include civil twilight—the period of light after the official sunset, then again before the official sunrise—we do enjoy "usable light" all night long during the peak of the summer.

That said, I still recommend carrying a small headlamp in your emergency kit year-round, because it's easy to get so used to the endless daylight that you get caught in the dark as the days shorten. Also, because the sun circles so low on the horizon, if you're traveling in mountain valleys you might find yourself suddenly in the dark—and cold—when the mountains block out the sun during the day.

Speaking of daylight, you won't see northern lights during the summer—it just doesn't get dark enough. But if you indulge in a night hike or are camping or just out after dark during the fall, winter, or spring, you might get lucky and see them. You need a clear, dark night and to be as far as possible from the light pollution of cities; as a general rule look to the northern horizon, although sometimes the lights shine overhead too. When the northern lights *aren't* out, the skies are usually dark enough for wonderful stargazing—just dress warmly.

ROAD AND TRAIL CONDITIONS

Most paved roads in Southcentral are in great condition during the summer, although on the highways you may encounter frequent road construction and ruts gouged out by the studded tires some locals use for extra traction during the winter. The condition of unpaved roads can vary widely, from roads "just as good as pavement" to those with car-eating holes, washouts, and downed trees.

Winter driving requires greater caution, even on maintained roads. I find the best winter drivers are those who subscribe to the "your brake pedal is the wreck pedal" school of thought. That doesn't mean not using your brakes—you definitely need them!—but instead driving so that you won't need to use them in the first place. Leave plenty of room between you and the vehicle ahead of you, and drive slowly enough to stay in control of your vehicle given the variable road conditions and visibility.

Some of the access roads to trails are closed seasonally, among them Herman Leirer Road (also known as Exit Glacier Road), the access road for Hikes 76 and 77; Archangel Road in Hatcher Pass, which is the access road for Hikes 7 through 10; and the road over Hatcher Pass itself, which is the access road for Hikes 2 through 5. Other roads may remain open but not necessarily plowed, such as Skilak Lake Road, which offers access for Hikes 90 through 96, or only be plowed partway to the trailhead, such as the access roads for Hikes 6, 33, and 68; I've let you know when you can expect to trek extra distance from the "winter" trailhead. Some trailheads are also gated off during the winter, but as a general rule, unless the land manager has posted a sign saying they're officially closed or warning of dangerous wildlife nearby, they are always open for walk-in use.

GENERAL SAFETY

One of the most common questions I get about hiking in Alaska is "Is it safe for me to go to such and such a place or do such and such a trail?" I struggle with the answer because Alaska is one big uncontrolled environment. That doesn't mean that you cannot have many, many safe hikes here—I sure have! But what it does mean is that you should always play an active role in ensuring your own safety.

Following a few safety "best practices" while hiking is really no different from remembering to look both ways before you cross the street, or looking behind you before you start backing up the car. Most of the time things would work out okay even if you didn't do those things, but you still make a habit of doing them just in case—right?—because on the rare occasion they do make a difference, it'll be a big one!

At a minimum, you should always carry the Ten Essentials (and know how to use what you're carrying; see later in this chapter); know what to do if you happen to encounter big wildlife like moose or bears (also later in this chapter); and know how to find your way back to the trailhead even in low visibility. Even if you don't need those safety skills yourself, you might end up in the perfect situation to help someone else.

SHOULD I CARRY A GUN?

Here's another very common question, and in most cases the answer is no. I am not anti-gun, but I am anti-bad-decisions-with-a-gun, and no matter how good you are with a gun in the city, if you're not fully informed of your gun's suitability and implications in a wildlife encounter, you are a bad decision waiting to happen. Also, moose are built to withstand bear attacks, and bears are built to take on moose. So while your little 9mm handgun might make you feel better, and while it might be handy as a *people* deterrent, all it's going to do to a moose or a bear is piss it off.

Studies have shown that you're less likely to be killed during a bear encounter if you use bear spray, and more likely to die if you're using a gun as your defense. And if you make a mistake in the stress of a crisis situation, you're more likely to permanently hurt another person with a gun than with bear

LEAVE NO TRACE

Perhaps you've heard of the seven principles of Leave No Trace adventuring? The idea is to leave the areas you visit just as pristine as they were when you arrived so that others can enjoy them in the same way. Here's a very quick look at the seven principles and ways they can apply to Alaska hikes.

1. **Plan ahead and prepare.** Be ready for extreme weather, pack to minimize waste, and stow ziplock baggies in your pack to carry out your own trash.

2. **Travel on durable surfaces.** Alaska's tundra can be exceptionally delicate and sensitive to your passage, as can riparian areas where water and land meet. Protect these sensitive areas by walking on durable surfaces such as rock, dry grass, and snow as much as possible when you're off-trail.

3. **Dispose of waste properly.** If you brought it in, you pack it out. Period. That includes toilet paper and other hygiene products. If you need to poop, bury it in a hole that's 6 to 8 inches deep and located at least 200 feet from water, camps, or trails. For more information, see Kathleen Meyer's delightful little volume *How to Shit in the Woods: An Environmentally Sound Approach to a Lost Art*, published by Ten Speed Press.

4. **Leave what you find.** Alaska is full of neat artifacts, from old mining equipment to pretty rocks. Admire them where you find them, then leave them in place for others to admire too.

5. **Minimize campfire impacts.** Bring a camp stove if you think you might want to cook during a long day hike. If you do make a fire, stick to established fire rings and gravel beaches or river bars below the high-water line—the only places where fires are permitted on most public lands—and make sure the fire is out and the ashes are completely cool before you leave. All it takes is one spark to start a catastrophic wildfire.

6. **Respect wildlife.** Keep a safe distance, never feed the wild animals or try to spray. So if you're going to carry, start from a position of humility—assume there are things you don't know—then educate yourself accordingly and treat shooting like the perishable skill it is (in other words, practice frequently and well). I really enjoy the bear and firearm safety training classes at Learn to Return.

WILDERNESS ETHICS

It may be tempting to toss your orange peels or toilet paper under a bush because Alaska is so sparsely populated, nobody will ever notice, right? Wrong. People go into Alaska's pristine wilds to see the beautiful land—not your trash—and our relatively cool climate means even organic material takes much

Photos make the perfect souvenir of a memorable hike (Hike 9).

touch them, don't let them get near your food, and never, ever get between a mother and child of any animal species.

7. **Be considerate to others.** This is easy; just do unto others as you'd have them do unto you. For example, don't throw rocks off of mountaintops (this used to be a popular pastime for unruly kids on Flattop), don't strew your gear all over the trail during rest stops, and take your turn yielding the right-of-way to other trail users.

longer to decompose than it would elsewhere. So if you bring it in, pack it out.

TRAIL ETIQUETTE

Trail etiquette is the easiest thing in the world! It boils down to being pleasant and treating others the way you want to be treated. Just think ahead and display a little common sense, and you'll be fine. Some examples of easy ways to be a fine human being on the trail include staying off soft trails during the spring, where your feet, wheels, or whatever can cause deep ruts and holes that will last all year long; and taking turns yielding with other trail users.

Good company turns a nice hike into a great adventure and even better memories (Hike 84).

There's no hard-and-fast rule about who gets priority, except for pack and saddle stock that are often so big or unwieldy they can't get out of your way. But as a general rule, the person who looks like they most need to maintain their momentum—whether they're suffering uphill or bombing downhill—should get priority.

DOGS

We Alaskans love our dogs! But loose pets, however beloved, can wreak havoc on everybody's wilderness experience. Dogs aren't allowed on the trails in Kenai Fjords National Park (see Hikes 76 and 77), but they're allowed almost everywhere else in Alaska's public lands, under a few conditions.

Most communities have leash laws, which extend to trails within their city or municipal boundaries. Even in areas where enforcement is known to be lax, if there is a problem and your pet was off leash, you'll come out in the wrong. In state parks, you must have your dog on leash in developed areas such as campgrounds and trailheads, then keep Fido under direct control in the backcountry—which can mean voice control, but only if it's truly effective.

If you find yourself futilely yelling after your dog as he races to chase ground squirrels or meet another pooch, he's not under voice control. In this situation, aside from annoying other people and dog owners that actually obey the rules, you also run the risk of having your dog harass a moose or bear, then bring the angry animal in tow when he comes running back to you for protection. Also, and very sadly, it's not unusual to see "lost dog" notices at trailheads because someone's unleashed pet got scared or distracted, ran away, and has never been seen again.

If that's not good enough motivation, consider this: hunting and trapping are allowed in some parts of Chugach State Park and in some wildlife refuges, and every once in a while you'll find a trap or snare where it shouldn't be. Even where trapping doesn't happen, it's not too hard to mistake a dog bounding out of the brush for a bear. Do you really want your dog subjected to bear spray or another hiker's handgun?

If your dog is new to hiking, be aware that their paws may be cut up on particularly rocky or icy hikes. If your dog has never hiked before, start with easy, short hikes and give their paws time to adapt. And don't forget to filter the water your dog drinks, just as you filter yours—they can get *Giardia* too.

Finally, while it's tempting to leave your dog's poop out in the wilds, they're not actually wild animals, and their feces can spread diseases. I suppose you could bury the poop, à la Leave No Trace, but most hikers choose to carry plastic bags and pack the poop out. Just don't drop the bag by the trail in hopes of picking it up later—that never works out. The best solution I've seen is a friend who would tie the poop bag to her dog's leash or tuck it into the dog's harness.

WILDLIFE

Southcentral's rich wildlife is a constant marvel for every hiker, on every trail. The basic rule for all animal encounters is the same: give them plenty of space and never, ever get between a mother and her young of any species. That said, there are a few things you should know about meeting bears, moose, and other animals in the wild.

Bears

Most bears will want nothing to do with you; as long as you make enough noise for them to hear you coming, they'll get out of the way. Making enough noise to give the bears a heads up to your presence is especially important in areas where sight, smell, or sound are obscured: in thick brush, when

If you can't see them, they might not know you're coming. Making noise (clapping, singing, talking, ringing a bear bell) is part of playing it safe when there's limited visibility in bear country (Hike 95).

you're downwind of the bear, or beside a rushing creek, for example.

If you do see a bear, don't run. If the bear isn't aware of your presence and is a safe distance away, you can continue around it at a distance without disturbing it. If the bear is aware of you and approaches, stay calm (easier said than done, I know, but you can do it!) and group close together with others to make yourselves look bigger. Speak calmly and firmly to the bear so it can tell you're human.

If the bear stands up, it's just trying to get a better look to figure out what you are. Usually once the bear determines you're human, it'll leave. You can also back slowly away; if the bear follows, stop and stand your ground again. If the bear continues approaching, you should become progressively louder and more insistent in your attempts to deter its interest and drive it off.

On very rare occasions—usually if you were unlucky enough to surprise a bear, come between a mother and her cubs, or come across a bear defending a food cache—a bear will charge. Again, as hard as it is to do, don't run! Much of the time these are bluff charges, so the bear will run right past you and keep going.

If the bear does make contact, experts suggest two courses of action. If you feel the attack was defensive in nature (i.e., you surprised the bear), play dead. Once it believes the threat is neutralized, it'll leave you alone. Lie facedown on the ground, legs splayed out for stability and hands protecting your head and neck, and try to stay calm and quiet until you're absolutely sure the bear has left the area.

If the bear continues to attack or you suspect you're involved in a predatory attack—which is enormously rare, but does happen on occasion—then you must fight back with everything at your disposal, aiming for the bear's sensitive eyes and nose.

Moose

These gigantic, half-ton ungulates are notorious for being cranky and unpredictable, and many locals will tell you that they're more dangerous than bears.

Unlike bears, you *do* run from a charging moose, because if you can get far enough away it'll generally leave you alone. That said, moose are much faster than you are, so your best option is usually to climb a tree when possible, or to get a tree between you and the moose; they can't corner around the obstacle as well as you can.

Other Wildlife

Although moose and bears get most of the attention in Alaska—and rightly so—there's plenty of other wonderful wildlife you can see, including a wealth of migratory waterfowl and songbirds that come and go through Southcentral every year. I highly recommend taking an educational birding walk with Audubon Alaska if you can. There are also a number of apps and bird identification books you can bring.

Pay particular attention to mischievous ravens, which are the focus of many Alaska Native legends and mythologies, and are responsible for many strange noises you might hear outside—they are accomplished mimics. These giant black birds are enormously intelligent and playful, so it's common to see them playing in the currents of wind created by rocky protuberances at high elevations.

There are a number of other land mammals you might see too. Porcupines are often slow moving, but they're a great example of when loose dogs can be a problem; many a curious Fido has come back with painful spines embedded in his nose, paws, and body.

Wolf and coyote sightings are rare, but possible. Just as with a bear or a strange dog, don't run in these encounters. Stand your ground, group together to look bigger, and make noise to scare them away. If a wolf or coyote attacks you or your pet, don't play dead—it's time to fight. Wolverine and lynx sightings are possible too, but incredibly rare; if you see either of these creatures in the wild, it's truly something special.

We also have three rodents that sometimes cause people confusion. Marmots are the biggest of our rock-dwelling rodents, roughly the size of a beaver, with a rough, silver- or white-tipped coat and a shrill whistle that sounds like a cross between a hiker's emergency whistle and a train. Ground squirrels are smaller—squirrel size, predictably enough—and tend to perch upright in the tundra and herald your arrival with chirps of warning and helicopter-like twirls of their little tails. Pikas are smaller yet, and look for all the world like tiny, miniature bunny rabbits. They usually live near the edge of boulder fields, and to me their call sounds like a hoarse squeaky toy.

Lightweight pants and long sleeves protect against cow parsnip and devil's club (Hike 59).

I've noted species of fish that you can catch on popular hikes in those hike descriptions, but it's up to you to double-check on the Alaska Department of Fish and Game's regulations, including open seasons, bag limits, and exactly where you can fish.

SNEAKY PLANTS

Although Southcentral Alaska doesn't have poison ivy or poison oak, we do have a few plants that can be . . . exciting. Two of them, devil's club and cow parsnip, are almost twins; the third, baneberry, is in a class of its own.

Devil's Club

You'll know this plant when you see it: the stems are covered in spiky thorns. When the broad, multilobed leaves open up, they're gorgeous and huge—easily bigger than your head. But they have spikes that will poke through any clothing (even three pairs of pants—don't ask!) and tend to break off in the skin and fester, so it's best to avoid touching this plant at all. On the occasion I do need to touch it, I wear gloves or, better yet, use a hiking pole to move it out of the way.

Cow Parsnip

Also known as wild celery or by its Russian name, *pushki*, this invasive plant looks like a thornless version of devil's club. But don't let that fool you: the sap contains a chemical that causes blistering burns that are worsened by exposure to sunlight. While not everybody is sensitive to cow parsnip sap, most hikers are, and just brushing up against one of these plants can yield a nasty surprise. Even if it's never irritated your skin before, a reaction can crop up without notice. The best protection is wearing long sleeves and long pants when around this plant so it never contacts your skin.

Baneberry

Although this berry looks sweet, it's actually very poisonous—so be sure to learn to recognize and avoid it. The white or red berries grow on a single upright stalk above leaves that have three to five parts, fine teeth, and narrow pointed ends. Protect your children by teaching them to show you berries still on the plant to find out if they're okay, instead of bringing the picked berries to you.

The poisonous baneberry produces spikes of all-white or all-red berries.

Who wins the muddy boot contest? Since they drain better, you might consider wearing sandals if you're in for horribly muddy or wet conditions, but most hikers opt for more sensible and protective footwear (Hike 67).

GEAR

What do you need for hiking in Alaska? Nothing that different from what you'd need for hiking elsewhere, as it turns out. Sturdy shoes or boots with good traction are a must; most people prefer the ankle support and all-around foot protection of hiking boots, but those with good ankle stability might enjoy the extra agility and light weight of hiking in trail-running shoes instead.

Aside from footwear, the most important component of your gear will be clothing. The key to being comfortable in Alaska's ever-changing weather is to dress in layers.

Learning to travel light is its own pleasure, but it takes some practice (Hike 90).

That doesn't mean putting on seven T-shirts! Instead, think in terms of a close-fitting base layer, a fluffy or puffy insulating layer (that could be down, noncotton fleece, or wool), and a weatherproof outer layer.

I also pack plenty of water and snacks or, if I know there'll be water sources along the trail, a water filter so I can safely replenish my supply. Never underestimate the value of a good snack for keeping the body warm or providing comfort in a tough situation.

You'll also want a pack that's capable of toting all that stuff. For me, the sweet spot for day hiking is between twenty-five and twenty-eight liters—enough room to carry everything I need, plus plenty of water, snacks, or extra layers for other people.

But, as in all things outdoors, your mileage may vary.

THE TEN ESSENTIALS

Every time you hike, you should carry enough gear to address emergencies that happen on the trail. That doesn't have to mean a kit full of stuff; my emergency kit fits in a quart-size to gallon-size ziplock bag, depending on the length of my hike. The point of the Ten Essentials, originated by The Mountaineers, has always been to answer two basic questions: Can you prevent emergencies and respond positively should one occur (items 1–5)? And can you safely spend a night—or more—outside (items 6–10)? When you build your own emergency kit, think in terms of satisfying the Ten

Essentials, or the ten basic needs you must be able to meet to stay comfortable and safe on the trail. These include:

1. **Navigation.** I prefer map and compass to GPS, because you can't break the screen or drain the batteries on a map.

2. **Sun protection.** Believe it or not, sunglasses and sunblock are both essential gear when traveling close to snowfields and glaciers.

3. **Insulation.** Extra clothing—this is self-explanatory.

4. **Illumination.** Don't depend on the flashlight mode in your phone; bring a headlamp and spare batteries.

5. **First-aid supplies.** Make sure you know how to use everything you carry.

6. **Fire-starting materials.** Ideally they should work even when wet.

7. **Repair kit and tools.** A knife, duct tape, and a bit of cordage usually do the job. Some people carry zip ties, dental floss to use as sewing thread, and a multitool.

8. **Nutrition.** Extra food—both for generating body heat and as a source of comfort.

9. **Hydration.** Extra water or, if you know other sources will be available, a filter or purification tablets to treat said water.

10. **Emergency shelter.** This could be anything from a bivy sack to a tarp or a garbage bag, depending on the nature of your hike.

For more information on the Ten Essentials—and a great many other topics related to safety in the wilderness—see

Lost Lake has become an enormously popular trail for mountain bikers (Hike 74).

Mountaineering: The Freedom of the Hills, published by Mountaineers Books.

Of these items, the ones I find myself using constantly are garbage bags, duct tape, my headlamp, and a map.

TRAILHEAD CONCERNS

Even Alaska's busiest trails aren't as busy as many trails in the Lower 48. Because of that relative remoteness, theft from cars is an issue. The best deterrent is to never leave anything valuable in your car at all. If you must leave something like a purse or wallet, hide it *before* you get to the trailhead, not after. Otherwise, if criminals happen to be watching, you've just shown them where to find your valuables.

For the most part, Alaska's hikes take place near nicely paved roads. But in a few cases, the access roads are unpaved gravel that varies from "no big deal" to almost undrivable. If you're not sure your car can make it up a given road, consider scouting the road on foot or with a bike, because there might not be a good place to turn your car around. The only thing worse than driving up a treacherous road is having to go back down it in reverse. Rest assured that as a general rule the more remote and difficult to reach, the more a hike is worth doing.

In the winter some trailheads are maintained, but others are not. Although I've done my best to note which is which, this may also fluctuate with funding and staff availability. You're still allowed to walk in and use closed trailheads, but be aware that there is avalanche hazard on many Alaska trails during the winter. I've tried to note known avalanche hazards, but just because I haven't written an explicit warning about avalanche hazards doesn't mean they're not there. Do your own due diligence!

HORSES AND BIKES

As a general rule, horses are allowed everywhere except the Flattop Mountain trails (see Hikes 43 and 44), the Turnagain Arm Trail (see Hike 53) and the Eagle River Valley hikes (see Hikes 36 and 37). Bike access is slightly more restricted, so check the "notes" section of a hike to see if two-wheeled travel is allowed. More trails are gradually opening to fat bike use during winter; when in doubt, check with local land managers about when and where they're allowed. In either case, be aware of the damage that horses and bikes can do to a soft trail, and stay off a melted-out trail in the spring until it has time to harden up. Just because you *can* bike or ride in a certain place doesn't always mean you should.

How to Use This Book

Each of the 100 trail descriptions in this book is designed to tell you how to get to the trail, how to find your way once you're there, and inform you of any relevant rules and regulations (including whether dogs and motorized access are allowed).

RATINGS

Each trail receives two ratings. The first, indicated by stars, is for the hike's enjoyability and beauty; think of it as a general "would I do this again?" ranking. Here's a rough guide to what I'm thinking when I assign the rankings:

***** This is so mind-splittingly beautiful, I'm staying and living here forever. Please arrange to have food delivered.

**** That was so gorgeous, I don't mind walking back in the dark just so I can linger and take more pictures.

*** Hey, this is really pretty! Better take some pictures.

** Hey, I love being outside in nature. That was educational/fun/a chance to stretch my legs and see some neat things.

* You won't find any one-star hikes in this book. Life's too short.

The other rating is for difficulty, indicated by numbers. If ranking a hike's enjoyability and beauty is subjective, I daresay that ranking its difficulty is just as personal. One person's uphill slog is another person's breezy warm-up. Here's the scale I developed to make sense of each hike's difficulty:

1 You could easily kick a soccer ball along this trail.

2 Still pretty easy to kick the ball, but you might spend some time chasing it because of hills or weird bounces.

3 Be ready to carry the soccer ball most of the way, whether because of hills or uneven ground.

4 Be ready to sweat a lot, and maybe cry a little, on the way up. Take selfie with soccer ball on top.

5 Leave the soccer ball at home.

DISTANCE

Every trail listing includes the roundtrip, loop, or one-way hiking distance. I used a GPS smartphone app to gauge mileage. If a hike is labeled as a roundtrip, it means you hike out, then retrace your steps on the return trip. If you only take the hike one way, starting and ending at different trailheads, I've labeled it as a one-way hike and sometimes use the words "thru hike" as well. And if the hike starts and ends at the same trailhead but takes a different route on the way back than what you used when outbound, it's a loop.

ELEVATION GAIN

I also used a GPS smartphone app to determine elevation gain for each hike. Elevation gain is cumulative, which is why on rare occasions the amount of elevation you gain is actually more than the height of the high point in the hike. (In other words, when there's a lot of up and down in a hike, I've included the total elevation gain of all the "up" portions.

HIGH POINT

The high point of each hike is, literally, the highest elevation you'll reach. This is almost always the culmination of the hike and the best viewpoint—we do love to hike uphill here in Alaska!—although in a few cases, such as Hike 72 (Ptarmigan Creek and Lake), a trail will sidehill up a valley wall and then back down again before arriving at the final destination.

SEASON

I've noted when trails are *usually* in their best hikable condition in a typical year. That doesn't necessarily mean a trail will be completely free of snow or mud or brush, but there'll usually be little enough of each of those that you can still enjoy a pleasant walk. With that said, trail conditions can vary enormously from year to year, with the primary determiner being what sort of winter and spring there was. In years with a lot of snow, it takes longer for avalanche hazard to fade and trails to melt out.

LEGEND

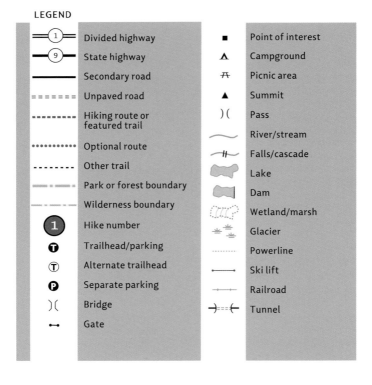

Divided highway	■ Point of interest
State highway	▲ Campground
Secondary road	⊼ Picnic area
Unpaved road	▲ Summit
Hiking route or featured trail	)(Pass
Optional route	River/stream
Other trail	Falls/cascade
Park or forest boundary	Lake
Wilderness boundary	Dam
Hike number	Wetland/marsh
Trailhead/parking	Glacier
Alternate trailhead	Powerline
Separate parking	Ski lift
Bridge	Railroad
Gate	Tunnel

Finally, wildlife threats can increase or diminish cyclically over the seasons, with moose cows being at their crankiest during the spring calving season in May and early June, and bears often the easiest to surprise when you hike near salmon-bearing streams in the summer or fall. I've done my best to note anywhere that wildlife encounters are known to be common, but they can happen anywhere and anytime in Alaska, so it's up to you to continue applying common sense and keep an eye out when you hike.

MAPS

I've listed the most relevant maps for each of the hikes, but keep in mind that even in Southcentral Alaska, which is the most densely populated part of the state, there aren't many topo maps that show hiking trails. Within Chugach State Park, you have two excellent options: Chugach State Park Anchorage from National Geographic, and Chugach State Park from Imus Geographics. Each shows a few trails the other doesn't, and both are excellent choices for most hikes. Outside of Chugach State Park, National Geographic topos are your only option aside from USGS quads. Most of the latter are far too old to show today's hiking trails, but sometimes trails built on old mining roads will be shown on the maps.

CONTACT

In the contact information for each hike, I identify the land manager for that trail. You'll find websites, mailing address, physical addresses (when available), and phone numbers for all of the land managers for these trails in Resources at the back of the book. If you have questions about the rules for a certain trail, contact the land manager.

With that said, some of Alaska's trails are managed and monitored quite closely; others, not so much. As a general rule, the biggest land managers, such as Chugach State Park or Chugach National Forest, will be well informed about current trail conditions, planned trail work, and the best season for hiking a given trail. For smaller land managers, such as ski clubs or rural towns, however, they may not have much information or even anyone whose job it is to answer the phone or monitor the trails year-round.

GPS

I used the smartphone app Gaia GPS (WGS84) to record the GPS tracks that eventually became my maps and to obtain the trailhead coordinates listed for each hike (in decimal degrees). It's a handy tool that made it easy to track mileage and elevation, annotate waypoints, append photos to those waypoints for future reference, and so on.

ICONS

Each hike has a series of icons to quickly clue you in to the trail's key characteristics. Here's what they mean:

Kid-Friendly

These trails are relatively easy, but they're not always a "gimme"! Instead, I focused on straightforward trails with an obvious payoff within a short distance (even if that's not necessarily the end of the trail). These trails also have decent or better visibility and good footing.

Dog-Friendly

A better question would be "which trails in Alaska *aren't* dog-friendly," but there are a few where dogs simply aren't allowed, or where even the best-trained dog must stay on a leash. If you see this icon it means well-behaved dogs are welcome, but still need to be under your direct control—so if Fido doesn't have perfect recall even when distracted by wildlife or another dog, please keep him on a leash.

Views
There is no such thing as bad scenery in Alaska. But when you see this icon, it means you're in for something special—so make sure you have your camera ready!

Wildlife
If you see this icon, it means some kind of critter is known to be common and frequently visible here. That can mean anything from migratory songbirds and waterfowl to bears and moose, so read the trail description for more details.

Lakes
Alaska's lakes come in an endless variety, from frigid alpine tarns to sprawling aquamarine giants. Some are fed by milky

TOP TEN ICONIC HIKES
You could argue that all hikes in Alaska are iconic in some way, and every single trail in this book has something major going for it. But a few stand out as true gems: these are the trails that are so well-known that they pop up everywhere, from social media to articles about hiking in Alaska, and they draw happy hikers back to them over and over again. If you were to ask locals for a short list of "don't miss this" hiking experiences in Alaska, I guarantee that most of these would be on the list.

3. **April Bowl**   A short, easy, and kid-friendly trail that yields totally outsized returns in views and adventure.

7. **Reed Lakes**   If you've seen photos of hikers posing by crystal-blue lakes or hopping over car-size boulders, the pictures were probably taken here.

24. **Eklutna Lakeside Trail and Eydlu Bena Loop**   It's the lakeside trail that makes this place such an icon; where else can you hike (or bike, or even ride an ATV on certain days) for 9 miles *one way* along the shore of one massive, gorgeous lake?

36. **Eagle and Symphony Lakes**   The lakes are a stunning reward for a hike that's surprisingly easy, despite its 11-mile length.

59. **Winner Creek**   Perhaps the best-known trail in Girdwood, an easy hike that starts right outside the Alyeska Resort but pays off big if you enjoy rushing, glacier-fed creeks or a thrilling hand-tram crossing.

60. **Raven Glacier**   Don't bother hiking the other 20 miles of the famous Crow Pass trail; the locals know these first 4 miles are where it's at.

66. **Portage Pass**   Gorgeous glacier views in less than a mile, and they only get better as you keep going.

74. **Lost Lake**   It's most famous for its backpacking, but hardy folks can take in this glorious, lake-dotted stretch of alpine tundra in one long day.

water melting out of glaciers, while others are the deep blue of natural spring water; but either way, they're always a big attraction for hikers.

Waterfalls

Waterfalls in Alaska usually aren't as grand or as openly visible as those you'll find in other states—but that makes the falls we do have that much more interesting, especially when they emerge from the depths of the forest or tumble down a rocky cliff in the tundra. If you see this icon, you'll get close enough to at least one waterfall to admire it.

Winter Hiking

I've used this icon to mark the trails that are known for being particularly popular or hospitable to winter travel. Winter hiking requires a little more skill and experience than summer hiking, and everyone's comfort level is a little different, but this is a good place to start.

The edge of Harding Icefield just coming into view (Hike 77)

76. **Exit Glacier**   Some of the best and easiest glacier views in the state, with great accessibility for all ability levels.
77. **Harding Icefield**   Exit Glacier's grown-up cousin. Some local hikers train all year to make it up this challenging trail with its overlooks of the sprawling icefield, and it's totally worth it.

Fishing

Southcentral Alaska is full of places you can pull your car up to the water and fish, but some anglers enjoy backcountry fishing as its own challenge. If you see this icon, it's worth packing your fishing pole—and fishing license!—for the hike.

Glaciers

Who doesn't love a glimpse of crystalline blue ice? If you see this icon, you'll know the hike gets you good views of at least one glacier, and in a few cases you can *almost* get close enough to touch.

A NOTE ABOUT SAFETY

Safety is an important concern in all outdoor activities. No guidebook can alert you to every hazard or anticipate the limitations of every reader. Therefore, the descriptions of roads, trails, routes, and natural features in this book are not representations that a particular place or excursion will be safe for your party. When you follow any of the routes described in this book, you assume responsibility for your own safety. Under normal conditions, such excursions require the usual attention to traffic, road and trail conditions, weather, terrain, the capabilities of your party, and other factors. Because many of the lands in this book are subject to development and/or change of ownership, conditions may have changed since this book was written that make your use of some of these routes unwise. Always check for current conditions, obey posted private property signs, and avoid confrontations with property owners or managers. Keeping informed on current conditions and exercising common sense are the keys to a safe, enjoyable outing.

—*Mountaineers Books*

Opposite: *This soaring singletrack along the Eska Creek Falls (Hike 1) trail epitomizes the best of the northern Mat-Su's multiuse trails; both hikers and bikers are welcome here.*

northern mat-su valley

The Northern Matanuska-Susitna Valley, or the Mat-Su Valley, as locals call it, is home to a few far-flung hikes, but most of the trails center around Hatcher Pass, an iconic region of vibrant green tundra and granite chunks deposited by glaciers. This place is often described as something straight out of the more misty, remote parts of Ireland or a *Lord of the Rings* set in New Zealand.

Eska Creek Falls

From Eska Falls Trailhead

RATING/ DIFFICULTY	ROUNDTRIP	ELEV GAIN/ HIGH POINT	SEASON
*****/3	8.3 miles	2096 feet/ 2960 feet	May–Oct

From mile 2.5 on Jonesville Mine Road

RATING/ DIFFICULTY	ROUNDTRIP	ELEV GAIN/ HIGH POINT	SEASON
****/3	11.8 miles	2745 feet/ 2960 feet	May–Oct

Maps: USGS Anchorage C6 NE, USGS Anchorage D6 SE; **Contact:** Matanuska-Susitna Borough; **Notes:** Open to mountain bikes. Motorized use allowed on the rough roads leading to the trailhead. Dogs must be on leash; **GPS:** 61.7506°, –148.9171°

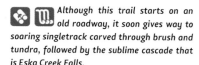 *Although this trail starts on an old roadway, it soon gives way to soaring singletrack carved through brush and tundra, followed by the sublime cascade that is Eska Creek Falls.*

GETTING THERE

From Anchorage, drive northeast on the Glenn Highway for about 55 miles, passing through Palmer and continuing on to the small town of Sutton. Turn left (north) onto Jonesville Mine Road, which turns to rough gravel at mile 2.5. Vehicles with low ground clearance may need to park here, in which case you can hike or bike the remaining 1.75 miles to the trailhead. Those with higher clearance can continue on this road, staying left at each fork (follow the small "hiker" signs). About 1000 feet from the trailhead, you'll find a few designated parking spots.

ON THE TRAIL

Even if you drove in with a high-clearance vehicle, it's still a short walk from the parking area to the actual trailhead (elevation 1430 feet). Walk another 1000 feet over rough gravel until the road forks. Take the left fork, which dead-ends in a small cul-de-sac with a trailhead sign.

Believe it or not, finding the trailhead is the hardest part of the hike. The rest is pretty straightforward, starting with a clear footpath that crosses a small footbridge over a creek, then leads you into the spruce and aspen trees that carpet the foothills below Eska Peak.

You'll cross another bridge at mile 1.25. From here the trail gets a little rockier, and the brush starts to open up so that when you arrive at a rough-hewn log bench at 1.4 miles (elevation 2000 feet) you have beautiful views of the Matanuska River valley to the right (east) and Eska Peak ahead of you.

From here, the trail is winding singletrack that zigzags back and forth in a series of swooping switchbacks—this must be great fun on a bike! You can hear a waterfall nearby but not see it; you still have a ways to go to Eska Creek Falls.

At 2.6 miles (elevation 2610 feet) look for especially gorgeous views out over the valley below you as the trail arcs along the

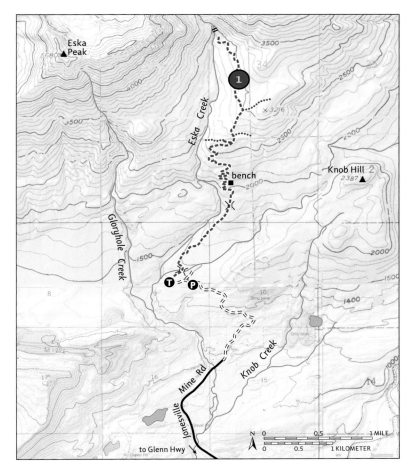

hillside above the treeline. The hillside itself is beautiful in the fall, when all the ground cover plants turn vibrant orange and red, a sharp contrast to the rocky summit of the mountain above you. At 2.75 miles you'll hit a T intersection; turn sharply right to stay on the hiking trail.

There's another intersection at 2.9 miles. The hiking trail continues straight ahead (left), but take a second to look around so you'll see which way to go when you come back this way.

At this point, the trail opens out into a broad valley crisscrossed with ATV trails.

Soaking in the view from the base of Eska Creek Falls

You can see the falls up at the head of the valley, but it's not immediately clear which trail will get you there. The easiest way is to trend right, following the ATV trail that climbs up an obvious bench. At 3.2 miles (elevation 2960 feet) the trail splits; take the left fork, which then heads down a gentle slope, straight toward the falls that come tumbling down the mountainside in a foamy white cascade.

If you really want to get close to the base of the falls—and who wouldn't?—you'll need to do some mild scrambling and rock hopping at about 4.1 miles, just before the trail ends underneath the falls. Take care in your exploration; as you might expect, the rocks around the falls are slippery when wet. Now that you've found your way here, it's relatively easy to retrace your steps on the way back.

2 Craigie Creek

RATING/ DIFFICULTY	ROUNDTRIP	ELEV GAIN/ HIGH POINT	SEASON
****/3	9 miles	1500 feet/ 4170 feet	June–Oct

Map: USGS Anchorage D7 SE; **Contact:** Alaska State Parks, Mat-Su Region; **Notes:** Road over the pass typically closes after first serious snowfall, usually in October. Open to mountain bikes, off-road vehicles. Dogs permitted under voice control in backcountry.

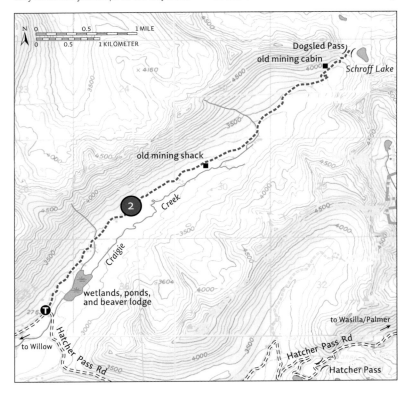

Bear and moose habitat; **GPS:** 61.77663°, –149.39850°

An old mining road runs up a broad valley roughly parallel to Craigie Creek, passing the remains of old mining shacks and equipment on its way to Schroff Lake in boulder-lined Dogsled Pass.

GETTING THERE

From Wasilla, take Trunk Road north about 6 miles. Continue straight through all the roundabouts until the road ends in a T intersection. Turn left at the T; this becomes Hatcher Pass Road. About 16 miles later, just before the road ends at Independence Mine State Historical Park, make a hairpin turn to the left onto the unpaved, sometimes rough road that actually leads up and over Hatcher Pass. Reset your odometer here. The unmarked Craigie Creek Trailhead is

6.2 miles from the start of that unpaved road; look for a rough pullout on the right, just as the road makes a sweeping bend to the left.

ON THE TRAIL

While this is a wonderful trail for both mountain biking and hiking, keep in mind that it's also open to off-road vehicles. That means two things: one, there's a constant possibility of meeting four-wheelers, jeeps, and the like on the trail; and two, you have the option of taking your own vehicle as far in as you like, although it's extremely rough driving with very few areas to pull out or turn around.

From the trailhead (elevation 2770 feet) take the immediate right fork to avoid private property. The rough dirt and rock road runs along the valley floor for several miles before starting its climb to the pass; at 0.3 mile, look to the right to see a beaver lodge

One of the rockier points in the old road alongside Craigie Creek

and extended views of the wetlands complex they've created with their dams. In late summer, the boggy meadows the beavers have built are covered in dark blue monkshood flowers.

Although Craigie Creek runs to the right of the trail and occasionally comes within arm's reach, I'm skeptical about using it as a water source; there's too much mining debris around here to be sure exactly what's in the water, so I prefer to pack in extra water or filter water from the lake at the top of the pass.

At 2.25 miles (elevation 3110 feet) look for the crumbling remains of an old mining shack in the near distance to the right. About a half-mile later there's a stretch of wet, rocky trail—you won't have to ford any streams, but you might appreciate having waterproof shoes, and the uneven surface could turn unwary ankles.

The real uphill push begins just shy of 4 miles (elevation 3700 feet) as the trail zags through two sharp switchbacks. Look for ruined mining equipment upstream in the creek. Just before 4.2 miles (elevation 3850 feet) you'll pass an old mining cabin. Look and take photos, but don't enter this or any of the other ruined buildings you see along this trail; they're very unstable. Also, there are still active mining claims in this area—so always respect any posted private property or mining claims you may see.

From the old shack, you can clearly trace the road's path up toward the pass, until it gets lost in a short stretch of boulders. The ascent looks a lot more intimidating than it really is. It's only just over another 0.3 mile and about 200 feet of elevation gain and, aside from some rock hopping or scrambling in that short stretch of boulders, it's pretty straightforward walking.

Your reward at the trail's end, 4.5 miles from the trailhead, is pretty blue-green Schroff Lake (elevation 4170 feet), cupped in the boulders to the right once you crest what's known as Dogsled Pass. The pass itself, studded with gigantic boulders and often shrouded in a light mist, is also quite a treat.

3 April Bowl

RATING/ DIFFICULTY	ROUNDTRIP	ELEV GAIN/ HIGH POINT	SEASON
****/3	2.7 miles	980 feet/ 4800 feet	July–Sept

Map: USGS Anchorage D7 SE; **Contact:** Alaska State Parks, Hatcher Pass Management Area; **Notes:** Hairpin turns on the sometimes rough road into the pass. Gate to the pass is generally open July 1 through September 15, depending on snow cover. Dogs permitted on leash in parking area, under direct control on trail. Bear habitat; **GPS:** 61.76490°, –149.31156°

 Find stunning tundra scenery in a short, relatively easy mountain hike that starts above treeline and often draws crowds. Follow switchbacks to a tranquil mountain bowl and a rocky ridge walk to the summit of Hatch Peak, with an optional loop down the far side.

GETTING THERE
From Wasilla, take Trunk Road north for about 6 miles. Continue straight through all the roundabouts until the road ends in a T intersection. Turn left at the T; this becomes Hatcher Pass Road. About 16 miles later, just before the road ends at Independence Mine State Historical Park, make a hairpin turn to

Looking back over the lakes in April Bowl.

the left onto the unpaved, sometimes rough road that actually leads up and over Hatcher Pass. Park in the obvious pullout at the top of the pass (elevation 3890 feet).

ON THE TRAIL

The start of the trail is marked by a small brown signpost on the opposite side of the road from the parking area; a pretty little cascade trickles down to the right of the trail. Because the entirety of this trail is above the treeline, you'll have a clear view of other hikers working their way up the sharply-cut switchbacks that make up the first 0.3 mile of trail and 180 feet of elevation gain.

This brings you to eye level with an alpine bowl that contains a small lake and a few smaller ponds, all enclosed within the circling arms of the ridges to either side of Hatch Peak. This lake is sometimes, confusingly, called Summit Lake; but Summit Lake is actually below you to the west. You'll get a good view of it as you keep hiking farther toward Hatch Peak.

At 0.5 mile (elevation 4200 feet) the trail forks; turn left. The right fork would take you into the bowl with the lakes before petering into nothing. At 0.6 mile, the trail departs the relatively flat tundra shelf around the lake and starts heading up the rocky ridge. Although the ridge is fairly narrow, it's hardly a knife-edge, and the footpath is clear; most hikers will have no problem here.

Just past 1.3 miles you'll reach 4800-foot Hatch Peak itself, directly across the cirque from where you began walking the ridge. That elevation may sound challenging, but since you started from almost 3900 feet at the trailhead, it's a reasonable 900-foot gain. In clear weather you also get sweeping views over Palmer in the distance, almost swallowed up by the vastness of the land around it.

For most people, this is the end of the trail; they'll tag the top of Hatch Peak and then return the way they came. However, if you don't mind some steep, loose terrain,

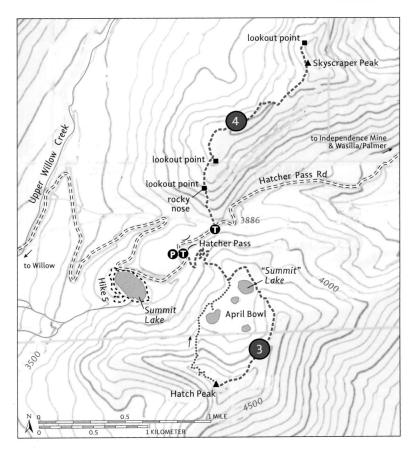

this can be a great loop hike. Follow a lightly defined footpath across Hatch Peak and down the ridge on the far side. Just past 1.5 miles from the trailhead (0.2 mile after the peak) you'll see a steep but manageable spine leading down and to the right, depositing you in the cirque below.

Take your time going down this spine; the footing is extremely steep and rocky, with little to no established trail, and the rocks may shift underfoot. Some people prefer to go up this section, doing the loop in reverse. Either way, once you're back on (relatively) flat ground, a short tundra walk takes you back to where you first emerged from those initial switchbacks. The total distance for the loop is just shy of 2.7 miles—about the same as a roundtrip to and from Hatch Peak.

4 Skyscraper Peak

RATING/ DIFFICULTY	ROUNDTRIP	ELEV GAIN/ HIGH POINT	SEASON
***/3	2.2 miles	1170 feet/ 4750 feet	July–Sept

Map: USGS Anchorage D7 SE; **Contact:** Alaska State Parks, Hatcher Pass Management Area; **Notes:** Hairpin turns on the road into the pass. Unmarked trailhead. Gate to the pass is generally open July 1 through September 15; may be open later if snow is late. Dogs permitted on leash at trailhead, under voice control in backcountry. Bear habitat; **GPS:** 61.76942°, –149.31218°

  A steep, eroded trail gives way to fantastic tundra walking while offering sweeping views over Independence Mine. Craggy rock outcroppings scattered across the ridge make Skyscraper, more than any other peak in the area, feel like something straight out of a Lord of the Rings *set.*

GETTING THERE

From Wasilla, take Trunk Road north for about 6 miles. Continue straight through all the roundabouts until the road ends in a T intersection. Turn left at the T; this becomes Hatcher Pass Road. About 16 miles later, just before the road ends at Independence Mine State Historical Park, make a hairpin turn to the left onto the unpaved, sometimes rough road that actually leads up and over Hatcher Pass. Park in the obvious pullout at the top of the pass (elevation 3890 feet) or in a much smaller pullout at the base of Skyscraper Peak, just before the bigger pullout.

ON THE TRAIL

This is another "you can't miss it" trail, even though the trailhead itself is not marked: look for the wide, eroded strip leading up the peak on the right side of the pass, just before the summit parking lot. The face of the mountain looks like something from the desert Southwest, but if you can stomach that first steep, loose 0.1 mile to almost 4100 feet in elevation, it settles down into a more walkable trail, with a few small clumps of flowers and diminutive alpine vegetation toughing it out between the rocks.

Just before 0.2 mile (elevation 4300 feet) you reach the first prominent rocky "nose" that you could see from the parking area, with a wonderful lookout point a short walk to the left. This is one of several spots where a pile of craggy rocks, seemingly dropped from the sky, makes the mountainside look for all the world like something from the mind of J. R. R. Tolkien. Feel free to bring your own orc costumes and stage a last stand.

At 0.3 mile (elevation 4470 feet) you'll reach another obvious lookout point, this one a rocky prow facing to the right, giving you great views down into the valley that holds Independence Mine. In getting here you've gained about 600 feet in 0.3 mile. My personal standard for "steep" is 100 feet of elevation gain per 0.1 mile and this is twice that so this is definitely a challenging stretch.

Happily, the slope gets much easier at this point, a mostly level ramble over loose tundra swells. The trail is faint and in spaces fades out altogether, but remember the lesson of that horribly eroded face and do your best to stick to the trail fragments when you can spot them. Small stacks of rocks help guide you in the most popular direction of travel.

A walk along Skyscraper Ridge under the midnight sun

By 0.6 mile (elevation 4570 feet) the trail becomes more defined as you go over a false high point in the ridge. As you walk, you're tracing the sky-scraping skyline that sits behind Independence Mine.

Just before 1 mile there's a short, steep push in loose gravel footing to the Army Corps marker, elevation 4750 feet. If you spend most of your time near or at sea level, the sudden transition to almost 5000 feet of elevation can feel a little heady. If you're feeling good, you can walk another 0.1 mile to yet another great lookout point that's only a few feet lower.

The ridge does go on from here but is no longer pleasant walking; instead, it's a drama of loose dirt and rock in unusually vivid colors for Alaska, falling steeply away from the ridge on both sides. Enjoy the great views down over Independence Mine on your right and glimpses of round Gold Cord Lake on the far side of the valley. Just have your hiking poles ready for the descent—especially that last 0.1 mile of loose terrain down to the parking lot.

5 Summit Lake

RATING/ DIFFICULTY	LOOP	ELEV GAIN/ HIGH POINT	SEASON
****/2	0.5 mile	75 feet/ 3830 feet	July–Sept

Map: USGS Anchorage D7 SE; **Contact:** Alaska State Parks, Mat-Su Region; **Notes:**

Hairpin turns on the sometimes rough road into the pass. Gate to the pass is generally open July 1 through September 15; may be open later if snow is late. Dogs permitted on leash in parking area, under direct control on trail. Bear habitat; **GPS:** 61.77917°, –149.19588°

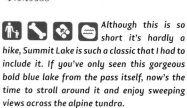 *Although this is so short it's hardly a hike, Summit Lake is such a classic that I had to include it. If you've only seen this gorgeous bold blue lake from the pass itself, now's the time to stroll around it and enjoy sweeping views across the alpine tundra.*

GETTING THERE

From Wasilla, take Trunk Road north for about 6 miles. Continue straight through all the roundabouts until the road ends in a T intersection. Turn left at the T; this becomes Hatcher Pass Road. After about 16 miles, just before the road ends at Independence Mine State Historical Park, make a hairpin turn to the left onto the unpaved, sometimes

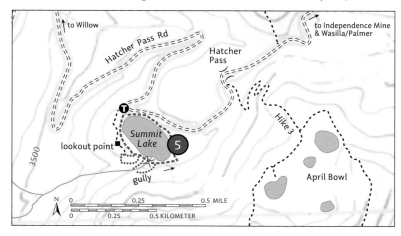

Walkers enjoying Summit Lake on a sunny summer day

rough road that actually leads up and over Hatcher Pass. Once you drive over the pass, you'll see Summit Lake close below you and to the left; park in the small but obvious pullout at its banks.

ON THE TRAIL

For the sake of convenience, let's assume that you're walking around the lake counterclockwise. You'll immediately see a web of trails leading uphill to a small lookout point on the right; but if you continue near the lakeshore, at 0.1 mile you'll walk down a small hill and cross a bridge over a lovely little outflow. You can turn right, either just before the outflowing creek or just after it, and explore a small, shale-lined gully that offers beautiful views out across the mountains toward Willow.

If you continue around the lake, it's easy walking until the trail peters to almost nothing at 0.25 mile. Kids have great fun scrambling up the nearby rocky slopes to find throwable stones, then hurling them into the water. But if you look a short distance ahead, there's a faint track that keeps going around the lake. Step across a small stream at 0.3 mile, and from there you can pick up a proper footpath that takes you back to the trailhead at 0.5 mile.

6 Gold Cord Lake

RATING/ DIFFICULTY	ROUNDTRIP	ELEV GAIN/ HIGH POINT	SEASON
****/3	1.6 miles	580 feet/ 4015 feet	July–Oct

Map: USGS Anchorage D6 SW; **Contact:** Alaska State Parks, Hatcher Pass Management Area; **Notes:** Alaska State Parks Pass or parking fee. No entry to upper parking lot after 5:00 PM. gate closes at 6:00 PM. Dogs permitted on leash in parking areas, under direct control on trail. Bear habitat; **GPS:** 61.79354°, –149.28091°

Despite this hike's short length, it's one of the best in the area. Starting well above the treeline, you'll cross tundra hummocks with burbling pools fed by underground streams, and hike up a steep stretch of rocky trail before gaining the surprisingly remote-feeling cirque that contains Gold Cord Lake.

GETTING THERE
From Wasilla, take Trunk Road north for about 6 miles. Continue straight through all the roundabouts until the road ends in a T intersection. Turn left at the T; this becomes Hatcher Pass Road. About 16 miles later the road ends in Independence Mine State Historical Park, where you have your choice of two parking lots. The upper lot is directly

across from the trailhead but involves an extra fee and is blocked by a gate that closes at 6:00 PM. The lower lot adds an extra mile and 400 feet of elevation gain to the trek, one-way, but does not invoke that extra fee or worry about your car being locked in.

ON THE TRAIL
If you parked in the upper lot, the Gold Cord Lake Trailhead (elevation 3500 feet) is just on the opposite side of the road. If you parked in the lower lot, walk the 1 mile past the gate and up the road, then look for the trailhead on the right, opposite the left turn that takes you into the parking lot.

From the trailhead, a clear dirt footpath immediately drops down to cross a short footbridge, then begins a gradual incline. At 0.3 mile (elevation 3670 feet) you'll pass a big, triangle-shaped boulder. It might not be immediately obvious, but the tundra around you is a relatively thin covering over many jumbled boulders like this one. That's what

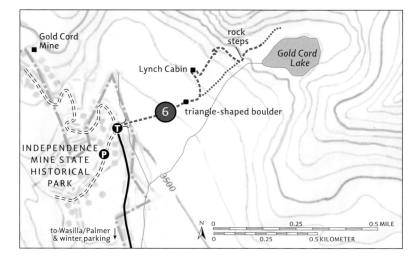

The historic Lynch Cabin along the trail to Gold Cord Lake

gives it such a hilly, hummocky feel, and in some places you can see the boulders being swallowed up by the slow-growing tundra plants.

Just past that rock, you'll see the old trail branch to the right and head directly up the side of the creek. Stick to the switchbacks on the left, which not only make for a nicer hike but also give the old trail a chance to recover from erosion.

At 0.4 mile you'll push up a short hill to pass around the historic but worn-down Lynch Cabin, circa 1930, a remnant of the mining activity in this area. The trail winds around the cabin and continues uphill, zig-zagging into rocky footing at 0.5 mile. By 0.7 mile you've climbed a series of rock steps and are just about level with the surprisingly gorgeous outflow of Gold Cord Lake (elevation 3960 feet).

For most, this will be the end of the hike. Agile hikers can follow a well-defined trail for another 0.1 mile through massive boulders

on the left side of the lake. By 0.8 mile you'll have reached the trail's high point at 4015 feet and have no easy way to continue, although if you're really determined—and careful—you could keep scrambling on the massive boulders.

Snow may linger on this trail well into June, but it's usually clear by July. This is a very popular hike when the mine is open, but once the mine closes in early September, it's a great short trail to solitude.

7 Reed Lakes

RATING/ DIFFICULTY	ROUNDTRIP	ELEV GAIN/ HIGH POINT	SEASON
*****/4	8.8 miles	2160 feet/ 4240 feet	July–Oct

Map: USGS Anchorage D6 SW; **Contact:** Alaska State Parks, Mat-Su Region; **Notes:** Alaska State Parks Pass or parking fee. Unmarked trailhead. Access road usually

Lower Reed Lake, seen from the trail to Upper Reed Lake

open July through September, longer if weather allows. Very rough driving. Dogs permitted on leash at trailhead, under direct control in backcountry. Bear habitat; moose sightings rare but possible. Avalanche hazard in winter; **GPS:** 61.80415°, –149.20274°

Find the most popular back-country hike in Hatcher Pass, and a perfect sampler platter of all things Alaska: easy walking on an old roadbed, boulder hopping across car-size stones, pretty alpine lakes, and a landscape of brooding, crumbling granite dotted with rich tundra.

GETTING THERE
From Wasilla, take Trunk Road north for about 6 miles. Continue straight through all the roundabouts until the road ends in a T intersection. Turn left at the T; this becomes Hatcher Pass Road. At about mile 14.4 of Hatcher Pass Road, make a sharp right turn onto unpaved, often rough Archangel Road. The trailhead is on the right, 2.4 miles in (elevation 2385 feet), and is extraordinarily rough; vehicles with low clearance can be parked in a gravel lot at about mile 2.1.

ON THE TRAIL
The first part of this trail traces a narrow roadbed along the left side of Reed Creek. The trail itself is lined with dense willows and fireweed, and is mostly flat for the first mile, with a few small creeks running across the trail. At 1.4 miles, hop rocks across a wide, placid stream.

Just past 1.5 miles the trail forks; there used to be a ruined cabin here, but it has been removed. The left fork heads uphill on a steep, muddy slope toward the defunct Snowbird Mine (see Hike 8). Stay right for Reed Lakes.

The trail crosses two branches of the same creek, then at 1.6 miles (elevation 2680 feet), a short 0.25-mile side trail leads through whip-tough willows to give you close-up views of a series of beaver-dammed ponds. Next, the trail ascends a series of rocky steps and several switchbacks, gaining a commanding lookout point at 1.9 miles (elevation 2940 feet). From here, you have great views back down the valley and of the Talkeetna Mountains around you.

At 2 miles the trail forks again; take the short side trail to the left for photo ops of a pretty cascade, or stay to the right to continue toward Reed Lakes. Shortly after this, you'll meet one more fork in the trail. Continuing straight ahead is the most direct route into the field of car-size boulders you must scramble through to reach the next part of your hike, but you can greatly shorten that boulder hopping by taking the right fork instead, heading up a short hill and traversing the slope above the boulder field on one of several clear footpaths.

At 2.4 miles (elevation 3360 feet) the trail descends to the edge of the boulder field and you can make the short, relatively easy crossing to the far side. There is no sign to guide you, but look for obvious weathering where many feet have crossed the boulders, and aim for the rough footpath on the far side.

You'll still have to scramble over a few rocks, and at 2.5 miles (elevation 3440 feet) you cross another short boulder field. Throughout the hike, these rocky areas are

great places to look for marmots—large, gray rodents the size of small dogs, with a shrieking, whistling call—and pikas, which look for all the world like tiny palm-size bunny rabbits.

At 2.6 miles the trail exits that second boulder field and crosses a series of wildflower-strewn meadows beside shallow ponds. At 3.1 miles there's a steep, often muddy section of trail; crest this and you'll be able to see Lower Reed Lake, a brilliant aquamarine jewel set in a tundra bowl at 3.3 miles (elevation 3770 feet).

The trail parallels the lakeshore for almost a quarter mile, but many people treat this as a picnic spot or a turnaround point, and some have even been known to swim or wade in the frigid water. The water feels very good on the hot summer days that are becoming increasingly common, but be careful if you go swimming—even strong swimmers weaken quickly in cold water.

It's well worth continuing on to the second lake. Follow the trail as it veers away from Lower Reed Lake, climbing steeply toward a lovely waterfall that gushes out of Upper Reed Lake. By 3.75 miles (elevation 4060 feet) you're level with the top of the waterfall. Be careful if you scramble around here or at the bottom of the falls; the granite boulders are very slippery when wet, and a slip or fall packs serious consequences.

From here, it's an easy stroll except for one last patch of boulders to cross through at 4.1 miles, and by 4.4 miles (elevation 4240 feet) you'll reach the trail's end at the shore of Upper Reed Lake, which is set in a desolately beautiful cirque lined with scree. The upper lake is often colder and windier than the lower lake, so an extra layer of clothing is usually in order here.

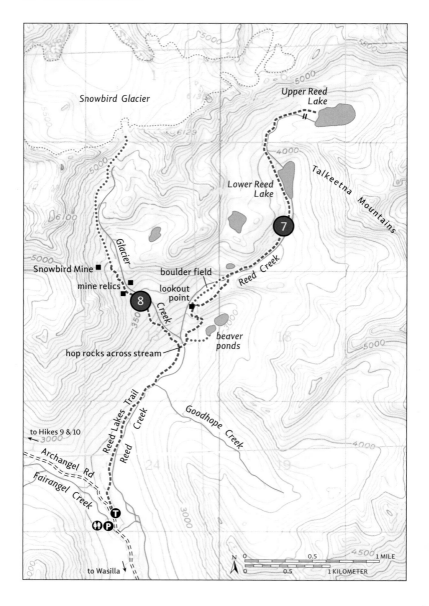

Snowbird Glacier

Upper Reed Lake

Lower Reed Lake

Talkeetna Mountains

Snowbird Mine

mine relics

Glacier

boulder field

lookout point

Reed Creek

beaver ponds

hop rocks across stream

Creek

Reed Lakes Trail

to Hikes 9 & 10

Archangel Rd

Fairangel Creek

Reed Creek

Goodhope Creek

to Wasilla

N

0   0.5   1 MILE

0   0.5   1 KILOMETER

8 Snowbird Mine

RATING/ DIFFICULTY	ROUNDTRIP	ELEV GAIN/ HIGH POINT	SEASON
***/4	4.7 miles	1640 feet 3870 feet	July–Oct

Map: USGS Anchorage D6 SW; **Contact:** Alaska State Parks, Mat-Su Region; **Notes:** Alaska State Parks Pass or parking fee. Unmarked trailhead. Access road usually open July through September, longer if weather allows. Very rough driving. Dogs permitted on leash at trailhead, under direct control in backcountry. Bear habitat; moose sightings rare but possible. Avalanche hazard in winter; **GPS:** 61.80415°, –149.20274°

For history and mining buffs, there's no better way to spend an afternoon than poking around in the rubble of an old mining claim. Just be careful; they call them ruins for a reason.

GETTING THERE
From Wasilla, take Trunk Road north. Continue straight through all the roundabouts until the road ends in a T intersection. Turn left at the T; this becomes Hatcher Pass Road. At about mile 14.4 of Hatcher Pass Road, make a sharp right turn onto unpaved, often rough Archangel Road. The trailhead is on the right, 2.4 miles in (elevation 2385 feet), and is extraordinarily rough; vehicles with low clearance can be parked in a gravel lot at about mile 2.1.

ON THE TRAIL
The first part of this trail coincides with the uber-popular Reed Lakes Trail (Hike 7). An old, relatively narrow roadbed makes

A refreshingly mud-free start along the trail to Snowbird Mine

for very easy walking. It's lined with dense willows and fireweed, and flanked by fields of flowers in the summer. At 1.4 miles (elevation 2620 feet) hop rocks across a wide, placid stream.

Just past 1.5 miles (elevation 2660 feet) the trail forks; there used to be a ruined cabin here, but it has been removed. The Reed Lakes Trail keeps going to the right, but for Snowbird Mine you turn left and start climbing up a steep slope. The trail here is often treacherously muddy, to the point that some people use ice cleats for more secure footing, even in the summer. Take the cleats off, when you can, to reduce erosion.

The slope is particularly steep at 1.9 miles (elevation 3040 feet) as you pass a rusting steel cable from the mine, along with a boulder field to your left. Just before 2.1 miles (elevation 3365 feet) the trail passes a few more relics, including a ruined cabin on the left, and briefly levels out. Enjoy the easy walking along the south side of the small gully that holds Glacier Creek.

At 2.2 miles (elevation 3650 feet) the keen-eyed hiker can spot more mining relics in the rocks to either side of the trail; leave them in place so that others can enjoy them too. At this point the trail becomes extremely rocky. Pick your way through the boulders and cross shallow, slow-moving streams until about 2.3 miles (elevation 3870 feet) and you'll be able to spot mine tunnels, cables, and other relics of the Snowbird Mine on the mountain slopes to your left.

A word about safety around old mines: don't go into ruined buildings or mine shafts. They're often dangerously fragile and unstable, and I can't think of a much more embarrassing way to go.

The established trail ends here but, if you're up for some advanced routefinding and serious boulder hopping, you can continue another 1.1 miles and 1300 feet in elevation to the obvious pass and overlooks of Snowbird Glacier. Don't venture onto the glacier itself unless you have training in glacier travel and rescue, and take care not to wander onto technical rock terrain by mistake. The general rule is that if you're not sure you can comfortably hike back down something, don't go up it in the first place.

9 Fairangel Lakes

RATING/ DIFFICULTY	ROUNDTRIP	ELEV GAIN/ HIGH POINT	SEASON
*****/3	2.6 miles	1180 feet/ 4060 feet	July–Sept

Maps: USGS Anchorage D6 SW, USGS Anchorage D7 SE; **Contact:** Alaska State Parks, Hatcher Pass Management Area; **Notes:** No fee. Unmarked trailhead. Access road usually open July through September, longer if weather allows. Very rough driving. Dogs permitted on leash in parking area, under voice control in backcountry. Moose and bear habitat. Requires fords; **GPS:** 61.81845°, –149.23993°

Explore a shorter, steeper, and wilder-feeling version of the uber-popular Reed Lakes hike and get all the beauty of remote, alpine lakes amid weathered, granite-studded tundra, with none of the crowds. After dropping into the brush you'll ford a frothing stream, then hike up, past the ruins of an old mine, to overlook two lakes set in the alpine quiet.

GETTING THERE

From Wasilla, take Trunk Road north for about 6 miles. Continue straight through all the roundabouts until the road ends in a T intersection. Turn left at the T; this becomes Hatcher Pass Road. At about mile 14.4 of Hatcher Pass Road, make a sharp right turn onto unpaved Archangel Road. The hike starts near the end of the road, 4 miles in, but the road gets extraordinarily rough beyond mile 2.4. SUVs and Subarus with good clearance can usually make it if carefully driven; vehicles with low clearance can be parked

Lower Fairangel Lake provides a perfect reflection of the sky.

in a wide gravel pullout on the left at mile 2.1 of Archangel Road; you'll then walk or bike the remainder of Archangel Road.

ON THE TRAIL

Some people think this hike starts at a ramshackle outhouse near the end of Archangel Road—but it doesn't. The easiest way to find the unmarked trailhead (elevation 3090 feet) is to start at the gate that marks the very end of Archangel Road and walk back along the road as if you were returning to the main road. Fairangel Lakes is the first clear (and again, unmarked) trail that drops down into the bushes on the right, only about 50 feet from the gate.

If you're on the right trail, within less than 0.1 mile you'll come to a pair of fords over a frothing stream. In most conditions, you can keep your feet dry with the aid of big

boulders and a little gymnastic ability. If the water is running high, as is common during the spring, or if you don't fancy the big, contorted steps it takes to get from one rock to the other, you may need to scout for a safer crossing spot or do a different hike, such as Lane Hut (see Hike 10).

Until 0.5 mile the trail is relatively easy, gaining a modest 100 feet until you reach a quiet, pooling stream with an enormous flat rock jutting into it. The trail fades into a reasonably level boulder field here; pick your way through the boulders and rejoin the trail on the other side.

Enjoy another stretch of relatively easy walking until 0.6 mile, with one more muddy stream crossing that can be cleared with a couple of agile hops, until you reach another flat, table-shaped rock to your left—this one situated in the middle of its pond. You'll

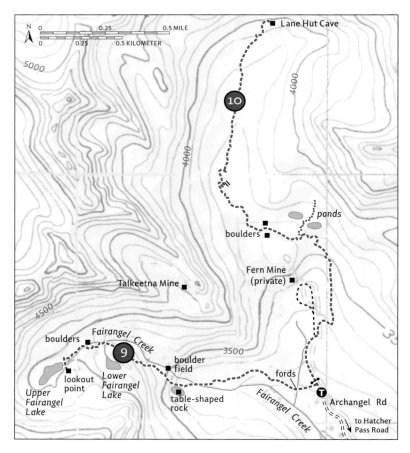

make one more easy crossing of a shallow stream; depending on water levels, you may be able to hop rocks across.

Next comes a steep, muddy scramble, traveling to the left of a boulder field. Some hikers like using trekking poles or spiky ice grippers for extra control on this type of slope, but I prefer keeping my hands free to use as extra points of contact.

Just before 0.8 mile the walking gets noticeably easier as you stroll atop a furrow of land that leads into an alpine meadow. Look for the pink plumes of Sitka burnet all around you, and beautiful valley views behind you.

At 1 mile, look to your left to see Lower Fairangel Lake just below you; it usually contains a perfect reflection of the sky. But don't stop yet: the trail continues more or less straight ahead past the lake, leading up and to the left of boulders that spill from an elevated bowl. Stay left as you hike up past the boulders, and look for the clear trail cutting the hillside above you.

At 1.2 miles the trail curves to the left, revealing Upper Fairangel Lake to your right. This lake is shaped like a narrow teardrop—almost a lollipop—so although what's left of the trail peters into nothing here, it's worth continuing another few hundred feet to the left and then scrambling about 100 feet to a high tundra lookout point for a better view of both lakes at once.

10 Lane Hut

RATING/ DIFFICULTY	ROUNDTRIP	ELEV GAIN/ HIGH POINT	SEASON
***/2	4.2 miles	910 feet/ 3870 feet	July– September

Maps: USGS Anchorage D6 SW, USGS Anchorage D7 NW; **Contact:** Alaska State Parks, Hatcher Pass Management Area; **Notes:** No parking fee. Unmarked trailhead. Approach road is extremely rough. Gate to Archangel Road is usually open July through September, sometimes into October if weather allows. Dogs permitted on leash at trailhead, under direct control on trail. Bear habitat; **GPS:** 61.81890°, –149.24030°

 A wildly popular trek, this trail follows an old road that once led to a backcountry hut. The hut has been removed, but you can still enjoy this easy, mostly flat stroll through the alpine tundra of Hatcher Pass. The trail can be a little muddy and boggy in spots, so consider wearing waterproof boots.

GETTING THERE
From Wasilla, take Trunk Road north. Continue straight through all the roundabouts until the road ends in a T intersection. Turn left at the T; this becomes Hatcher Pass Road. At about mile 14.4 of Hatcher Pass Road, make a sharp right turn onto unpaved Archangel Road. The hike starts at the end of the road, 4 miles in, but the road is extraordinarily rough beyond mile 2.4. SUVs and Subarus with good clearance can usually make it if carefully driven; vehicles with low clearance can be parked in a wide gravel pullout on the left at mile 2.1 of Archangel Road, then walk or bike the remainder of Archangel Road.

ON THE TRAIL
If you weren't able to drive to the end of the road, you now have a pleasant 1.7-mile stroll or mountain bike ride from the last parking area on Archangel Road, the Reed Lakes Trailhead at mile 2.4, to the end of the road. The road gradually gains 650 feet of elevation along the way, stopping at a gate.

The unmarked Lane Hut Trail begins as a continuation of the old roadbed that was Archangel Road. Stay on said roadbed, steering clear of the private, well-marked Fern Mine, until 0.25 mile in. At this point, take the trail that bends to the right then makes another sharp jog to the left, leading you up into the mouth of the valley. You'll sometimes see adventurous rock climbers scaling the stern-faced granite slopes on either side of the valley.

Things start getting muddy just before 0.6 mile, where a creek briefly runs through the trail, although you can usually step across on small rocks. This is the first of a series of such "step-across" crossings—and

An unusual little waterfall along the way to the Lane Hut Cave

goop—that will crop up continuously along the trail.

At 0.7 mile you'll pass by a series of ponds to the right side of the trail; they remain your constant companions for the rest of the hike and are a lovely place to wade or rinse your feet on a hot summer day.

At 0.9 mile the trail forks. Go left, following a twin-track trail into the tundra. At 1 mile you'll cross a boulder field that stretches about a hundred feet, with a small stream trickling through the middle. The boulders are relatively small and easy to navigate—think on par with Eagle and Symphony lakes (see Hike 36)—as opposed to the car-size behemoths you'll encounter on the nearby Reed Lakes Trail (see Hike 7).

At 1.4 miles, you'll pass a short but exceedingly pretty waterfall that cascades down the face of an angled rock slab to the right of the trail. At 1.9 miles, you can start to barely pick out the unnatural colors of spray-painted graffiti on rocks near the head of the valley. This is all that's left of the Lane Hut, which was removed because it attracted too many partiers and vandals. You'll cover almost 100 feet of elevation gain in the remaining 0.2 mile of trail, which gets you right up to the "Lane Hut Cave," a series of crevices in the boulders that once backed the hut.

11 Marmot Mountain

RATING/ DIFFICULTY	ROUNDTRIP	ELEV GAIN/ HIGH POINT	SEASON
***/4	3.2 miles	2170 feet/ 4690 feet	May–Oct

Map: USGS Anchorage D7 SE; **Contact:** Alaska State Parks, Mat-Su Region; **Notes:** Alaska State Parks pass or parking fee. Dogs permitted on leash in parking lot, under direct control on trail. Bear and moose habitat. Popular for berry picking and paragliding in summer. Popular for skiing, sledding, and snowmachining in the winter. Bring hiking poles for the descent; **GPS:** 61.76703°, –149.26549°

This short, challenging hike unlocks sweeping views over almost every peak in Hatcher Pass. Although the first part of the trail is well traveled, you probably won't see many people on the summit.

GETTING THERE

From Wasilla, take Trunk Road north for about 6 miles. Continue straight through all the roundabouts until the road ends in a T intersection. Turn left at the T; this becomes Hatcher Pass Road. Park at the Fishhook Trailhead (elevation 2700 feet), which will be on your right at mile 16.5 of Hatcher Pass Road.

ON THE TRAIL

You can't miss the well-worn trail that starts just behind the brown wooden trail kiosk, although the peak you can see from the trailhead is not Marmot Mountain: it's Fish Peak, the first of two false summits on your way to the top of Marmot. The first 0.1 mile of trail through short, wiry willows is a gimme, but

A view well earned: surveying the mountains of Hatcher Pass from atop Marmot Mountain

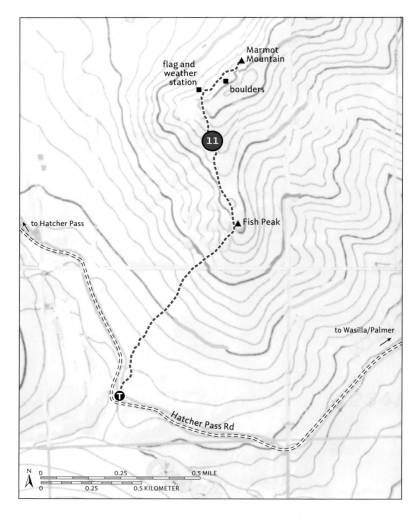

after that it's time to sweat for your views, gaining 1300 feet on a steep, eroded mix of loose dirt and rock until you reach Fish Peak (elevation 4020 feet) just past 0.8 mile.

This is a popular launching point for paragliders; on busy summer days there may be up to a dozen of them soaring and swooping in the sky. Even without taking to the sky, the views are amazing. If you turn around and look out from the mountain at any point on the way to Fish Peak, Hatcher Pass itself is clearly visible just to your right, a road-clad furrow in the mountains with Hatch Peak (see Hike 3) on its left side and Skyscraper Peak (see Hike 4) on the right. Once you gain the summit ridge, you'll have bird's-eye views down into Independence Mine State Historical Park too.

From Fish Peak, stroll along an easy ridge-line on a clear footpath. At 1 mile the trail starts climbing again, and at 1.4 miles you'll reach the second false summit (elevation 4585 feet), which is marked by an American flag, a tripod weather station, and the satis-faction of knowing the hard part of the hike is behind you.

You have only another 100 feet or so of elevation to gain in the final 0.2 mile to the peak of Marmot Mountain (elevation 4690 feet). This peak isn't always marked correctly on maps, but it's the obvious high point. The trail to it is a clear, easy-to-follow footpath, although you'll need to pick your way over a few small stretches of boulders to get there. If you reach a steep downhill stretch with nothing but boulders in front of you, and beyond them an unusually rocky zigzag ridge, you've arrived.

12 Gold Mint

RATING/ DIFFICULTY	ROUNDTRIP	ELEV GAIN/ HIGH POINT	SEASON
*****/4	16.6 miles	2530 feet/ 4040 feet	June–Sep

Map: USGS Anchorage D6 SW; **Contact:** Alaska State Parks, Mat-Su Region; **Notes:** Alaska State Parks Pass or parking fee. Park-ing lot shared by snowmachiners traveling

toward Hatcher Pass during winter. Popular for cross-country and backcountry skiing. Dogs permitted on leash at trailhead, under direct control in backcountry. Bear and moose habitat; **GPS:** 61.77917°, –149.19588°

 Gold Mint gains almost all of its elevation at the very end, in a steep push toward the Mountaineering Club of Alaska's iconic red hut. Until then, it's a shockingly beautiful walk along a brushy, flower-filled valley floor toward the head-waters of the Little Susitna River.

GETTING THERE

From Wasilla, take Trunk Road north for about 6 miles. Continue straight through all the roundabouts until the road ends in a T intersection. Turn left at the T; this becomes Hatcher Pass Road. At mile 13.7 of Hatcher Pass Road, the trailhead (elevation 1810 feet) will be on your right.

ON THE TRAIL

The first mile of this trail is a pleasant, level walk along a narrow old roadbed, tracing one of Southcentral's prettiest rivers—the Little Susitna—toward its source. You're sur-rounded by dense growth of alders, willows, and the occasional cottonwood tree, and wildflowers that grow almost as thick as the brush: look for monkshood, fireweed, wild geraniums, false hellebore, the brush-like Sitka burnet, and even the erect white flow-ers of devil's club and cow parsnip—both of which are very unpleasant if touched.

In the absence of other landmarks, mile markers on posts make it easy to gauge your progress along the trail. At 1.1 miles (elevation 1975 feet) the trail narrows and the brush closes in, but it doesn't get really bad until about mile 2 (elevation 2200 feet),

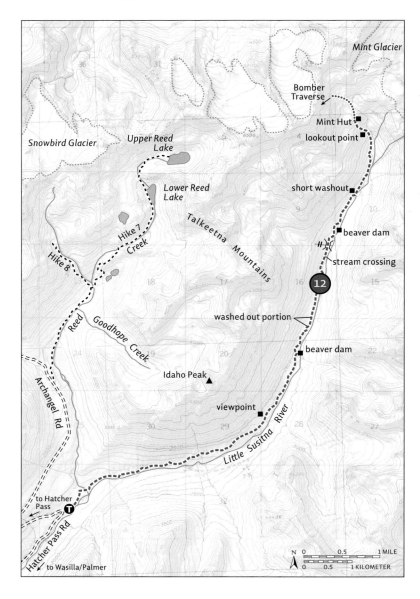

when there's barely room for one person to walk through the corridor between branches.

The Little Susitna River makes a stunning, picture-worthy companion that's in close view for most of the walk, but at 3.25 miles (elevation 2340 feet) you'll have a particularly lovely viewpoint over a bend in the river as it winds along the valley floor against a dramatic downvalley backdrop. Because you're so close to the water, you'll periodically have to step over small streams that come down to feed the river, and some stretches of trail can be muddy.

Just before mile 4.4 (elevation 2440 feet) look for a beaver dam right beside the trail. These busy animal architects are forever engineering their surroundings, and they're probably part of the reason the trail is washed out between 4.9 and 5 miles in. You can still pass through here, but, depending on water levels, you may have to do some shallow wading, and beware the copious amounts of devil's club and cow parsnip.

Stick to the most-traveled path (which heads to the left of the washed-out area, leaving the river behind for a little while) and don't fret about not seeing the 5-mile marker, which is lost in the washed-out portion. From here on out, you can look forward to sporadic patches of wet, muddy trail, although they're generally easy to get around.

At 5.3 miles (elevation 2550 feet) the brush reaches epic, head-high levels, but opens up again at mile 5.6 for great lookouts up and down the valley. By now you've made enough progress that, on anything but a sunny weekend day, it's easy to feel like you're alone in the remote wilderness.

At 6.1 miles (elevation 2690 feet) there's a large enough stream crossing that, when it runs high, you might have to wade through. At 6.2 miles (elevation 2700 feet) you'll cross a bridged stream with a pretty waterfall on the left and, shortly after, another beaver dam. You should always filter water in the Alaska backcountry, but the silty water of the Little Susitna will clog a filter quickly, and as for the beaver dams—well, there's a reason that *Giardia* is called "beaver fever." So try to get your water from clear, running tributaries such as this waterfall, and make sure you filter it, no matter how clean the water looks.

At 6.3 miles, the ferns, willows, and fireweed are so thick that you can barely see the trail. But keep going, because at 6.5 miles (elevation 2780 feet), after scrambling through a short stretch of large boulders, you'll get breathtaking views of the river and more waterfalls cascading down the valley wall.

From here the trail is generally wet and eroded until it veers away from the river again at 6.9 miles, followed by more boulder hopping and another short washout. At 7.6 miles (elevation 3160 feet) you'll burst into the open again, with views of waterfalls cascading down the far side of the valley.

This is where the trail makes up for having been so flat for so long and starts gaining elevation in earnest, pushing almost straight up the valley wall to the left. The trail is rocky, steep, and often muddy too, but at 8.1 miles (elevation 3630 feet) you get a wonderful, commanding lookout point over the valley.

From here, the trail gets so rocky that it's a half-scramble, and the trail comes and goes in the boulders; look for occasional cairns to help keep you on track. At 8.3 miles (elevation 4040 feet) you'll see the bright

The Little Susitna River flows alongside much of the Gold Mint trail.

red Mint Hut on your right, one of the more iconic of Alaska's backcountry photo ops. The hut marks the end of the Gold Mint Trail, and is maintained by the Mountaineering Club of Alaska and reserved for use by its members (memberships are extremely inexpensive; see mtnclubak.org).

If you want views of the Mint Glacier to the northeast, keep scrambling for another 0.6 mile and 700 feet of elevation gain. Some people use this as the start of the so-called Bomber Traverse, a circuit that links the Gold Mint hike to the Reed Lakes Trail (see Hike 7), going past the remains of a bomber that crashed in 1957.

The Bomber Traverse includes glacier travel, so only go if you're experienced in routefinding and managing the hazards presented by glacier travel, technical terrain, and loose rock. The Mountaineering Club of Alaska is a good place to start gathering route information.

13 Government Peak

Government Peak

RATING/ DIFFICULTY	ROUNDTRIP	ELEV GAIN/ HIGH POINT	SEASON
*****/5	6.5 miles	3800 feet/ 4781 feet	June–Oct

Blueberry Knoll

RATING/ DIFFICULTY	ROUNDTRIP	ELEV GAIN/ HIGH POINT	SEASON
****/4	3.2 miles	1450 feet/ 2550 feet	June–Oct

Map: USGS Anchorage C7 NE; **Contact:** Matanuska-Susitna Borough; **Notes:** Mat-Su Borough parking pass or parking fee. Access gate is open from 8:00 PM to 10:00 PM. This

complex becomes a dedicated ski area in winter. Main hiking trail is not open to mountain bikes or horses, but there are dedicated single-track and equestrian trails in the complex. Dogs must be on leash. Bear and moose habitat. Avalanche hazard in winter; **GPS:** 61.70550°, –149.27791°

On one of the most iconic peaks in the Mat-Su Valley, a surprisingly doable combination of steep trail and even steeper tundra scrambling leads you to commanding views over Knik Arm, the Knik Glacier, and the Talkeetna Mountains.

GETTING THERE
From Wasilla, take Trunk Road north for about 6 miles. Continue straight through all the roundabouts until the road ends in a T intersection. Turn left at the T; this becomes Hatcher Pass Road. At mile 7 of Hatcher Pass Road, turn left onto Edgerton Parks Road. After 1 mile, turn right on Mountain Trails Drive, which leads you straight into the large parking area for Government Peak Recreation Area (elevation 1030 feet).

ON THE TRAIL
The Government Peak Recreation Area is a wonderful, sometimes confusing web of ski trails, hiking trails, and single-track bike trails. When you first drive into the parking lot, look for the large, wooden sign on your right. This marks the best place for hikers to enter the trail network.

Once you step onto the trails, you'll spot another sign marking the start of the Blueberry Knoll Trail. Blueberry Knoll is a fine destination in its own right, and also the start of the most civilized route up to Government Peak. (Your other option is the Government Peak race trail, the sort of fiendishly steep and treacherous uphill slog that's par for the course during mountain races in Alaska. Unless you're comfortable in steep, loose technical terrain, stick to the hiking trail.)

Stay on this narrow footpath as it crosses the wide ski trails and, at roughly 0.1 mile, hangs a sharp right. This section of trail tends to be muddy, but a lot of hard work has gone into making it walkable. By 0.5 mile the trail has settled into a nice wide footpath.

Just before 1 mile (elevation 1640 feet) the trail angle steepens, and tree roots—always ready to stub an unwary toe—get more prominent.

Just after the 1-mile mark the spruce and birch trees start giving way to grass, which can get thick enough that it's easy to walk right past the signed "Government Peak" Trail to the left, at 1.25 miles (elevation 2125 feet). This trail devolves into an over-grown scramble that turns disappointed hikers back, so keep going uphill instead,

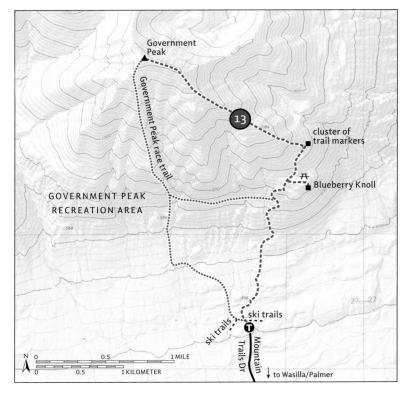

This is the sign that steers you to the summit.

watching for slick spots in the steep, muddy trail.

By 1.4 miles (elevation 2390 feet) you'll reach beautiful lookouts over the valley below, but the views get even better if you keep going just another 400 yards, turning right at the signed intersection to reach Blueberry Knoll (elevation 2550 feet), an obvious protuberance with a picnic table. This is the perfect destination for adventurous families or anyone who wants to drink in views of the valley below.

If you'd like to go all the way up Government Peak, go back to the intersection where you turned off for Blueberry Knoll and turn north to continue uphill through the bushes, gaining the toe of an obvious ridge at 1.8 miles (elevation 2730 feet). As you exit the bushes onto the tundra ridge, you'll see a small cluster of trail markers.

The defined trail ends here, but the rest of the hike is straightforward. Turn left and clamber straight up the ridgeline, using scattered, reflective trail markers as your guides. The trail fades in and out, so stick to the trail when you can see it and, when you can't, walk on the more durable surfaces (e.g., rocks) available to you.

There will be no shortage of said rocks as you continue another 1.5 miles to the mountain's rocky, 4781-foot peak, where you'll enjoy the fruits of your labors: vast, sweeping views of Knik Arm, the Knik Glacier and its floodplains, and the corrugated ridges of the Talkeetna Mountains rolling into the distance behind you.

At times the trail is so steep, you can reach out and touch it without bending over—and with no established trail, it's up to you to choose the easiest route as you wind up the ridgeline. Be kind to the tundra by sticking to fragments of worn trail whenever you see them; eventually, these will consolidate into a so-called social trail all the way to the peak.

Also, leave yourself plenty of time for a safe descent. The grass and tundra can be very slippery when wet, so I have absolutely no qualms about butt-scooting or crab-walking down this terrain as needed. Safety first; dignity later.

Opposite: *The trails closest to Wasilla may be chill, but they're no less beautiful for that laid-back nature. Here, sun, sky, and clouds reflect off the ever-changing waters of Reflections Lake (Hike 18).*

wasilla area

With the exception of Hatcher Pass, most of the trails around the Matanuska-Susitna Valley town of Wasilla (population about 10,000) tend toward the short, flat, and easy side of things, so they make for great family outings or rambling afternoon explorations. Several of these trails access the Palmer Hay Flats State Game Refuge, a sprawling, 28,000-acre area of grassy wetlands that create some truly unusual, almost pastoral scenery for Alaska.

14 Red Shirt Lake

RATING/ DIFFICULTY	ROUNDTRIP	ELEV GAIN/ HIGH POINT	SEASON
***/3	5.6 miles	750 feet/ 320 feet	May–Oct

Map: USGS Tyonek C1 NE; **Contact:** Alaska State Parks, Mat-Su Region; **Notes:** Alaska State Parks pass or parking fee. During the winter, vehicle access is restricted to mile 2.2 of Nancy Lake Parkway. Popular for cross-country skiing, snowshoeing, snow-machining, and dog mushing in the winter. Dogs permitted on leash at trailhead, under direct control in backcountry. Bear and moose habitat. Pike fishing in the lake. Canoe rentals available by prearrangement; contact Tippecanoe Rentals in Willow; **GPS:** 61.66711°, −150.14142°

 *Ramble through rolling terrain in a forest of spruce, birch, and aspen trees, all jumbled together with berry bushes and wildflowers. This is a great family hike or afternoon stroll to the grassy lakeshore, where you can pick up a prearranged canoe rental.*

GETTING THERE

From Wasilla, drive northwest on the Parks Highway for about 25 miles. There are, confusingly, two left turns off the highway marked for Nancy Lake. Take the second, which is also signed for South Rolly Lake Campground, at mile 67.3 of the highway. Continue on Nancy Lake Parkway for about 6.5 miles, where it ends at South Rolly Lake Campground and the Red Shirt Lake Trailhead (elevation 250 feet). In winter, road access is limited to the winter trailhead at mile 2.2 of Nancy Lake Parkway.

ON THE TRAIL

There's a lot to enjoy here in the forest: the rolling terrain is easy for the entire family, and the rich jumble of black and white spruce trees, peeling birch, and slim aspens is home to many birds. Bring a plant book if you want to pick your way through the understory, which is a jumble of devil's club, horsetail, and fiddlehead ferns, plus a lot of flowers, including fireweed, wild roses, violets, and bluebells, and a variety of wild berries starting in late July.

From the trailhead, take the obvious, tree-lined trail to the west and, when it forks just before 0.1 mile, bear left. Just before 0.5 mile you'll hit the trail's high point—a whopping 320 feet—and at about 0.8 mile you might get a few peeks at small Arc Lake to the left of the trail. At 1.5 miles you have a pretty view of the two Twin Shirt Lakes to your left, set against a backdrop of wetlands and forested hills.

From here, the trail starts a rolling descent until at 2 miles (elevation 240 feet) you can catch glimpses of Red Shirt Lake ahead and to your left. Sometimes you'll hear

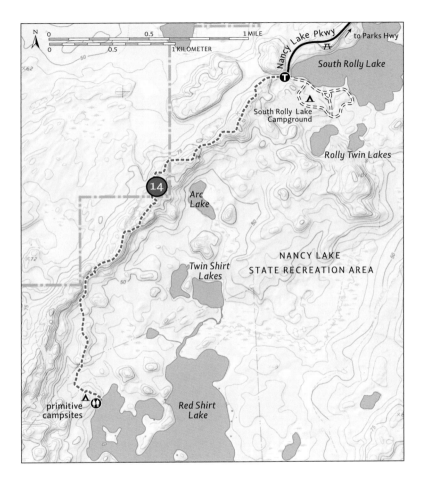

the strange, lonely laugh of loons calling from the water. Both black-headed common loons and gray-headed Pacific loons are known to nest here, and Arctic terns are common here as well.

At 2.2 miles you'll start to encounter some muddy patches in the otherwise firm, easy dirt trail; sporadic boardwalks help you keep your feet dry. This mud and all the water nearby make a great breeding ground for

A hiker surveys Red Shirt Lake, the terminus of this trail.

mosquitoes. Bring your insect repellent or hike on a windy day, when the breeze will help keep the bugs off—although not much of it penetrates through the trees.

At 2.6 miles (elevation 140 feet) the trail seems to bottom out, but you actually have to crest one more small rise before arriving at the grassy lakeshore, 2.8 miles from the trailhead. There are primitive backcountry campsites and an outhouse at the lake. There are also canoes for rent, but you must arrange the rental in advance by calling Tippecanoe Rentals in Willow.

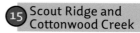

15 Scout Ridge and Cottonwood Creek

Scout Ridge Loop

RATING/ DIFFICULTY	LOOP	ELEV GAIN/ HIGH POINT	SEASON
***/2	1.2 miles	180 feet/ 160 feet	Year-round

Wetlands Out-and-Back

RATING/ DIFFICULTY	ROUNDTRIP	ELEV GAIN/ HIGH POINT	SEASON
**/2	1.4 miles	15 feet/ 40 feet	Year-round

Maps: USGS Anchorage B7 NW, USGS Anchorage C7 SW; **Contact:** Alaska Department of Fish and Game, Palmer office; **Notes:** Wetlands Out-and-Back Trail is open to ATV use. Scout Ridge viewing deck is handicap accessible. Dogs must be on leash. Rubber boots or hip waders are a must on the Wetlands Out-and-Back Trail. Beware of tidal fluctuations in the creek and mud; do not travel on barren mud. Moose and bear habitat. Popular spot for birding during spring migration and waterfowl hunting in fall. The lower 1 mile of Cottonwood Creek is open to weekend salmon fishing (primarily sockeye) from mid-June onward; check Alaska Department of Fish and Game for

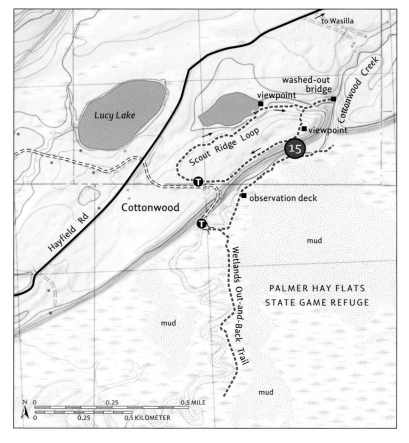

latest regulations; **GPS:** Upper trailhead: 61.51305°, −149.55856°; lower trailhead: 61.51098°, −149.55839°

 *Enjoy a pleasant stroll along a modest wooded ridge or, if you've brought your rubber boots, a gleeful romp through the mud puddles along a wetland trail. The wetlands portions are especially great for kids, but be aware of tidal fluctuations and stay off the barren mud.*

GETTING THERE

From the Glenn/Parks Highway interchange, travel about 2 miles west on the Parks Highway. Take the Hyer Road/Fairview Loop exit and turn left onto East Fairview Loop Road. Stay on this road, which winds outrageously and becomes West Fairview Loop. After about 9.4 miles, make a sharp left onto Hayfield Road and follow the brown signs for Palmer Hay Flats parking. The Scout Ridge Loop starts from this upper parking lot. If you continue past this lot and down a sizable hill on a one-lane dirt road, you'll reach the lower parking lot and the start of the Wetlands Out-and-Back Trail.

ON THE TRAIL

You have two hiking trails to choose from in this little corner of the Palmer Hay Flats State Game Refuge. The 1.2-mile Scout Ridge Loop starts and ends from the upper trailhead; look for a small footpath and small brown "trail" sign on the left as you enter the lot. This leads to an old, forested ATV trail.

Continue following small brown "trail" signs. Just before 0.1 mile you'll take a right fork in the road; just before 0.3 mile you'll get peeks of a pretty, unnamed lake on the left side through the trees, and at 0.4 mile there's a nice lookout over the lake.

At 0.6 mile the trail forks. Straight ahead the trail dead-ends at the remains of a washed-out bridge over rushing Cottonwood Creek. Instead, turn right (look for the small brown "trail" sign) and climb a short, steep hill to gain Scout Ridge. The next 0.4 mile of this walk is a narrow, root-filled, but pleasant trail with views of the expansive hay flats through the trees. Look for plants such as wild roses, high-bush cranberries, and currants. This is also a good place to listen and watch for migratory waterfowl on the flats, including sandhill cranes.

At 1 mile you'll hit a lovely wheelchair-accessible observation deck overlooking the Palmer Hay Flats State Game Refuge below you. The remaining 0.2-mile walk back to the car is also wheelchair-accessible, depositing you at the opposite end of the parking lot from where you started.

The Wetlands Out-and-Back Trail starts from the lower trailhead, and you'll need tall rubber boots to negotiate it. After you cross the bridge, ignore a left fork and continue straight, following the trail grids and upright brown trail markers through numerous muddy puddles. This stretch of track is open to ATVs, but at 0.7 mile it passes a plastic fence that bars further ATV track; then the trail itself braids into soggy nothing.

During the winter, if conditions are just right, the flooded and frozen portions of the trail make for great ice skating. And on any day with good visibility, the expanse of the hay flats, framed by the wooded ridge on one side and craggy mountains on the other, forms a very pretty picture that's not at all what people usually imagine when they think of Alaska.

If you walk back to the lower trailhead (a 1.4-mile roundtrip), you can explore another

A hiker exploring the broad flatlands of the Palmer Hay Flats State Game Refuge.

section of this out-and-back trail. Turn right at the trail intersection just before the trailhead, or, if you're coming *from* the trailhead, turn left at the obvious intersection. This chunk of hardened trail meanders for 0.5 mile along the creek until it starts fading into the grass.

This trail parallels the edge of the creek and is a great place for kids to explore, but keep a close eye on them—the mud is slippery and sticky, and the water levels in the creek fluctuate enormously with the tide. In fact the entire flats can be subject to tidal flooding, so stay off areas of barren mud that can turn to treacherous quicksand as the water level rises. The tidal channels in this area are constantly shifting with the influx and departure of water.

Two final notes: This is a popular haunt for waterfowl hunters during the fall; if you hike during duck hunting season, wear an obnoxiously bright "I'm not a duck, don't shoot me!" hat or vest. Finally, the state has plans for some fairly major trail upgrades here in the next few years, but the trail's general orientation should remain the same.

16 Long Lake Loop

RATING/ DIFFICULTY	LOOP	ELEV GAIN/ HIGH POINT	SEASON
***/2	5.7 miles	840 feet/ 240 feet	Year-round

Maps: USGS Anchorage C6 SW and USGS Anchorage C6 NW, but the trails are too new

Flat doesn't mean boring; check out the views on a fall day at the University of Alaska Fairbanks Experimental Farm.

to be on these maps. Matanuska-greenbelt .org has the most useful (and up-to-date) trail maps. **Contact:** Matanuska-Susitna Borough; **Notes:** Most, but not all, trails open to mountain bikes and horses once trails have hardened in spring. Dogs must be on leash. Moose sightings are frequent, bear sightings less common but possible; **GPS:** 61.56640°, −149.25162°

This easy out-and-back hike from the University of Alaska Fairbanks Experimental Farm Trailhead showcases the easy walking and interesting landscapes that characterize the Matanuska Greenbelt.

GETTING THERE

From the Parks/Glenn Highway interchange, drive northwest on the Parks Highway for less than a mile. Exit for Trunk Road and turn right (north). After just 0.3 mile, turn right onto Georgeson Road. Make a quick left turn onto East Cottrell-Campus Drive, then right onto South Trunk Road. Look for a small gravel parking area and trailhead sign on the left of the road (elevation 190 feet) just before you would drive into the farm complex proper.

ON THE TRAIL

The Matanuska Experiment Farm & Extension Center (aka the University of Alaska

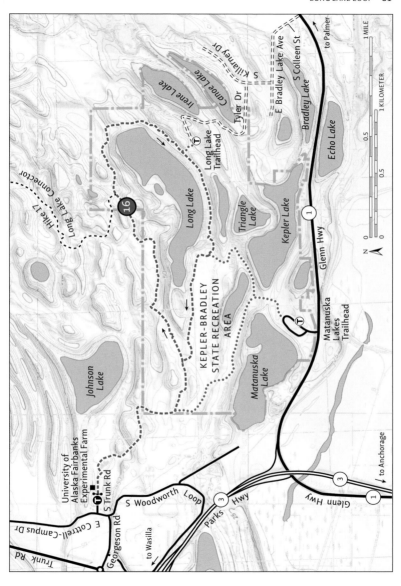

Fairbanks Experimental Farm) is one of four cooperative landowners that, together, have created more than 30 miles of trails in this greenbelt area. Be aware that although the trails are generally in wonderful condition, they're not specifically maintained for public use; you're there by the grace of the farm, so please yield to farm equipment and operations, stay off the fields, keep your dog on a leash, and clean up after your pet.

Park in the small gravel lot reserved for hikers, then follow the main road (on foot) into the farm complex and through a gate that has a pedestrian walkaround to the right. When the road forks, you can go either straight or left. Whichever way you go, once on the far side of the buildings you'll arrive at your first signed intersection, already 0.3 mile from the trailhead. Turn right for an easy stroll along a wide road that passes between the farm's fields.

At 0.7 mile turn right and go up a short, 50-foot hill, then continue straight until you reach a sign advertising the Long Lake Connector to the left. Make that left turn then, at about 1.1 miles, continue straight ahead—again, following signs for the Long Lake Connector. Keep following the same signs with a right turn at 1.5 miles, which puts you on a narrow footpath along an interesting little ridge to the north side of Long Lake, then make another right turn just shy of 2 miles.

Just past 2.2 miles you'll pass the actual Long Lake Connector trail, which veers off into the trees on the left and is part of Hike 17. But for now your mission is to continue straight ahead, veering right at signed intersections when possible, to finish your loop around the lake, passing by first the Long Lake Trailhead, then the Matanuska Lakes

trailhead, before following signs to retrace your steps to the UAF Experimental Farm Trailhead—a total loop of 5.7 miles, with only 840 feet of elevation gain along its entire distance.

17 Crevasse Moraine to Long Lake

RATING/ DIFFICULTY	ONE-WAY	ELEV GAIN/ HIGH POINT	SEASON
***/2	3.7 miles	535 feet/ 275 feet	Year-round

Maps: USGS Anchorage C6 SW and USGS Anchorage C6 NW, but the trails are too new to be on these maps. The most useful (and up-to-date) trail maps are available at matanuska-greenbelt.org; **Contact:** Matanuska-Susitna Borough; **Notes:** Mat-Su Borough parking pass or parking fee at Crevasse Moraine Trailhead. Many, but not all, trails are open to mountain bikes and horses once trails have hardened in spring. Dogs must be on leash. Moose sightings frequent, bear sightings less common but possible; **GPS:** Crevasse Moraine Trailhead: 61.59187°, –149.19326°; Long Lake Trailhead: 61.55986°, –149.19922°

  Another one of my favorite trails in the Matanuska Greenbelt—because how often can you pull off a forested, 3.7-mile traverse in an "urban" setting? An optional extension to the Matanuska Lakes Trailhead makes it just under 5 miles total, or do it as an out-and-back stroll.

GETTING THERE
Crevasse Moraine Trailhead: From the Parks/ Glenn Highway interchange, drive northwest

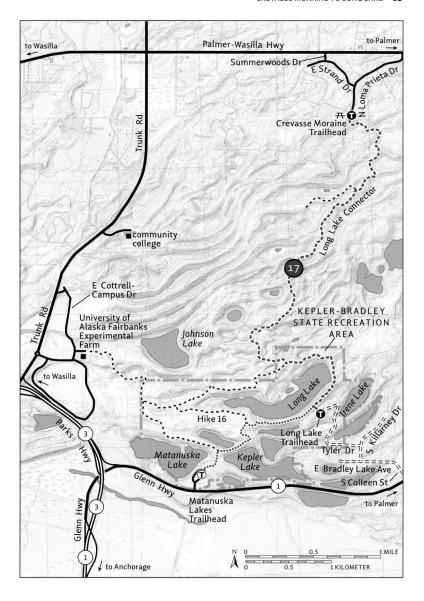

Sterling signage is the key to navigating the web of trails in the Matanuska Greenbelt.

on the Parks Highway. Exit for Trunk Road and turn right. Continue on Trunk Road for about 3 miles until it intersects the Palmer-Wasilla Highway. Turn right here and continue for just over 1 mile. Then turn right again onto the neighborhood street Summerwoods Drive, left onto East Strand Drive, and right onto North Loma Prieta Drive, which ends at the Crevasse Moraine Trailhead (elevation 300 feet).

Long Lake Trailhead: From the Parks/ Glenn Highway interchange, drive east on the Glenn Highway for about 3.5 miles, then turn left onto South Colleen Street. Make a series of quick turns: left onto East Bradley Lake Avenue, then right onto South Killarney Drive, and left onto Tyler Drive. The trailhead (elevation 160 feet) is at the end of Tyler Drive. The rough gravel roads here can be hard on low-clearance vehicles.

ON THE TRAIL

Aside from their pleasant setting, one of the best things about these greenbelt trails is the hundreds of directional signs placed by the four cooperative land agencies that, together, own and maintain the heavily forested greenbelt trails. As long as you pay attention to the signs and have a rough idea of your destination, it's hard to get lost. That said, on your first few visits it pays to check the Matanuska Greenbelt Trails website and download or print one of the trail maps to help you stay oriented.

Because of all that signage, hiking this trail from the Long Lake Trailhead is very straightforward: turn right at the first intersection, then continue on part of the Long Lake Loop (see Hike 16) around the east side of the lake until you reach the Long Lake Connector at 1 mile. From there, it's a

2.7-mile traverse to the Crevasse Moraine Trailhead, with plenty of directional signs to guide you through the interlocking loops of trails at Crevasse Moraine.

Now, if you start from the Crevasse Moraine Trailhead: this park houses so many interlocking loops of trails that getting on the right trail can be a challenge. But once you *are* on the right trail, the excellent signage makes the rest of your journey straightforward.

From the first parking lot, go through the gate and take the obvious, wide road down to a second parking area. Look for blue metal fencing and a covered picnic shelter on your left. Walk through a gap in the fencing and past the picnic shelter, then look to your right for a directional signpost that points the way to the Long Lake Connector. From there, all you have to do is follow the signs for the Long Lake Connector. At 2.7 miles from the Crevasse Moraine Trailhead, you'll reach Long Lake itself; turn left and follow the trail around the lake until you reach the trailhead of your choice.

Alternate Route

You can also start this hike from the Matanuska Lakes Trailhead, located just north of mile 36.4 off the Glenn Highway, making this a 5-mile traverse. The turns are just a little more complicated—but again, excellent signage makes it easy to find your way. From the trailhead, turn left at the first intersection, then right, then left again, followed by another right, following signs for the Long Lake Trailhead. Once you pass the trailhead turnoff, follow the Long Lake Loop Trail around the east side of the lake until you intersect the Long Lake Connector.

One word about the Matanuska Lakes Trailhead: although a 5-mile traverse is more worthy of the effort it takes to set up a car shuttle, this trailhead is run by a private contractor, and as I write there's an ongoing question of whether the trailhead will be open during the winter, and rumors are that the access fees might skyrocket. So, it never hurts to check online before you go. Keep in mind that if you want extra miles without a car shuttle, you can easily make this an out-and-back from any of the other trailheads mentioned, or explore to create your own loops on the greenbelt trails.

18 Reflections Lake

RATING/ DIFFICULTY	LOOP	ELEV GAIN/ HIGH POINT	SEASON
***/1	1.2 miles	20 feet/ 40 feet	Year-round

Map: USGS Anchorage B7 NE; **Contact:** Alaska Department of Fish and Game, Palmer office; **Notes:** Open year-round. Restrooms and picnic shelter near trailhead. Lakeside loop is handicap accessible. Dogs must be on leash. Occasional waterfowl hunting during the fall. Bear and moose habitat. Wetland flats tidally affected; do not walk on barren mud; **GPS:** 61.48699°, –149.24846°

 On calm days this little lake lives up to its name, reflecting the mountain vistas around it. This short walk is perfect for families, with a wildlife-viewing tower and a side trip onto the flats where the Matanuska and Knik rivers come together—as long as you're mindful of the mud and tides.

GETTING THERE

From Anchorage, drive about 32 miles northeast on the Glenn Highway to the marked

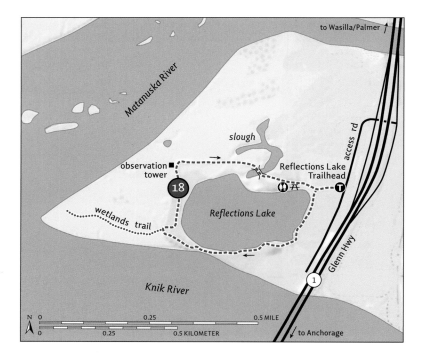

exit for the Knik River access. After exiting, turn left and drive under the highway, then follow the road as it bends to the left. The small trailhead is on your right, with space for four or five cars. Additional parking is sometimes available on the road shoulder and near the Knik River access at the end of the road, but be careful not to block the road or boat trailers.

ON THE TRAIL

Reflections Lake is what nature made of an empty construction gravel pit. Now it's the perfect place for a family stroll, a naturalist outing onto the tidally affected hay flats, or watching for birds and wildlife from the lakeside trail and observation tower.

From the trailhead, make an immediate left turn onto a boardwalk that leads around the lake. The boardwalk quickly gives way to a hardened dirt trail that's broad enough for a couple of people to walk comfortably side by side. The broad, strong flow of water on your left is the Knik River.

The entire trail is handicap accessible; at steep hills it splits and then rejoins, with one fork offering a wheelchair-friendly grade that sticks closer to the water, so you don't lose your views. Benches dotted sporadically along the trail make great places to sit and

Make sure you bring your binoculars, spotting scope, or zoom lens to the Reflections Lake observation tower.

take in views or watch for waterfowl, raptors, and songbirds near the lake.

At 0.4 mile from the trailhead, a small sign marks a turnoff to the left for the wetlands trail. A fairly well-established foot track leads out onto the flats, then peters out near the shores of the Matanuska River as it flows to meet the Knik, sometimes depositing weathered trees, stripped of their bark and turned to driftwood, on the flats.

Be aware that these flats are tidally affected, and Turnagain Arm has one of the steepest tidal differentials in the world. Don't travel on the mudflats that are barren of vegetation (near the rivers); they can turn to treacherous quicksand as the water table rises, and during high tides other portions of the flats can flood. It's also easy to lose the

trail as you approach the banks of the Matanuska River, so make sure to look behind you so you know where to reenter the trees on your way back.

If you do go on the flats—which is well worth it, as long as you mind the tides—watch for tiny, elegant orchids, the white plumes of cotton grass, and tracks in the mud from moose and, more occasionally, bears. You might even see the tiny wood frog, one of just two frog species that live in Alaska. This natural marvel survives winter by burying itself in the mud and freezing solid, then thawing out and going on about its business in the spring.

Back on the main trail, at 0.7 mile around the lake you'll reach a multilevel observation tower that offers sweeping views over the hay flats, the convergence of the two rivers, and of course Reflections Lake. If you've brought your binoculars, this is the perfect place for spotting birds and wildlife.

At 0.8 mile you'll pass along the edge of a tranquil slough that, if it freezes solid, makes for decent ice skating. A short footbridge crosses the slough, taking you to a finger of land that juts into the lake from the trailhead. Turn left to follow that little spit back to the trailhead, passing a picnic shelter and a pair of pit toilets along the way.

Opposite: *The trails around Palmer tend toward the dramatic. Even diminutive, 850-foot-high Bodenburg Butte (Hike 22) can put on quite a show.*

palmer area

Like Wasilla, Palmer (population about 7000) sits in the Matanuska-Susitna Valley, but its hikes tend to head straight for the sky, with a couple of the toughest (and most rewarding) mountain trails in Southcentral. But you'll find mellow trails here too, including the much-beloved Bodenburg Butte and a lesser-known, rambling trail that takes you along the banks of the ever-shifting Matanuska River. (In fact, that's the first trail in this section.)

19 Palmer–Moose Creek

RATING/ DIFFICULTY	ONE-WAY	ELEV GAIN/ HIGH POINT	SEASON
***/3	6.9 miles	355 feet/ 420 feet	Year-round

Maps: USGS Anchorage C6 NW, USGS Anchorage C6 NE; **Contact:** Matanuska-Susitna Borough; **Notes:** Extremely limited parking at Palmer Trailhead. Pit toilet available at Moose Creek Trailhead. Open to mountain bikes and horses during summer. Snowshoeing, cross-country skiing, and skijoring in winter. Dogs permitted on leash. Bear and moose habitat. Watch for falling rocks, especially after rain; **GPS:** Palmer Trailhead: 61.61401°, –149.10711°; Moose Creek Trailhead: 61.68177°, –149.04986°

Alaskans sometimes consider "flat" trails boring—but this walk along an old railway bed is anything but! On one side you have the mighty Matanuska River, which changes its channels on a whim. On the other is a steep bluff that sometimes drops landslides across the trail. As unlikely as it seems, the result is an utterly charming, interesting walk.

GETTING THERE
Palmer Trailhead: From Anchorage, drive 43 miles northeast on the Glenn Highway into Palmer. Shortly after crossing East Bogard Road, turn right onto East Eagle Avenue, a neighborhood street. Turn right onto North Valley Way, then look for the designated curbside parking area on your right. It's marked with a small sign and has space for only three or four cars. The trail starts behind a bright yellow concrete barrier on the far (north) side of East Eagle Avenue, between North Valley Way and North Denali Street.

Moose Creek Trailhead: From Anchorage, drive 50 miles northeast on the Glenn Highway, passing through Palmer, until you reach the Moose Creek Campground. The campground will be on your left, between miles 54 and 55 of the Glenn Highway.

ON THE TRAIL
Although you can do this hike as a long out-and-back, the description here is a thru-hike starting from the parking area in Moose Creek Campground. The trail starts in the trees on the opposite side of the Glenn Highway; be extremely careful when you cross the road. Although the starting point is not marked, the trail is easy to see, nestled in the U of the highway's sharp right turn.

Once you're on the trail—an easy, broad path through birch, spruce, and cottonwood trees—you'll see Moose Creek gurgling along to your left, and sporadic brown trail markers that show your distance from Palmer in feet (a mile is 5280 feet). At 0.5 mile you cross a washed-out scree slope. On this and the many other washouts you'll cross, look for where the trail resumes on the far side, then cross carefully. Hiking poles will be handy for some, but shoes or boots with

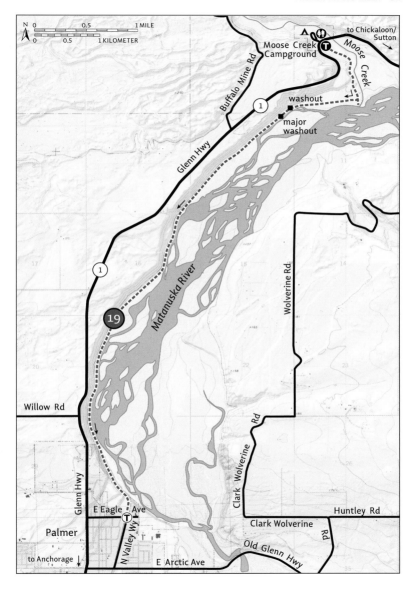

A hiker enjoys fresh air, fallen leaves, and the arrow-straight corridor left by old railroad tracks.

aggressive traction are even more important on this sort of terrain.

At about 0.8 mile you'll see a grid of upright wooden posts on your right: old pilings left over from a railroad bridge. The trail forks here. Take the right fork, which makes a hard bend around the bridge pilings and peels off away from the creek. From this point on you'll see very few brown trail markers, but it's impossible to miss the arrow-straight, tree-lined trail that would only have been created by a railroad. Ignore periodic side trails and continue straight ahead.

At 1.5 miles the trail goes through a washout, followed closely by a much bigger washout. That second, major washout can be a little confusing when the trail unexpectedly dumps you onto a broad stretch of silty, rocky mud. Assuming the wash stays dry, walk along its base and look for the straight line of the trail cutting into the hillside above you. Then either retrace your route onto the hillside and find your way through the trees, or find a slope you don't mind scrambling up to get back to the trail.

At 1.75 miles the trail starts following the north bank of the glacier-fed Matanuska River, offering gorgeous views up and down the broad river valley. The rest of the trail remains a pretty, mostly level footpath through light forest, occasionally veering just a little too close to the crumbling riverbank. When this happens, stay inland and pick the trail back up when you can.

You'll also pass a number of rocky landslides, with rocks ranging from fist-size to as large as bowling balls. On my most recent visit, I counted seven landslides between miles 1.75 and 3.1, with another set between miles 5.3 and 5.5. The bluffs above the trail are at their most unstable after a rainfall,

so save this hike for a sunny day and, even then, keep one eye out for the possibility of falling rocks.

At 4 miles the trail starts to peel away from the riverbank, taking you on another stroll through the leafy forest, but returns to the river at mile 5. At 6.8 miles the trail curves decisively inland once more, emerging from behind a bright yellow concrete barrier that marks the Palmer trailhead.

20 Lazy Moose and Lazy Mountain

RATING/ DIFFICULTY	ROUNDTRIP	ELEV GAIN/ HIGH POINT	SEASON
****/4	8 miles	3100 feet/ 3640 feet	May–Oct

Map: USGS Anchorage C6 SE; **Contact:** Matanuska-Susitna Borough; **Notes:** Dogs permitted on leash. Bear and moose habitat; **GPS:** 61.61143°, –149.01631°

The Lazy Mountain Trail is a true rite of passage for Southcentral hikers, gaining 3000 feet of elevation in just 2.5 miles of steep, eroded trail. But it's crumbling under the onslaught of many feet. The Lazy Moose Trail gets you to the same place at a gentler incline, and skips the horrible erosion of the main trail.

GETTING THERE
From Palmer, drive east on the Old Glenn Highway for 2.5 miles. Turn left onto Clark-Wolverine Road. After 0.5 mile, turn right onto Huntley Road and follow it about 1 mile more to the end. The Lazy Mountain Trailhead (elevation 660 feet) will be on the right.

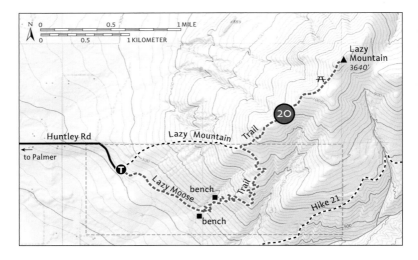

ON THE TRAIL

The trail splits immediately out of the trail-head, with the "old" Lazy Mountain Trail going straight up, while the Lazy Moose Trail cuts off to the right at an angle through a rough arch. The two trails rejoin farther up the mountain, so if you're in the mood to recontour your quads and calves, go ahead and head straight up the Lazy Mountain Trail from that first intersection. The two trails rejoin at about mile 1.1 on the Lazy Mountain Trail (elevation 2400 feet), which, all told, gains 3000 feet of elevation in just 2.5 miles (one way) on a very eroded trail.

But my preferred route is the gentler walk up the beautifully carved switchbacks of the Lazy Moose Trail, following a gentle incline that runs through a forest of cottonwood, aspen, spruce, and birch trees, all jumbled together with fireweed at their feet.

Following the Lazy Moose Trail, at about 0.8 mile (elevation 910 feet) you'll find a bench that looks out to the south,

showcasing the twin summits of Pioneer Peak on the far side of the Knik River. Then the trail starts switchbacking up the mountain. Please don't cut the switchbacks, or this will end up the same sort of eroded mess as the old trail, which is a victim of its own popularity and the ravages of water coursing down the path of least resistance—which happens to be the trail.

At 1.2 miles (elevation 1220 feet) there's a second bench with pretty views. Despite the continuing switchbacks, the trail climbs at a moderately stiff incline. By 2.3 miles you've reached almost 2000 feet in elevation, and the mix of grass and cottonwood trees is very reminiscent of the McHugh Creek section of the Turnagain Arm Trail (see Hike 53).

From here, the trail exits the treeline in favor of alpine tundra and bends left (west) through the brush, rejoining the old Lazy Mountain Trail at 2.9 miles (elevation 2400 feet). From this point, the remaining trail uphill is very steep and eroded, braiding

Walking the last rocky stretch toward the summit of Lazy Mountain

through rocky stretches and patches of tough brush.

There is no such thing as a bad viewpoint on this mountain—especially once you're above the treeline—but don't get too excited about the false peak you see at 3 miles (elevation 2700 feet). You'll know the true peak of Lazy Mountain because it has an American flag mounted on it.

Once you reach 3.6 miles (3270 feet) the trail levels out to a more civilized, albeit relatively barren, slope; small cairns help you find the right path on your way back down. At 3.8 miles (elevation 3360 feet) you'll pass a picnic table, and from there it's a last steep push—with just a touch of exposure and one or two scrambling moves—to the summit at 4 miles (elevation 3640 feet). Watch your footing on the way down.

21 Matanuska Peak

RATING/ DIFFICULTY	ROUNDTRIP	ELEV GAIN/ HIGH POINT	SEASON
*****/5	10.6 miles	5910 feet/ 6063 feet	June–Oct

Map: USGS Anchorage C6 SE; **Contact:** Alaska State Parks, Mat-Su Region; **Notes:** Dogs permitted on leash. Moose and bear habitat. Bring gloves (for human hands) and booties (for dogs) for protection from sharp rocks during the summit scramble; **GPS:** 61.59944°, –149.00035°

Although it doesn't look like much at first, this trail soon delivers you into a massive alpine bowl with the rakish tilt of Matanuska Peak presiding over the far end.

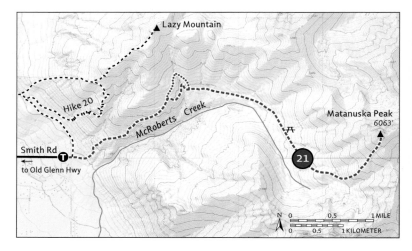

Never-ending views of the Chugach Mountains, Cook Inlet, and the Knik and Matanuska rivers await those bold enough for the steep, rocky summit scramble.

GETTING THERE

From Palmer, drive east on the Old Glenn Highway for 3.5 miles. Turn left onto Smith Road. After 1.5 miles, find the small parking lot for the Matanuska Peak Trailhead at the end of the road. Hikers often park (carefully) on the shoulder.

ON THE TRAIL

From the trailhead, follow the obvious hardened trail as at 0.1 mile it crosses the Morgan Horse Trail, a level, and easy—but grassy—pathway that connects with the trailhead for Lazy Mountain (see Hike 20). Continue straight ahead until a marked left turn for the Matanuska Peak Trail at 0.3 mile (elevation 640 feet).

The trail incline here is steep, taking you quickly uphill through light forest and

brush until at 0.8 mile (elevation 1300 feet) you crest over the lip of an enormous, shallow valley, with the unmistakable, off-kilter point of Matanuska Peak—also called Byers Peak—presiding over the far rim.

From here, enjoy a relatively flat stroll along the valley floor among big birch trees and brushy alders until just past 1.8 miles, where there is an obvious but unmarked fork in the trail. The "old" trail to the right washed out, and the left fork was meant to be an improvement—but I still prefer the right fork, as do many of the locals.

That's because the left fork adds on about a half mile of extra distance (each way) and goes up a short but miserably steep hill, whereas the old trail is "only" somewhat eroded, and in a couple of places you end up tiptoeing across the trunks of alder trees—which conveniently grow out from the slope at an angle—because the trail has eroded away around them.

Anyway, it's a case of pick your poison. If you take my preferred route—the old trail,

Although the summit scramble on Matanuska Peak is brutal, the valley approach is very pleasant.

which is usually marked with brightly colored flagging tape—the two trails rejoin at 2 miles from the trailhead (elevation 2250 feet). From there, follow the brown "fence-post" trail markers as they lead down a short incline and into a stretch of head-high grass, although the trail itself is usually brushed out.

At about 2.5 miles the grass becomes patchy, alternating with stretches of alders, until you emerge into the clear at 3.2 miles (elevation 2700 feet) with lovely views of Matanuska Peak's rakish slant ahead of you and the McRoberts Creek valley behind you.

At 3.6 miles (elevation 3000 feet) you'll pass a beat-up picnic table conveniently situated at the foot of Matanuska Peak. The table is a good stopping point for anyone who's not prepared for the final steep, rock-hopping scramble to the peak. From here, the trail continues for almost another mile over tundra swells, until at 4.4 miles (elevation 3850 feet) it hooks left and kicks in the afterburners, gaining more than 2000 feet in less than a mile.

This last mile of trail is nothing but a steep scramble over rocky debris, and the rocks get extremely sharp toward the top. Bring gloves to protect your hands—which most hikers will need as much as their feet to make forward progress—and if you're hiking with a dog, make sure he or she wears protective booties. Otherwise, the sharp rocks will cut up Fido's paws. The trail ends atop 6063-foot Matanuska Peak, about 5.3 miles from the trailhead.

22 Bodenburg Butte

RATING/ DIFFICULTY	ROUNDTRIP	ELEV GAIN/ HIGH POINT	SEASON
***/2	2.6 miles	720 feet/ 850 feet	Year-round

Maps: USGS Anchorage C6 SE, USGS Anchorage C6 SW; **Contact:** Matanuska-Susitna Borough; **Notes:** Matanuska-Susitna Borough parking pass or parking fee. Dogs permitted on leash. Bear and moose habitat; **GPS:** 61.55207°, −149.05370°

This hike up a big, rocky butte plunked down in the middle of rich farmland is a pilgrimage for new hikers and a perennial favorite of anyone seeking 360-degree views of Pioneer Peak, Matanuska Peak, the Matanuska River, and Knik Glacier.

GETTING THERE

From Palmer, take the Old Glenn Highway south to the first intersection for Bodenburg Loop Road and turn right. If you're coming from Anchorage, take the Old Glenn Highway north to the second intersection for Bodenburg Loop Road. After about 0.5 mile turn left on Mothershead Lane, which is signed for "West Butte" trail. Look for the new trailhead on your left after a big curve.

ON THE TRAIL

This trail (sometimes called the West Butte Trail) has seen a lot of improvements in the last few years, including a new parking area, new interpretive signs, and a few new stairs. The broad, hardened gravel trail starts just across the road from the parking area.

There are a few social side trails here; just stay on the main trail, which gains 260 feet in elevation until it reaches three benches

A rocky summit, happy hikers, and gusty winds grace the top of Bodenburg Butte.

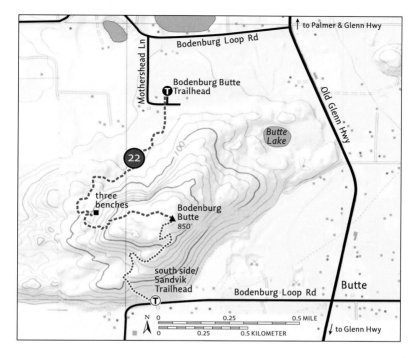

clustered at 0.75 mile, offering great look-outs over the floodplain of the Matanuska River. At 0.8 mile the seemingly endless stairs start. There are several hundred stairs on this side of the butte, both buttressing the land against erosion and improving traction on what was once a slippery, steep incline. During the winter the steps can get icy, so bring ice grippers or cleats, just in case.

Just before 1 mile you scramble over a large rock in the trail, then it's back to the stairs for another 0.1 mile. Leave the stairs behind as the trail loops around to the left, ascending the rocky knob atop the butte. From here you have amazing views over the Knik Glacier and the farmland around you.

You might spy what look like caribou in the fields below you. Those are reindeer (basically, domesticated caribou) that belong to the Reindeer Farm (reindeerfarm.com).

The remaining 0.2-mile trail to the top leads through a mix of alders and birch trees, but the vegetation on top of the butte is very different: you'll even find sage among the rocks, and if you're lucky you might see ravens or paragliders playing in the swirling currents of air.

Alternate Route

There is another way up the Butte. This "south trail" crosses property owned by the Sandvik family, with a fee for using the trailhead. To reach the south side/Sandvik Trailhead from Palmer, take the Old Glenn Highway to the second Bodenburg Loop intersection and turn right. (If you're coming from Anchorage, this would be a left turn at the first Bodenburg Loop intersection.) After a little more than half a mile on Bodenburg Loop, look for the small, unpaved parking lot on the right. The trail starts steeply uphill from the left side of the trailhead.

Be aware that this trail is so steep and eroded, full of loose sandy soil, that it's a horrible place to be on a windy day. However, if you take it on a calm day, at 0.2 mile you might get lucky and see horses grazing beyond the fence to your left. Just past 0.3 mile you get nice views of the Matanuska River, also to the left. The trail ends after 0.75 mile with a little low-angle rock scrambling to gain the top of the butte.

23 Pioneer Ridge and Pioneer Peak

RATING/ DIFFICULTY	ROUNDTRIP	ELEV GAIN/ HIGH POINT	SEASON
*****/5	9.6 miles	5330 feet/ 5300 feet	June–Sept

Maps: USGS Anchorage B6 NE, National Geographic Chugach State Park, Imus Geographics Chugach State Park; **Contact:** Matanuska-Susitna Borough; **Notes:** Mat-Su Borough parking pass or parking fee. Dogs permitted on leash. Moose and bear habitat; **GPS:** 61.49430°, –148.92747°

This hike up the northeast ridge of Pioneer Peak showcases big country at its finest, with commanding views over the Knik River to the north, Knik Glacier to the east, and Knik Arm to the west. This is one of those hikes that you train all year to do, then dream of doing all over again.

GETTING THERE

From Palmer, take the Old Glenn Highway south for 9.5 miles, crossing the Knik River Bridge. Turn left on Knik River Road. After 3.5 miles the trailhead (elevation 100 feet) will be on your right. The trail sign is parallel to the road, so it's very easy to miss the first time by.

ON THE TRAIL

This hike doesn't mess around. Straight from the start, it climbs through a birch forest lined with fireweed and grass; by 0.6 mile (elevation 660 feet) your views start opening up over the Knik River floodplain to the north, a broad plain of silt that harbors the river's constantly shifting braided channels.

As you climb, you'll encounter many small rivulets that flow across the trail, some of them bridged by short boardwalks; the others you just step across. Keep an eye out for brown "fencepost"-style markers too. They tell you how far you've gone in feet. (Remember: a mile is 5280 feet.) Here's one more warning to the wise: just past 1.2 miles (elevation 1550 feet) there's almost always a hornet nest located between two footbridges. So if you hear a strange buzzing, don't stop to investigate the cause!

The next half mile is steep and often muddy, but by mile 1.8 (elevation 2220 feet) a series of switchbacks starts. This is also where you'll find the first picnic table out of three—great landmarks for gauging your progress, and of course a great place to rest and enjoy sweeping views over the Knik River and, in the distance, Knik Glacier as well.

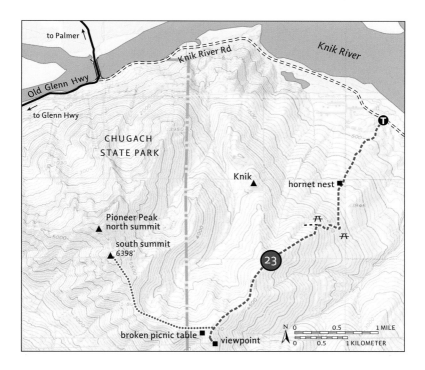

By this point you're above treeline, but still traveling through some fairly thick brush and grass. At 2.2 miles (elevation 2800 feet) you'll pass the second picnic table; it's down and slightly to the right of the trail. Just past the picnic table, the trail splits; ignore the right fork and go straight ahead. From this point the trail gets steeper and rockier, pushing through wiry, whippy willows until you exit brushline at 2.6 miles (elevation 3400 feet).

By 3.1 miles (elevation 4300 feet) you crest a false peak and the trail starts to level out, opening into a wide ridge that quite

simply dwarfs you and your party. That feeling—of being so tiny against such a vast land—is one of the best things about hiking in Alaska. The hardest part of the hike is now behind you, and sporadic cairns and occasional trail markers help keep you on track.

By about mile 3.6 you've crested another false peak. Walk an easy, gently sloping ridge to the southwest until 4.5 miles (elevation 5300 feet), where you'll find the broken remains of the third picnic table. It was, no doubt, squashed by heavy snow accumulation, but it looks for all the world as if a giant sat on it.

Where the gates of Mordor lie . . . oh, my bad, it's just the twin summits of Pioneer Peak.

Just over 0.1 mile to the south, there's a stupendous viewpoint. From various places on the ridge you can see all the way to the sprawling Eklutna Glacier to the south, the Matanuska River valley to the north, the Talkeetna Mountains to the northwest, and the distant bulk of the Denali massif on clear days.

For many people, this is the ideal turn-around point. But if you're okay with some serious scrambling and routefinding, you can follow the obvious ridge west toward the 6398-foot south summit of Pioneer Peak.

The first 0.6 mile of the ridge isn't too bad, and packs some wonderful views over the water to the west. But after that it gets progressively more exposed, and you'll need both hands and feet to make progress through the notoriously loose and crumbly "Chugach crud," a brittle type of shale that passes for rock here. I don't recommend doing this part of the hike if you have a dog along.

Even strong hikers can easily take a dozen hours for the 12-mile round-trip hike from trailhead to south summit and back again, so keep the sunset time in mind, and remember that sometimes picking your way down a steep, rocky slope is harder—and slower—than finding your way up.

If you've made it to the south summit, it's tempting to keep going to the north summit, which is very slightly higher. But one look at the treacherous terrain between the summits should dissuade you: the passage is extremely sketchy and I don't recommend it.

Opposite: *Eklutna Lake (Hike 24) is, without a doubt, the centerpiece of this region.*

eklutna area

The centerpiece of these trails is massive Eklutna Lake, which also happens to serve as a water reservoir for the Anchorage municipality. This area is a hot spot of recreation, with cycling, paddling, and—most important for our purposes—hiking trails along the lakeshore and into neighboring peaks.

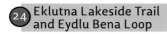

24 Eklutna Lakeside Trail and Eydlu Bena Loop

Eklutna Lakeside Trail

RATING/ DIFFICULTY	ROUNDTRIP	ELEV GAIN/ HIGH POINT	SEASON
*****/3	25.4 miles	1385 feet/ 1080 feet	Year-round

Eydlu Bena Loop

RATING/ DIFFICULTY	LOOP	ELEV GAIN/ HIGH POINT	SEASON
***/2	2.1 miles	360 feet/ 1160 feet	Year–Round

Maps: USGS Anchorage B6 NW, USGS Anchorage B6 NE, USGS Anchorage B6 SE; National Geographic Chugach State Park; Imus Geographics Chugach State Park; **Contact:** Chugach State Park; **Notes:** Alaska State Parks pass or parking fee. Lakeside Trail is open to mountain bikes, horses. Lakeside Trail is open to ATVs March 31 through December 1, Sunday–Wednesday only, speed limit 15 mph. Snowmachines allowed on lakeside trail when snow cover is sufficient. Dogs permitted on leash at trailhead, under direct control in backcountry. Bear and moose habitat; **GPS:** 61.41041°,–149.13519°

 *Eklutna Lake is an icon of outdoor recreation in Southcentral, drawing hikers,*

bikers, fishermen, kayakers, and during the Sunday-to-Wednesday motorized opening, ATV users. The lakeside trail is far too long to hike in a day, but you can pair biking with hiking, or just go as far as you like.

GETTING THERE
From Anchorage, drive northeast on the Glenn Highway to the marked exit for Eklutna Lake—about 25 miles. Turn right, followed by another right onto the Old Glenn Highway, then a left onto Eklutna Lake Road. Leave yourself at least 20 minutes to drive the last 10 miles on winding, narrow Eklutna Lake Road. Park in the Eklutna Lake Campground's day use area and cross the pedestrian bridge at its east end, then turn right to access the trailhead (elevation 890 feet). Turning left instead would get you to the trailhead for Twin Peaks/Pepper Peak (Hike 25).

ON THE TRAIL
Obviously, most people won't hike the entire Eklutna Lakeside Trail in a day. But walking the broad trail along the shore of this blue-green gem is a great way to spend the day. This is one of those rare hikes that's actually best at the start: by 0.2 mile (elevation 875 feet) you're strolling the old roadbed right at the lakeside, alternating open views of the water with short screens of trees.

Occasionally the trail splits, with the roadbed continuing very slightly inland. At these intersections combination bike/hike trails—for people who want to avoid motorized users—split off to the right, sticking even closer to the water than the old road.

The water level in Eklutna Lake varies enormously, and it can generate ocean-size waves on extremely windy afternoons, so these hike/bike sections are subject to

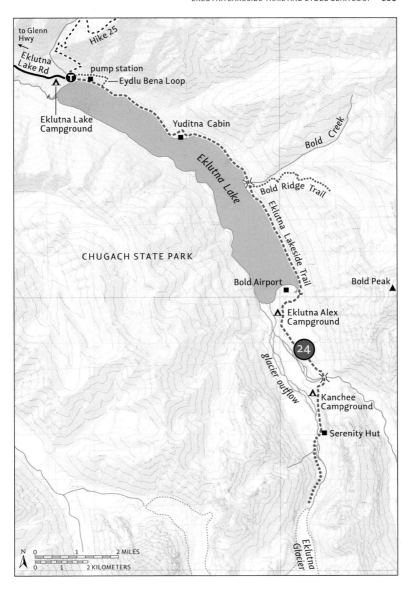

to Glenn Hwy

Hike 25

Eklutna Lake Rd

pump station

Eydlu Bena Loop

Eklutna Lake Campground

Yuditna Cabin

Bold Creek

Eklutna Lake

Bold Ridge Trail

Eklutna Lakeside Trail

CHUGACH STATE PARK

Bold Airport

Bold Peak ▲

Eklutna Alex Campground

24

glacier outflow

Kanchee Campground

Serenity Hut

N

0   1   2 MILES

0   1   2 KILOMETERS

Eklutna Glacier

The Eklutna Lakeside Trail is a haven for winter hiking, biking, and more.

frequent washouts; you're free to stay on the road if you'd rather. Sometimes you can walk right along the lake's loose, gravelly shore, but that also depends on the water level.

At mile 2.8, look for a signed turn-off to Yuditna Cabin, a public use shelter that must be reserved in advance. Make reservations online, for a fee, at reserve america.com.

At 5.2 miles (elevation 930 feet) cross a bridge over Bold Creek, and at 5.3 miles reach a signed turnoff to the left for the Bold Ridge Trail, a very brushy, overgrown 5-mile roundtrip hike that winds uphill through the forest. At 1.2 miles (elevation 1990 feet) from the turnoff you start getting views of the lake through the brush.

The Bold Ridge Trail peters out shortly after 2 miles (elevation 2950 feet), but the ridgeline offers easy walking and spectacular views along the lake and to nearby peaks. Do not confuse this hike with 7522-foot Bold *Peak*, which is a technical climb.

At 8.5 miles, the trail departs the lakeside and passes by the small Bold "Airport," a small landing strip on the far end of the lake. The trail narrows and gets brushy here, and wildlife encounters are common. Just past 9.3 miles the trail passes the primitive first-come, first-served Eklutna Alex Campground, along with braided outflow from the Eklutna Glacier. At 11.5 miles you'll pass the primitive Kanchee Campground, and at about 12.7 miles you'll hit the Serenity Hut, which is meant to be shared by multiple parties, but bunks must be reserved in advance with reserveamerica.com.

For all intents and purposes, this marks the end of the lakeside trail. Once upon a time you could hike about a mile farther from here to a viewpoint over Eklutna Glacier, but the glacier has now receded so far that this becomes a find-your-own-route of boulder hopping, river crossing, and scrambling. Make sure you don't accidentally scramble yourself into technical terrain.

A few notes about this trail: it's understandably popular with mountain bikers, and ATVs are allowed on Sunday through Wednesday. Usually there's no problem at all, because there's plenty of room for the different groups to pass each other, and everyone's just happy to be out there. But loose dogs could cause a serious problem if they dart in front of a fast-moving bike or ATV, so keep your dogs close and under direct control.

You can also fish the lake for Dolly Varden and rainbow trout, and paddling is a popular pastime here. You can rent mountain bikes or kayaks from Lifetime Adventures, which maintains a rental hut near the trailhead during the summer. If you kayak, take this lake seriously: it's enormous and cold, and on windy days it can generate ocean-size waves. Often in the afternoon, stiff winds kick up that can make it extra challenging to paddle back toward the trailhead.

Eydlu Bena Loop:
If you want some relative solitude, this mellow, 2.1-mile loop is just the trick. Starting from the same trailhead as Eklutna Lake, the trail trends gently uphill on an old maintenance road. At 0.4 mile (elevation 1000 feet) the trail passes a pump station and becomes a narrow foot trail through grassy spruce and birch forest. You'll find a lot of berries here in late summer, so it's no surprise that black bear sightings are common.

The trail continues gently uphill until its high point at 1 mile (elevation 1160 feet), at which point it bends sharply to the right and descends quickly to rejoin the lakeside trail at 1.3 miles (elevation 920 feet). From there, it's an easy stroll back on the broad, well-trafficked lakeside trail.

25 Twin Peaks to Pepper Peak

RATING/ DIFFICULTY	ROUNDTRIP	ELEV GAIN/ HIGH POINT	SEASON
*****/5	8.6 miles	4550 feet/ 5440 feet	May–Oct

Maps: USGS Anchorage B6 NW, National Geographic Chugach State Park, Imus Geographics Chugach State Park; **Contact:** Chugach State Park; **Notes:** Alaska State Parks pass or parking fee. Dogs permitted on leash in parking area, under direct control in backcountry. Bear and moose habitat; black bear sightings especially common. Some loose scrambling near the top; **GPS:** 61.40985°, −149.13463°

This steep hike is on straightforward terrain, except for one nasty section of scrambling. This would be a great hike anywhere, but its surroundings—from the craggy Twin Peaks to brooding Pioneer Peak, distant Knik Arm, and spectacular Eklutna Lake—make it truly spectacular.

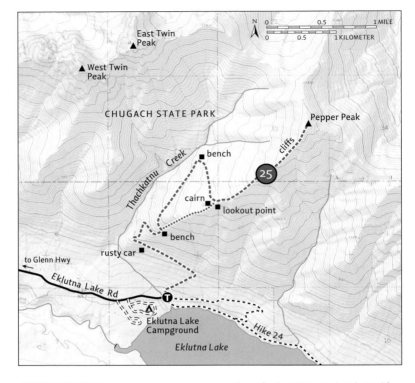

GETTING THERE

From Anchorage, drive northeast on the Glenn Highway to the marked exit for Eklutna Lake—about 25 miles. Turn right, followed by another right onto the Old Glenn Highway, then a left onto Eklutna Lake Road. Leave yourself at least 20 minutes to drive the last 10 miles on winding, narrow Eklutna Lake Road. Park in the Eklutna Lake Campground's day use area and cross the pedestrian bridge at its east end, then turn left to access the Twin Peaks/ Pepper Peak Trailhead (elevation 950 feet). Turning right instead would take you to the trailhead for the Eklutna Lakeside Trail (see Hike 24).

ON THE TRAIL

The first 2.5 miles of this trail take place on the well-maintained Twin Peaks Trail, which climbs steeply through a dense forest of spruce, birch, and alders. During the summer, keep an eye out for wildflowers such as monkshood, fireweed, lupine, Sitka burnet, and wild geraniums, along with the pretty but burn-inducing cow parsnip.

The trail is a constant, but manageable uphill grade. Just before 1 mile (elevation

1500 feet) you might just be able to see an old, rusty car down the slope to the left, mostly hidden by the undergrowth. From here the trail ascends a couple of switchbacks until at 1.6 miles (elevation 2020 feet) the trees open up to views of Eklutna Lake down below. There's a bench here, which people often use to measure their progress up the trail; for example, "I made it to the first bench." There's also an extremely steep footpath that continues straight ahead here and can serve as a shortcut to a later point on the trail; in some years, it's snow-free by April. But the (relatively) easy main trail continues to the left.

At 2.1 miles (elevation 2500 feet) the trail levels out briefly, giving you nice views of the Mordor-like Twin Peaks on your left. They look intriguing but have so much loose, crumbling rock that they're an unpleasant, dangerous scramble.

At 2.5 miles (elevation 2780 feet) you'll reach the second bench, which also marks the end of the maintained Twin Peaks Trail. This bench doesn't offer views over the lake. But if you take the rough (and sometimes steep) dirt footpath leading up and to the right, straight out of brushline, at just past 3 miles (elevation 3315 feet) you'll reach a wonderful lookout point over the lake.

If you want to continue on to Pepper Peak, backtrack about 300 feet from the lookout point. You'll see a clear footpath leading straight up into the tundra on your right, marked by a wide, shallow cairn. When it's very foggy, I get sketched out by this patchy path—but it's easy to follow on clear days, leading straight up the southwest ridge of Pepper Peak, one false peak at a time.

At 3.75 miles (elevation 4550 feet) you'll have particularly good views of Eklutna Lake

The first bench on the Twin Peaks Trail offers hard-to-beat views over Eklutna Lake.

down below, but at 4 miles (elevation 4960 feet) the trail gets really sketchy, ascending ridiculously steep "cliffs" made of the crumbling, loose and slippery shale that's known locally as Chugach crud. No technical climbing is needed to get to the top, but you do need some routefinding skill—and a tolerance for scrambling exposure—to pick your way through, using the bits and pieces of "trail" you can find to make the passage easier.

If you make it through this horrible section, at just past mile 4.1 (elevation 5270 feet) you're rewarded with a return to easier—if still steep—tundra walking, until the trail ends at mile 4.3 (elevation 5440 feet) with heart-pounding views of the Twin Peaks and Knik Arm to the west, Pioneer Peak to the northeast, and all the way down the length of Eklutna Lake.

26 Thunderbird Falls

RATING/ DIFFICULTY	ROUNDTRIP	ELEV GAIN/ HIGH POINT	SEASON
***/2	1.75 miles	680 feet/ 320 feet	Year-round

Maps: USGS Anchorage B7 NE, National Geographics Chugach State Park, Imus Geographics Chugach State Park; **Contact:** Chugach State Park; **Notes:** Alaska State Parks pass or parking fee. Dogs permitted on leash. Bear and moose habitat. Steep drop-offs hidden near path; **GPS:** 61.44938°, −149.37086°

An iconic, family-friendly hike, this route culminates in an overlook of Thunderbird Falls as it skips 200 feet down the steep walls of Eklutna Canyon. A well-groomed side trail takes you to a charming pool at the waterfall's base.

GETTING THERE
From Anchorage, take the Glenn Highway about 27 miles northeast and exit for Thunderbird Falls. Turn right and follow signs for another 0.2 mile to reach the clearly marked trailhead (elevation 135 feet).

ON THE TRAIL
This sweet, mostly flat trail isn't very long, but it's so iconic that I couldn't leave it out. It's a broad, old roadbed that runs near the lip of Eklutna Canyon. On either side of the trail you'll see the ubiquitous Southcentral Alaska mix of birch trees, alders, and underbrush, including thorny devil's club. There are some steep drop-offs hidden in that underbrush, so stay on the trail.

At 0.5 mile you'll find a wooden viewing platform that offers great views into steep-walled Eklutna Canyon, with the Eklutna River snaking along its floor.

You'll crest the trail's very modest high point at 0.6 mile (elevation 320 feet). From here there's a slight dip to 0.7 mile (elevation 280 feet), where a side trail branches down and to the left. You should explore this, but first continue on to the viewing deck at 0.75 mile (elevation 300 feet), where you'll get the big-picture view of Thunderbird Falls as it comes leaping and skipping down the steep canyon wall. During the winter, the falls often freeze into fantastical ice sculptures.

It's tempting to explore off-trail here, but don't do it. People have been seriously hurt doing exactly that: the rocks are unstable, the slippery vegetation hides some steep drop-offs, and it can take a long time for the technical rescue required to retrieve a person from that sort of situation.

When you're ready, backtrack to the aforementioned side trail and follow it down the canyon wall at a moderate slope. The

Thunderbird Falls splashes down into a peaceful, misty grotto.

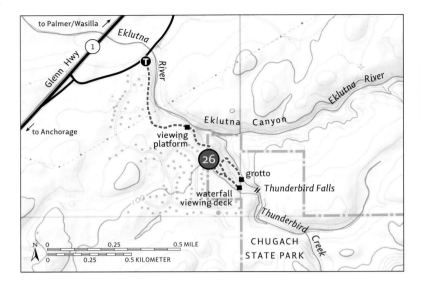

trail emerges on the canyon floor within arm's reach of Thunderbird Creek, which at this point is a shallow, wide sheet of water. But if you follow the trail around to the right you can enjoy a misty grotto at the base of Thunderbird Falls (1 mile from the trailhead, elevation 195 feet), where the water's boisterous plunge into the pool is a marked contrast to the calm creek. If you choose to scramble around on the rocks at the bottom of the falls, be careful—they're slippery when wet.

Although wildlife such as bears and moose can pop up anywhere in Alaska, this trail receives so much traffic that sightings are rare—so it's a great beginner hike for anyone looking to build confidence or just enjoy a quick stroll.

Opposite: *Eagle River is home to some of the prettiest and most accessible hikes in Southcentral Alaska. Here, the Alaska flag flies atop Mount Tucker, a peak on the way to Mount Magnificent (Hike 32).*

eagle river and vicinity

Eagle River is the name of both a river and a town; the town is Anchorage's one and only true suburb, with a population of about 22,000 people. Some of Southcentral's best hiking trails are here or in small communities just to the north, clustering around the river's various forks or taking to the hills for a series of lovely ridgewalks that ambitious hikers sometimes link together for grueling, day-long traverses.

27 Big Peters Creek

RATING/ DIFFICULTY	LOOP	ELEV GAIN/ HIGH POINT	SEASON
**/2	6.5 miles	1110 feet/ 1690 feet	Year-round

Maps: USGS Anchorage B7 NE, USGS Anchorage B7 SE, National Geographic Chugach State Park, Imus Geographics Chugach State Park; **Contact:** Chugach State Park; **Notes:** Open to mountain bikes. Open to cross-country skiing, snowmachines, and trapping during winter months. Can be very buggy. Dogs permitted on leash at trailhead, under direct control in backcountry. Moose and bear habitat. Optional ford; **GPS:** 61.39737°, –149.41251°

Part tranquil woodland get-away and also part neighborhood dog walk for the residents of Peters Creek, this relatively untraveled trail is a pleasant stroll for families looking to picnic by the banks of Four-Mile Creek in the summer. It's also popular with mountain bikers during the summer, and cross-country skiers in the winter.

GETTING THERE

From Anchorage, drive north on the Glenn Highway about 21 miles. Take the Peters Creek exit and turn right onto Ski Road. Turn

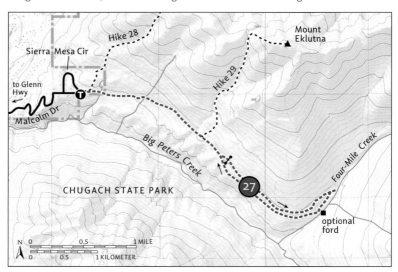

It's over the river, through the woods, and onto Peters Creek Trail you'll go during an early winter hike.

right onto Whaley Avenue, then left onto Chugach Park Drive. Follow Chugach Park Drive until it ends at Kullberg Drive. Turn left on Kullberg Drive, then right on Sullins Drive and, after several switchbacks, turn right on Malcolm Drive. A big brown sign marks the trailhead (elevation 1200 feet) just before the road makes a sharp left turn and becomes Sierra Mesa Circle, just under 3 miles from the highway exit. Park carefully on the side of the road.

ON THE TRAIL

This quiet woodland trail occupies an old roadbed that passes through very brushy terrain but is generally well cleared up until mile 3. All that brush, combined with birch and spruce trees standing just off the trail, makes a great place to listen for birdsong.

From the trailhead, the trail starts off on a steep little hill. At 0.1 mile, a clear but unmarked track veers into the trees to the left; this is the trail to Bear Mountain (see Hike 28). At mile 1, you'll head up a moderate but easily managed hill, gaining 400 feet in one mile. Watch for enthusiastic mountain bikers bombing down this slope, and be considerate of the noise you make because although you can't see them, there are houses hidden in the woods along the first mile of trail.

At 1.3 miles you'll hit the trail's modest high point—1690 feet—and also a signed turnoff for the trail to Mount Eklutna (see Hike 29).

Just before 2 miles the trail forks, which is what allows this to be a loop hike. The Big Peters Creek Trail continues along the right fork; during the winter, snowmachines are allowed on this trail. The left fork passes through a gate designed to block motorized vehicles and becomes a narrow but clear and well-brushed footpath.

I prefer to go left first, leaving the old roadbed of the Big Peters Creek Trail behind and following a gently rolling footpath through the brush. The trail forks again at mile 2.8; take the left fork to reach the shores of pretty Four-Mile Creek at mile 2.9. There's a broad, grassy area that is perfect for picnicking, along with a lot of social side trails and game trails to explore in this area. Heads up: bear and moose encounters are very common along the entirety of this trail.

When you're ready to go back to your loop hike, backtrack to the clear fork at mile 2.8 and take the unmarked but very clearly defined "other" trail: it's a left turn if you're coming from the creek, or a right turn if you never went down to the banks of the creek. This narrow footpath winds 0.4 mile through the forest before rejoining the Big Peters Creek Trail at a signed intersection. At this point you've hiked 3.4 miles, thanks to that connector trail. If you turn left, after 0.1 mile you'll reach a tributary to Peters Creek that can be forded at normal water levels; expect the water to be at least knee-deep.

That said, there's not much point in making the crossing. Technically the old roadbed that is the Big Peters Creek Trail continues another 2 miles on the other side of the creek, but leave that to the snowmachiners. As soon as you ford the creek the trail swings south, becoming a narrow, overgrown single-track path that receives very little sun for most of the year.

Instead, turn back and follow the Big Peters Creek Trail all the way back to the trailhead, closing a long, skinny loop. The old roadbed makes for easy walking or biking, and during the winter it's also great for cross-country skiing.

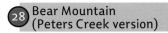

28 Bear Mountain (Peters Creek version)

RATING/ DIFFICULTY	ROUNDTRIP	ELEV GAIN/ HIGH POINT	SEASON
****/4	4 miles	1980 feet/ 3140 feet	May–Oct

Maps: USGS Anchorage B7 NE, National Geographic Chugach State Park, Imus Geographics Chugach State Park; **Contact:** Chugach State Park; **Notes:** The first 0.25 mile is open to mountain bikes and cross-country skiing. Snowmachines allowed on first 0.25 mile (Big Peters Creek Trail) when snow cover is sufficient. Area subject to trapping in winter months. Dogs permitted on leash at trailhead, under direct control in backcountry. Bear and moose habitat; **GPS:** 61.39737°, –149.41251°

Often done as a loop hike with Mount Eklutna, Bear Mountain (called Bear Point on some maps) is half grueling uphill hike and half lazy stroll along a broad tundra plateau, culminating in the modest summit of Bear Mountain.

GETTING THERE

From Anchorage, drive north on the Glenn Highway about 21 miles. Take the Peters Creek exit and turn right onto Ski Road. Turn right onto Whaley Avenue, then left onto Chugach Park Drive. Follow Chugach Park Drive until it ends at Kullberg Drive. Turn left on Kullberg Drive, then right on Sullins Drive and, after several switchbacks, turn right on Malcolm Drive. A big brown sign marks the trailhead (elevation 1200 feet) just before the road makes a sharp left turn and becomes Sierra Mesa Circle, just under

Hikers chase the sun back down from the summit of Bear Mountain.

3 miles from the highway exit. Park carefully on the side of the road.

ON THE TRAIL

Start your hike on the Big Peters Creek Trail (see Hike 27), a broad, old roadbed that's also open to mountain bikers during the summer. At 0.1 mile, turn left onto a clear but unmarked side trail; this is the path to Bear Mountain. The trail starts off at a steep uphill slope, passing through a mix of grass-lined birch, spruce, and alder trees, with a few spots of thick, goopy mud.

At 0.4 mile (elevation 1400 feet) the grade really steepens, gaining more than 1200 feet in the next 0.8 mile. Starting at 1.2 miles (elevation 2640 feet) you'll tackle the steepest, most eroded part of the trail. Your quads will burn and your feet might slip a bit, but at least the steep climb doesn't last long. By 1.4 miles (elevation 3020 feet) the trail rolls over onto the broad, sloping tundra plateau that makes up Bear Mountain. Pay close attention to where the trail crests over the lip of that shelf, because there's no marker to help you find it on the way back.

When people pair this hike with Mount Eklutna (see Hike 29) to create a big loop, they usually turn right here, following a patchy trail east onto an obvious ridge that leads to the other mountain. But if you do that, you'll miss out on the easy walking and spectacular views to the west over Knik Arm.

As you head north, the trail roughly parallels the western edge of the tundra shelf; the farther you go, the better the views get. At 2 miles (elevation 3140 feet) you'll reach the small point that serves as the summit. Some maps mark this as Bear Point. This is a popular trail, but because so many hikers use Bear Mountain as the lead-in to a Mount Eklutna Loop, the summit point is quieter than you might expect—a great place to pause and reflect on the grand sweep of the world below you.

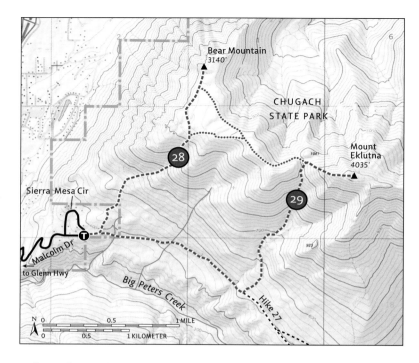

If you still want to do the loop with Mount Eklutna, you can follow a faint foot track southeast from the summit point, intersecting the ridge trail that leads to the other mountain. All told, the loop is about 6.9 miles and is best started from this direction, because it's much easier to go up the very steep slopes of Bear Mountain than down.

Otherwise, take your time working back down the steep Bear Mountain Trail, and don't be shy about using hiking poles or even scrambling on hands and feet, as I've seen many people do, to make the descent easier. (I like to pack light gloves, even at the peak of summer, to protect my hands when things get really steep going up *or* down.) Here's a

hidden perk of going down Bear Mountain: you get a first-class look at the great views that were behind you all the time, but might have gone unnoticed as you toiled to make it uphill.

29 Mount Eklutna

RATING/ DIFFICULTY	ROUNDTRIP	ELEV GAIN/ HIGH POINT	SEASON
***/4	6 miles	2960 feet/ 4035 feet	May–Oct

Maps: USGS Anchorage B7 NE, National Geographic Chugach State Park, Imus Geographics Chugach State Park; **Contact:**

A hiker works her way down from the saddle after descending Eklutna Peak.

Chugach State Park; **Notes:** First part of trail (Big Peters Creek Trail) is open to mountain bikes and, during winter, snowmachines. Can be very buggy. Dogs permitted on leash at trailhead, under direct control in backcountry. Bear and moose habitat. Final summit ridge is dangerous when icy; **GPS:** 61.39737°, –149.41251°

A broad, easy trail along the forested valley floor gives way to a winding footpath through the brush and, finally, a walk along a sometimes-rocky summit ridge to a lofty, lonely-feeling peak. That last ridge walk feels more daring than it is, but make no mistake: you're going to sweat for your views.

GETTING THERE

From Anchorage, drive north on the Glenn Highway about 21 miles. Take the Peters Creek exit and turn right onto Ski Road. Turn right onto Whaley Avenue, then left onto Chugach Park Drive. Follow Chugach Park Drive until it ends at Kullberg Drive. Turn left on Kullberg Drive, then right on Sullins Drive and, after several switchbacks, turn right on Malcolm Drive. A big brown sign marks the trailhead (elevation 1200 feet) just before the road makes a sharp left turn and becomes Sierra Mesa Circle, just under 3 miles from the highway exit. Park carefully on the side of the road.

ON THE TRAIL

The first 1.3 miles of this trail take place on the Big Peters Creek Trail (see Hike 27), a quiet woodland walk along an old roadbed. Bear and moose sightings are common here, and the plentiful spruce and birch trees make excellent habitat for migratory songbirds.

At 0.1 mile a clear but unmarked track veers into the trees to the left; this is the trail to Bear Mountain (see Hike 28), which can be part of a loop hike including Mount Eklutna. At 1 mile the Peters Creek Trail heads up a moderate hill, and at 1.3 miles you hit its modest high point—1690 feet—and a signed left turn for the trail to Mount Eklutna.

From here the trail becomes a narrow footpath that snakes steadily uphill through the brush and trees. Beware—this portion of trail can be very buggy! At 2.1 miles (elevation 2440 feet) you'll start to emerge from the brush as the trail transitions into braided dirt and rocks, with occasional muddy stretches.

The hike is especially steep from mile 2.2 (elevation 2650 feet) onward, gaining a whopping 750 feet on sometimes loose, rocky, and muddy trail until at mile 2.6 (elevation 3400 feet) it gains the saddle just below Mount Eklutna's peak.

From here, turn right (east) and head up the obvious steep, eroded, and sometimes rocky ridgeline, gaining another 635 feet before hitting the peak of Mount Eklutna (elevation 4035 feet) at mile 3. The ridge walk feels more daring than it really is; most hikers will do fine as long as they take it

slowly and carefully, and consider carrying hiking poles to aid your descent. That said, the ridge can be genuinely dangerous when it's icy or snowy. So when conditions are borderline, always pack a healthy dose of common sense.

If you're considering making a loop between Mount Eklutna and Bear Mountain (Hike 28), you could turn left at the saddle. However, it's extremely difficult to find the unmarked descent trail on Bear Mountain if you didn't come up it, so this loop is best started from Bear Mountain.

③⓪ Ptarmigan Valley

RATING/ DIFFICULTY	ROUNDTRIP	ELEV GAIN/ HIGH POINT	SEASON
**/3	9 miles	2410 feet/ 2300 feet	June–Oct

Maps: USGS Anchorage B7 NW, USGS Anchorage B7 SW, USGS Anchorage B7 SE, National Geographic Chugach State Park, Imus Geographics Chugach State Park; **Contact:** Chugach State Park; **Notes:** Snowshoeing, cross-country skiing, and snowmachining during the winter. Open to horseback riding. Dogs permitted on leash at trailhead, under direct control on trail. Bear and moose sightings are very common here; **GPS:** 61.39017°, –149.47047°

Hike a pretty woodland trail and easy ascent into an alpine bowl, although you'll have to tiptoe through some persistently muddy patches along the way. It's no secret: this is a great trail for berry picking if you don't mind the approach, although that may be why animals like this valley so much too.

GETTING THERE

From Anchorage, take the Glenn Highway northeast about 17 miles to the South Birchwood exit. Turn right, then turn left onto the Old Glenn Highway. After about 3 miles, you'll see the large trailhead (elevation 410 feet) on your right.

ON THE TRAIL

If you're looking for online resources (or even maps) for this hike, be warned that it's frequently confused with the Big Peters Creek Trail (Hike 27), probably because some people also call this hike the *Little Peters Creek Trail*.

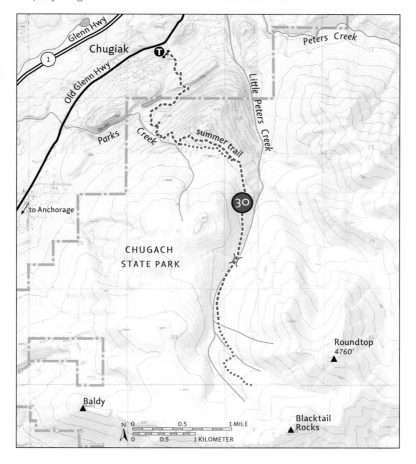

The trees open up and so do the mountains; you're on your way to "berry heaven."

With that said, at least the trail itself is easy to find. From the trailhead, a little brown hiker sign points you through the brush to an old roadway. It's amusing to see speed limit signs on a hiking trail; they're meant for the snowmachiners that use this trail in winter.

Go around a gate at 0.1 mile, then follow the moderately steep incline through thick birch, spruce, and cottonwood forest until 0.6 mile (elevation 790 feet), where the trail hooks sharply to the right. This is a good time to mention that bear and moose sightings are very frequent in this valley.

So far, my personal record is three moose, three grizzly bears, and one black bear—all in a single visit. So always mind your wildlife manners, especially in places with limited visibility.

At 1 mile in, depending on how the weather has been, things could get muddy. When the trail is softened by fall rains, mud all but swallows the logs and planks that have been laid down to help you through it. When at 2 miles you have the opportunity to veer left onto a narrow summer trail, take it. If you stick to the "main" motorized trail, you'd better have rubber boots and a good attitude.

Once you turn left onto the summer/hiker's trail, push through sporadic stands of tall grass until about 2.1 miles, where you'll find yourself walking a moderate uphill grade on a pretty woodland path, with beautiful views over Knik Arm behind you.

Watch for tree roots in the trail, and don't get distracted by the game trails that wander into the bushes; stick to the obviously more traveled path. The hiker's trail rejoins the motorized trail at just past 2.8 miles (elevation 1590 feet) then bends sharply to the right. The first part of this trail does not match what some maps have labeled as the Ptarmigan Valley Trail, but at this point they should all coincide.

At 3.1 miles the trail gets very grassy, and by 3.5 miles the left side starts to drop away, giving you glimpses into a broad valley below you. At 3.8 miles you cross a small creek on a solid bridge. By about 4.2 miles the trail opens up to pretty views of Roundtop on your left; on the right, tundra swells rise toward the flanks of Baldy. And by 4.5 miles, you're completely free of the brushy alders and can enter berry-filled tundra to either side of the trail, which quickly devolves into a web of social trails linking into hikes on the nearby peaks.

This is where many people linger before turning around, but you can also scramble up the neighboring peaks to link this hike with Baldy (Hike 31) or with Roundtop to the east or Blacktail Rocks to the southeast (all extensions of Hike 31). All of these involve some tundra walking, but there's also a cobweb of informal social trails throughout the valley, worn by the passage of many feet—so practice your best Leave No Trace principles by walking on the trails that already exist, or on rocky surfaces that won't be damaged by your passage, as much as you can.

31 Baldy and Blacktail Rocks

Baldy—Front Side

RATING/ DIFFICULTY	ROUNDTRIP	ELEV GAIN/ HIGH POINT	SEASON
****/3	2.5 miles	1200 feet/ 3020 feet	May–Oct

Blacktail Rocks

RATING/ DIFFICULTY	ROUNDTRIP	ELEV GAIN/ HIGH POINT	SEASON
*****/4	7.6 miles	3030 feet/ 4390 feet	May–Oct

Maps: USGS Anchorage B7 SW, USGS Anchorage B7 SE, National Geographic Chugach State Park, Imus Geographics Chugach State Park; **Contact:** Chugach State Park; **Notes:** Dogs permitted on leash at trailhead, under direct control in backcountry. Bear and moose habitat. Popular "back side" trail crosses private land; **GPS:** 61.33789°, –149.51280°

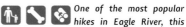 *One of the most popular hikes in Eagle River, this little mountain sees an awful lot of traffic, but with good reason. A newly cut trail turns what was once a steep scramble into a much more civilized walk that you can extend for miles along neighboring ridges.*

GETTING THERE

From Anchorage, drive northeast on the Glenn Highway. After about 11 miles, take the marked exit for Eagle River Loop/Hiland Road. Turn right onto Eagle River Loop. After about 3.5 miles, turn right onto West Skyline Road. Follow this road through numerous name changes as it switchbacks uphill for another 2.5 miles, changing names repeatedly, finally ending as Golden Eagle Drive.

The trailhead (elevation 1840 feet) is at the end of the road.

ON THE TRAIL

To access the public trail up Baldy, which some locals call the "front side" of the mountain, look for the two unpaved roads at the east (uphill) end of the trailhead parking area. Take the rightmost of these roads, a gated, gravel maintenance road that immediately heads steeply uphill. The road quickly shrinks to a broad, well-built footpath.

At about 0.4 mile (elevation 2120 feet) the trail splits. The track that scrambles straight uphill over very rocky, eroded terrain is the old trail, which had a rightly earned reputation for being a steep, sometimes treacherous scramble. Instead, continue on a wide switchback to the right, which rejoins the old trail at 0.7 mile (elevation 2325 feet). These switchbacks were recently built by Chugach State Park, alleviating that fierce scramble and creating a trail that can stand up to constant foot traffic. As a nice bonus, as the switchbacks curl around the mountain they also show off pretty views of Eagle River to the south and Knik Arm to the west.

The same pattern continues all the way to the top of the mountain: every time you're faced with the steep, eroded rock and dirt of the old trail, stay on the switchbacks for much easier walking and, as a bonus, reducing the eroding impact of foot traffic on this beloved mountain.

Some serious trail work has turned what used to be a steep, loose scramble into a series of lovely switchbacks.

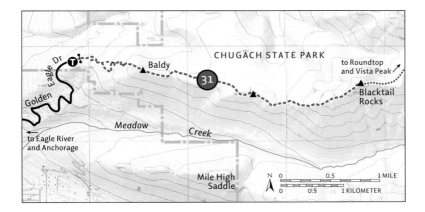

As of 2018, at the 1-mile point, the switchbacks end and you are left to scramble the last quarter-mile up to the peak on the old trail. But another set of switchbacks leading all the way to the top is slated for the next year or two, so by the time you read this, they may already be in place.

At 1.25 miles (elevation 3020 feet) you'll reach the top of Baldy. Some maps show this as Dowling Peak, with "Baldy" situated farther back on the ridge; but at least according to the many hikers that walk here (and most maps), the first and obviously highest patch of rocks is in fact the summit of Baldy.

Families and those out for a short day hike tend to turn back here, satisfied with having tagged the summit of one of Southcentral's most beloved mountains. But if you have more time, you may enjoy following the long, broad ridge behind Baldy a while longer.

At 3.8 miles you'll reach the next most likely stopping point, the 4390-foot summit of Blacktail Rocks (marked on some maps as Blacktail Ptarmigan Rocks). The walking is easy, if a little steep, but you might have

to piece together bits of trail in the tundra as you get to the top. When in doubt, stay to the left, which is a reasonable tundra slope; there's absolutely no need to walk near the exposed, rocky drop-offs on the right.

This is as far as most hikers will go. But if you started early enough and are comfortable with basic land navigation, you can walk down the back side of Blacktail Rocks and continue east, then northeast until the ridge splits. From there, follow the ridgeline north for the summit of 4760-foot Roundtop (a total of 5.2 miles from the trailhead, 3470 feet of elevation gain) or turn southeast on the ridge to reach 5011-foot Vista Peak (a total of 6 miles and 3980 feet of elevation gain from the trailhead). Or, of course, you could tag both in one very long, challenging hike of about 12 miles roundtrip.

Last but not least, there is another way up Baldy that is colloquially known as the "back side" route. It's noticeably gentler, but crosses private land on an old homestead owned by the Wallace family, with potential for trespassing issues, so it's not recommended.

32 Mile Hi Saddle and Mount Magnificent

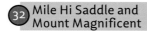

RATING/ DIFFICULTY	ROUNDTRIP	ELEV GAIN/ HIGH POINT	SEASON
****/4	6.4 miles	3470 feet/ 4230 feet	June–Oct

Maps: USGS Anchorage B7 SW, USGS Anchorage B7 SE, National Geographic Chugach State Park, Imus Geographics Chugach State Park; **Contact:** Chugach State Park; **Notes:** Trailhead parking is very limited. Dogs permitted on leash at trailhead, under direct control on trails. Bear and moose habitat; **GPS:** 61.31343°, –149.46530°

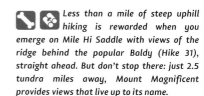

Less than a mile of steep uphill hiking is rewarded when you emerge on Mile Hi Saddle with views of the ridge behind the popular Baldy (Hike 31), straight ahead. But don't stop there: just 2.5 tundra miles away, Mount Magnificent provides views that live up to its name.

GETTING THERE

From Anchorage, take the Glenn Highway northeast. After about 11 miles, take the marked exit for Hiland Road/Eagle River Loop Road. Turn right onto Eagle River Loop Road, then turn right onto Eagle River Road. About 2 miles after the last turn, look for Mile Hi Avenue on the left; it veers left

Taking in the view from atop Mount Magnificent's unlikely grass-topped peak

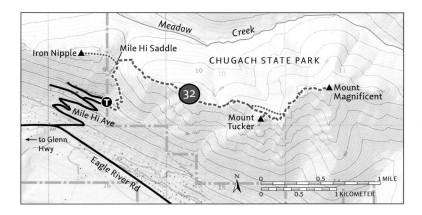

just as Eagle River Road curves to the right for the first time. Stay on Mile Hi Avenue as it switchbacks uphill for another 1.7 miles, going through multiple name changes. The tiny trailhead (elevation 1550 feet) is on the right at a sharp bend just before the end of the road.

ON THE TRAIL

Follow the obvious trail as it passes to the left of an antenna tower. From there it's a steep uphill hustle through lush greenery, gaining 800 feet in just 0.75 mile. As of 2018 there are no switchbacks here—just a loose, eroded dirt trail on the steepest parts—but because this trail is so popular, it might not be long before they're added. Keep an eye out for wild roses, protect your skin from the plentiful cow parsnip, and be aware of browsing moose hidden by the thick summer growth.

At 0.75 mile you pop out onto the Mile Hi Saddle (elevation 2350 feet). Although it's not actually a mile high, it does offer some nice views of the Mount Baldy ridge straight ahead (Hike 31). The trail to your left leads onto a vaguely mammary-shaped mountain that has received many names over the years; of those, "Iron Nipple" is the most genteel.

But the best walking is to the right. From the saddle, turn right and head up a couple stretches of steep, loose dirt. By about 1.1 miles (elevation 2915 feet) you'll hit the first of several false peaks. Keep following the clear tundra footpath along the ridge until at 1.9 miles (elevation 3060 feet) it dips down and shoots up another peak; this is Mount Tucker.

Veer right to the top of Mount Tucker (about 2.3 miles, elevation 3560 feet) to take a picture with the Alaska flag, which confuses many hikers into thinking this is Mount Magnificent. But it's not, so pick your way down the east side of Mount Tucker and back up the ridge to the northeast. The trail fades in and out, but by about 2.6 miles (elevation 3750 feet) you'll start to pick it up again, usually just to the left and slightly downhill of the ridge crest.

If you look straight ahead on this ridge, you can spot your next goal: a straight slash of trail cutting near the top of a steep grassy ramp, the last high point before the ridge veers sharply to the right. This is a false peak, and at just shy of 3 miles (peak elevation 4230) you can pick your way around it to the north, then down into the obvious saddle.

Once you've turned that literal corner, keep following a somewhat loose, mildly exposed trail through the rocks (and sometimes also mud) on the north side of the ridge. Just before 3.2 miles some very mild scrambling gets you to the top of Mount Magnificent, which is, strangely enough, crowned with a big tuft of grass.

On your way back, you can skip the summit of Mount Tucker; look for a clear path that sidehills past it, then rejoins the footpath along the ridge.

33 Barbara Falls

RATING/ DIFFICULTY	ROUNDTRIP	ELEV GAIN/ HIGH POINT	SEASON
***/2	6.2 miles	715 feet/ 600 feet	Year-round

Maps: USGS Anchorage B7 SW, National Geographic Chugach State Park, Imus Geographics Chugach State Park; **Contact:** Chugach State Park; **Notes:** Chugach State Parks pass or parking fee. Open to snowmachine use when snow cover is adequate. Cross-country skiing and snowshoeing during winter. Dogs permitted on leash in parking area, under direct control on trail. Bear and moose habitat. Bear encounters very likely when fish are running in the river. Requires a shallow ford; **GPS:** 61.29695°, −149.53268°

   ❄ *Variously known as South Fork Falls, Lower Eagle River Trail, and the River Woods Trail, this pleasant, easy walk through lowland forest and boardwalk ends at 60-foot-tall Barbara Falls.*

GETTING THERE

From Anchorage, drive northeast on the Glenn Highway. After about 11 miles, take the marked exit for the Eagle River Loop Road/Hiland Road. Turn right onto Eagle River Loop. After 1.5 miles, look for an unmarked, unpaved road that cuts to the right and downhill, just before the Briggs Bridge. The hike starts from the Greenbelt Access/Briggs Bridge Trailhead at the end of this road. Depending on snow conditions, the access gate may be closed during winter; hikers can park in a small turnout (don't block the gate) and walk the remaining 0.2 mile to the trailhead.

ON THE TRAIL

This trail has many names; Chugach State Park rangers call it the Lower Eagle River Trail, but hikers seem to have adopted Barbara Falls as the most popular name. Access the trail from the east end of the parking lot, or take either of several access paths down to the river, then turn right at the railing and walk along an old gravel roadbed as it enters the forest. At 0.1 mile, ignore a right fork and continue straight on the roadbed.

As a general rule this trail offers very easy, mostly level walking year-round. But during winter, watch for overflow that pours over the trail then freezes into a virtual skating rink. Bring ice cleats or spikes for better footing during the winter and spring, and brace yourself for big muddy patches during

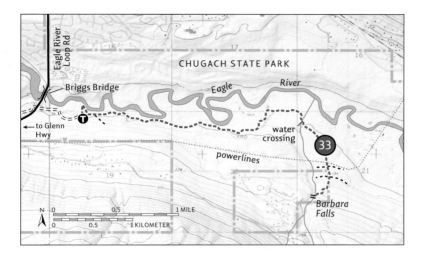

the summer. On the nicer end of things, it's common to see signs of snowshoe hares and moose on this stretch of trail.

Salmon also spawn in the river here. Although Chugach State Park doesn't officially close this trail for the salmon

These boardwalks are beautiful but can get slippery in winter; wear good winter boots or ice grippers.

run, consider skipping this trail, or at least being extra bear aware, when the salmon are running—typically mid-August to mid-October, the same time frame in which Chugach State Park officials close the Albert Loop Trail (see Hike 34) at Eagle River Nature Center.

At 1.6 miles the trail bends to the left, following a series of lovely new boardwalks through lowland meadows that give surprisingly good views of the mountains around you. This is the section of trail that goes closer to the river than before; it was rerouted to avoid a corner of private homestead land.

Then at just past 2.1 miles, trail and river meet. There's no bridge, and the river's pretty wide—but it usually flows gently here, and is only around knee-deep, which makes crossing very easy. During the winter, the river eventually freezes into a solid ice bridge that you can walk to the other side. Exactly when this happens—and when the ice melts—depends on the weather.

At 2.7 miles the trail crosses under a set of powerlines, then reaches a large four-way intersection. Go right, followed by a quick jog to the left, to stay on the trail to the falls. The trail ends at a concrete barrier, 3.1 miles from the trailhead. Just beyond the barrier you'll find a small viewing platform for the falls, which pour out over a rocky knob before tumbling some 60 feet to the ground.

34 Albert and Rodak Loops

Albert Loop

RATING/ DIFFICULTY	LOOP	ELEV GAIN/ HIGH POINT	SEASON
***/2	3.2 miles	230 feet/ 510 feet	Year-round

Rodak Loop

RATING/ DIFFICULTY	LOOP	ELEV GAIN/ HIGH POINT	SEASON
***/2	0.8 mile	130 feet/ 510 feet	Year-round

Maps: USGS Anchorage A7 NE, National Geographic Chugach State Park, Imus Geographics Chugach State Park; **Contact:** Eagle River Nature Center or Chugach State Park; **Notes:** Eagle River Nature Center parking pass or parking fee; Alaska State Parks pass not valid here. Albert Loop is closed during salmon runs—usually in mid-August—to reduce bear encounters. Dogs permitted on leash. Bear and moose habitat. Wet ground; consider wearing rubber boots; **GPS:** 61.23342°, –149.27086°

  Here you'll find a lovely introduction to Alaska for visitors, or an afternoon stroll for the whole family. Often overlooked in favor of more grandiose hikes, this is a fun place to stomp through mud puddles, watch for swans, and learn how beaver ponds and river flooding shape the land.

GETTING THERE

From Anchorage, drive northeast on the Glenn Highway. After about 11 miles, take the marked exit for the Eagle River Loop Road/Hiland Road. Turn right onto Eagle River Loop. After about 4 miles, turn right onto Eagle River Road. Continue almost 11 miles until the road ends at the Eagle River Nature Center (elevation 510 feet).

ON THE TRAIL

The Eagle River Nature Center is a wonderful place for both visitors and residents, with a wealth of educational activities and a small

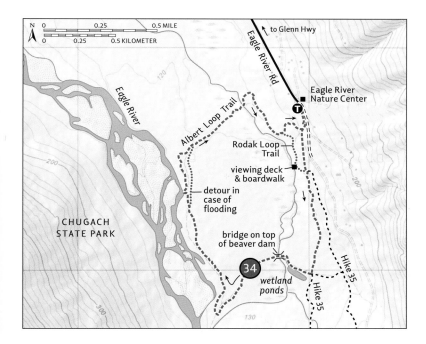

"petting zoo" of animal artifacts that will enchant children and the young at heart; see the Eagle River Nature Center website (ernc .org) for hours. But even when the nature center itself is closed, the trails remain open. The sole exception is Albert Loop, which is closed every year when the salmon start running, usually around mid-August. This is done to reduce the likelihood of dangerous bear encounters, and the trail is reopened once the salmon run ends.

Albert Loop: From the back deck of the Nature Center, walk straight down the largest, most obvious hiking trail. As you descend the hill into spruce and birch forest, you'll pass a signed right turn for the Rodak Loop at 0.1 mile. This is also where you'll

emerge when you finish Albert Loop. But for now, continue straight.

At 0.3 mile you'll reach the bottom of the hill and see a signed right turn for a viewing deck to the right; this is a great place to watch salmon spawning or to watch for beavers that are actively at work in the wetlands around the nature center. A left turn here would lead you onto the Dew Mound Loop (see Hike 35).

Continue straight and, when you reach another four-way intersection at 0.8 mile, turn right to stay on Albert Loop. Swans and other migratory waterfowl are often sighted in the wetland ponds here, which were created by hardworking beavers that still actively shape the valley's topography. At

Watch for wildlife, including beavers, from viewing decks along the short Rodak Loop.

1 mile (elevation 405 feet) you get to walk across a footbridge that's actually built on top of the remains of a beaver dam.

At 1.4 miles the trail veers to the right and roughly parallels the shore of Eagle River. The river's shallow, braided channels are prone to flooding and regularly shift their path, so it's common to find wet or flooded ground here. A cheerful attitude and willingness to stomp through a few mud puddles is recommended, and wearing rubber boots never hurts.

Sometimes the main trail becomes completely impassable due to flooding from the nearby river channel, but a signed detour just shy of 2 miles cuts inland, rejoining the trail at 2.3 miles, so you should have no problem continuing the loop. At 3 miles you'll pass another signed right turn for the Rodak Loop, and at about 3.1 miles you'll intersect with the trail where you started; turn left to return to the nature center at 3.2 miles.

The numbered stations along Albert Loop are part of a self-guided geology tour. I recommend getting the inexpensive tour pamphlet, which is available inside the nature center.

Rodak Loop: The first part of this much shorter loop coincides with the Albert Loop Trail. Starting from behind the Eagle River Nature Center, take the most obvious hiking trail down a forested hill. At 0.1 mile continue straight past a signed intersection for Rodak Loop.

At 0.3 mile, turn right at another signed intersection for Rodak Loop. This takes you on a lovely quarter-mile stroll past a series of viewing decks, benches, and interpretive signs, all of which give you great perspectives on the wetland habitat that occupies the valley floor. This is a nice place to pause

and watch for beavers, moose, and other wildlife in the water. Although the nearby Albert Loop Trail is closed seasonally when salmon spawn, the observation decks usually stay open.

When you're ready to continue, at about 0.5 mile you'll reach a marked intersection with Albert Loop. Turn right and start up a short, but stiff hill—the only thing that bumps this hike from "easy" to "moderate" for some people. At 0.7 mile you'll rejoin the main trail that departs from the nature center; turn left to get back to the center, completing the 0.8-mile loop.

35 Dew Mound

RATING/ DIFFICULTY	LOOP	ELEV GAIN/ HIGH POINT	SEASON
***/3	6.1 miles	880 feet/ 800 feet	Year-round

Maps: USGS Anchorage A7 NE, USGS Anchorage A6 NW, National Geographic Chugach State Park, Imus Geographics Chugach State Park; **Contact:** Eagle River Nature Center or Chugach State Park; **Notes:** Eagle River Nature Center parking pass or parking fee; Alaska State Parks pass not valid here. Dogs permitted on leash at Albert/Rodak Loop trails, under direct control elsewhere. Bear and moose habitat; **GPS:** 61.23342°, –149.27086°

  Friendly enough for beginners but also interesting enough to be a fun outing for any hiker, this 6.1-mile loop takes you past a small, pleasant lake and several exciting sections of Eagle River, then back to its starting point along a rehabilitated portion of the Historic Iditarod Trail.

Working along the shores of frozen, snow-covered Dew Lake

GETTING THERE

From Anchorage, drive northeast on the Glenn Highway. After about 11 miles, take the marked exit for the Eagle River Loop Road/Hiland Road. Turn right onto Eagle River Loop. After about 4 miles, turn right onto Eagle River Road. Continue almost 11 miles until the road ends at the Eagle River Nature Center (elevation 510 feet).

ON THE TRAIL

With the exception of seasonally closed Albert Loop (see Hike 34), the trails at Eagle River Nature Center are always open—even when the center itself is closed. That makes this relatively gentle, rolling trail a perfect getaway on any morning. If you hike it in the evening, be aware that this part of the valley tends to fall into shadow relatively early, and gets markedly colder when that happens.

From the back deck of the nature center, start hiking on the largest, most obvious trail, which leads into the forest and down a moderate hill. At this point you're on the main trail through the Eagle River valley, sometimes called the Historic Iditarod Trail because it did, in fact, serve as part of the life-saving serum run in 1925. The trail passes a couple of signed intersections with the Rodak Loop Trail (part of Hike 34) until a marked left turn for the Dew Mound Trail at 0.3 mile (elevation 415 feet).

From here, the trail is a narrow footpath that can get grassy until trail crews come through, but is usually in good shape. At 0.75 mile, 1.5 miles, and 1.7 miles you'll pass signed shortcuts that would, if you turned right, take you back to the main valley trail. Instead, continue straight ahead to stay on the Dew Mound Trail.

Once past this point the trail scales a short hill, gaining about 200 feet. From there it's easy cruising over rocky ground until 2.5 miles, at which point it descends slightly toward the banks of a small stream. Depending on how the water's running you

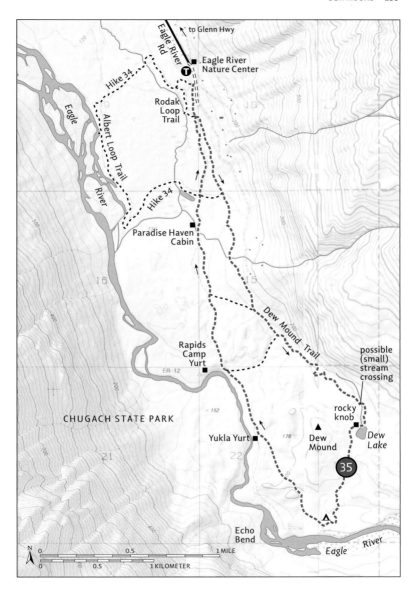

may need to step across it, but you shouldn't have to wade. At 2.6 miles (elevation 750 feet) the trail passes to the right of a small, reed-lined lake: Dew Lake. Look to your right for an obvious rocky knob that many hikers use as a lookout point, photo op, or picnic spot. The knob is part of the lower flanks of the Dew Mound itself, a huge, rocky pile that's hidden in the trees.

As you depart the lake, the trail climbs to its high point of 800 feet, then dips down to the shores of Eagle River at 3.3 miles (elevation 580 feet). This area is known as Echo Bend, and you'll find designated first-come, first-served backcountry campsites in the trees, along with great views along the riverbanks that showcase the immensity and quiet, hushed feel of this grand river valley.

The trail curves back to the right here, rejoining the main trail on its way back to the nature center. After one more small hill, the hiking is mostly level or downhill. You'll pass two signed turnoffs for public use shelters that must be reserved in advance for a fee (for details, see the Eagle River Nature Center website at ernc.org): they are the Yukla Yurt at 4 miles and the Rapids Camp Yurt at 4.5 miles.

As you continue straight ahead on the main trail, you'll pass signed cutoffs for the shortcut trails that link you to the first leg of the Dew Mound Loop. Then at 5.4 miles (elevation 415 feet) you'll reach a signed turnoff for one last reservable public use shelter, the Paradise Haven Cabin. You're in the home stretch now: at 5.6 miles (elevation 415 feet) you'll see a signed left turn for the Albert Loop Trail (another part of Hike 34). Continue straight ahead, and at just past 6 miles you'll start the last moderate hill back up to the nature center.

36 Eagle and Symphony Lakes

RATING/ DIFFICULTY	ROUNDTRIP	ELEV GAIN/ HIGH POINT	SEASON
****/3	11.4 miles	1515 feet/ 2750 feet	May–Oct

Maps: USGS Anchorage A7 NW, USGS Anchorage A7 NE, National Geographic Chugach State Park, Imus Geographics Chugach State Park; **Contact:** Chugach State Park; **Notes:** Chugach State Parks Pass or parking fee required; cash/check, bring a pen to fill out the form. You will be ticketed if you park on the side of the road. Dogs permitted on leash at trailhead, under direct control on trail. Bear and moose habitat. Grayling fishing in Symphony Lake. Some boulder hopping. Avalanche hazard in winter; **GPS:** 61.2326°, –149.4562°

 A great first long hike for kids or a stunning, day-long outing for adults, this trail parallels South Fork Eagle River to its source, milk-blue Eagle Lake. Its color is a marked contrast to nearby indigo-blue Symphony Lake, which you can reach with boulder hopping.

GETTING THERE

From Anchorage, drive northeast on the Glenn Highway. After about 11 miles, take the marked exit for Hiland Road, turn right, then turn right again onto Hiland Road. Stay on Hiland as it changes names multiple times; after about 7.5 miles turn right on South Creek Road, followed by a right onto West River Drive. The trailhead (elevation 1960 feet) is on your left. The parking area is often crowded, but resist the temptation to park on the side of the road. You'll limit

Periodic cairns are semi-helpful in finding your way through the boulder field alongside blue-green Eagle Lake.

emergency vehicle access to nearby homes and may get a ticket.

ON THE TRAIL

This well-maintained trail starts on a sequence of boardwalk and hardened gravel, offering firm footing through a forest of spindly spruce trees and marshy ground. The trail quickly leaves the wet ground behind and zigzags up the mountainside for about 100 feet in the first 0.2 mile. At 0.4 mile (elevation 2140 feet) you'll pass a signed intersection for Hunter Pass, an optional side trail that leads you up a brutally steep ridge for views, berry picking, or to connect with the Rendezvous Ridge Trail (see Hike 41).

From here, the trail is a long, mostly level stroll along the side of the valley until 1.75 miles (elevation 2400 feet). Here, a right turn would take you up to an unnamed pass, another access point to Rendezvous Ridge. But you'll want to stay on the main trail as it descends slowly to the valley floor and at 2.3 miles (elevation 2200 feet) crosses South Fork Eagle River on a sturdy footbridge—one of the most iconic photo ops on this hike. Note how the bottom of the valley is a broad U; that's how you know it was carved by a glacier instead of a stream, which would have turned it into a sharp V.

At 2.7 miles (elevation 2330 feet) you'll pass an unmarked footpath that veers uphill into Hanging Valley (Hike 37). The main trail continues winding along the valley floor, companionably near the river, until at 4.9 miles (elevation 2600 feet) you meet another bridge—this time over the outlet of Eagle Lake, which gets its milky blue-green coloring from silt shed by Eagle Glacier.

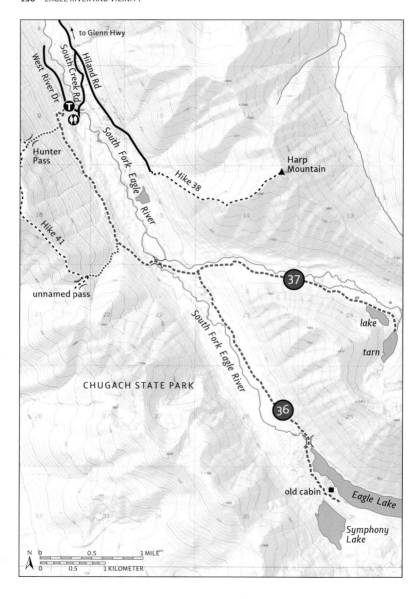

Once you cross the bridge, the terrain is all boulders deposited by the retreating glacier. You can hop boulders down to the rocky shore of Eagle Lake or continue south, boulder-hopping your way to the shores of Symphony Lake, a popular backcountry fishing destination for small grayling. The boulder-hopping is mild by Alaska standards, and you'll find smatterings of trail fragments scattered among the rocks. Watch out for seagulls that, strangely, nest in the middle of the boulder field every year; they're notorious for dive-bombing unwary hikers.

The difference in color between these lakes is very striking. Symphony Lake is fed by snowmelt and streams, which render it a vivid indigo blue in sharp contrast to Eagle Lake's mild aquamarine. My favorite picnic destination—which I'll call the endpoint of this hike—is a brushy spine at 5.7 miles (elevation 2750 feet) that runs between the two lakes, marked by the remains of an old, ramshackle cabin.

37 Hanging Valley

RATING/ DIFFICULTY	ROUNDTRIP	ELEV GAIN/ HIGH POINT	SEASON
****/3	10 miles	1960 feet/ 3420 feet	May–Oct

Maps: USGS Anchorage A7 NW, USGS Anchorage A7 NE, National Geographic Chugach State Park, Imus Geographics Chugach State Park; **Contact:** Chugach State Park; **Notes:** Chugach State Parks Pass or parking fee required. You will be ticketed if you park on the side of the road. Dogs permitted on leash at trailhead, under direct control on trail. Bear and moose habitat. Some boulder hopping. Avalanche hazard in winter; **GPS:** 61.2326°, –149.4562°

Looking down to the lower of two alpine lakes along the Hanging Valley trail

 *No matter how crowded the trails along the valley floor may get, this peaceful retreat in an isolated alpine valley always feels like a world unto itself. By summer it's a lush green alpine wonderland; in fall, it paints itself in a riot of bright reds and oranges.*

GETTING THERE

From Anchorage, drive northeast on the Glenn Highway. After about 11 miles, take the marked exit for Eagle River Loop Road/ Hiland Road, turn right, then turn right again onto Hiland Road. Stay on Hiland as it changes names multiple times; after about 7.5 miles turn right on South Creek Road, followed by a right onto West River Drive. The trailhead (elevation 1960 feet) is on your left. The parking area is often crowded, but resist the temptation to park on the side of the road. You'll limit emergency vehicle access to nearby homes and may get a ticket.

ON THE TRAIL

This trail shares its first 2.7 miles with Eagle and Symphony Lakes (Hike 36). Both trails start on a short stretch of boardwalk and hardened gravel, work up a few short switchbacks until mile 0.2, then at 0.4 mile cross a signed intersection with Hunter Pass, a brutally steep side trail leading up to Rendezvous Ridge (Hike 41).

From that point, the wide, rock-studded dirt trail winds lazily along the side of this glacier-carved valley, giving you great views over South Fork Eagle River and, during the fall, stands of slim, straight aspen trees clad in bright yellow leaves—a beautiful contrast to the rich reds and oranges of the fall tundra. During the summer, look for wildflowers and thick berry patches, and listen for birds.

At 1.75 miles (elevation 2400 feet) you'll pass another optional right turn leading up to Rendezvous Ridge. Stay on the main trail as it descends to the valley floor and at 2.3 miles (elevation 2200 feet) crosses South Fork Eagle River on a sturdy footbridge.

The turnoff for Hanging Valley comes at 2.7 miles (elevation 2330 feet), just as the Eagle and Symphony Lakes Trail makes a sharp turn to the right—almost a U-turn. Just at the apex of that turn, look for an unassuming, unmarked footpath that cuts sharply up and to the left through some grass, leading into the obvious hanging valley in front of you. By mile 3 (elevation 2700 feet) you've "topped out" in the valley.

Several thready footpaths lead through the scrubby tundra bushes; just pick one that heads straight into the hanging valley you've already entered. This stretch of trail wades through whip-tough, knee-high willows that can get very wet, so waterproof boots, waterproof pants, and gaiters can all make for a more comfortable hike in the spring or after a good rain. Looming to your left is 5001-foot Harp Mountain (Hike 38).

From here you can enjoy a solid mile of easy, mostly level strolling along the valley floor. At about mile 4.5 (elevation 3080 feet) you'll see a pretty, placid lake to the right of the trail, but this isn't the end of the hike. Continue past the lake and look for an obvious steep-sided bowl to your right, with a creek trickling down the middle of the wall that forms the bowl. Hike the narrow, often muddy trail that leads up and to the right of that creek, gaining another 300 feet in just 0.2 mile until at mile 5 you reach an alpine tarn that often holds sheets of ice well into the summer (elevation 3420 feet).

Heads up: wildlife sightings aren't terribly common along the heavily trafficked South

Fork Eagle River Valley (see Hike 36). But because Hanging Valley receives much less traffic, you're more likely to find wild critters here who, just like you, are seeking respite from the (relative) crowds down below.

38 Harp Mountain

RATING/ DIFFICULTY	ROUNDTRIP	ELEV GAIN/ HIGH POINT	SEASON
***/4	3.5 miles	2650 feet/ 5001 feet	June–Oct

Maps: USGS Anchorage A7 NE, National Geographic Chugach State Park, Imus Geographics Chugach State Park; **Contact:** Chugach State Park; **Notes:** Limited parking; no fee. Dogs permitted on leash in parking area, under direct control on trail. Bear and moose habitat. Bring hiking poles for the descent. Respect private property.

Cornicing, avalanche hazard in winter; **GPS:** 61.22322°, –149.43138°

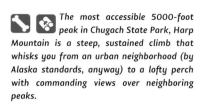 *The most accessible 5000-foot peak in Chugach State Park, Harp Mountain is a steep, sustained climb that whisks you from an urban neighborhood (by Alaska standards, anyway) to a lofty perch with commanding views over neighboring peaks.*

GETTING THERE

From Anchorage, drive northeast on the Glenn Highway. After about 11 miles, take the marked exit for Eagle River Loop Road/ Hiland Road, turn right, then turn right again onto Hiland Road. Stay on Hiland Road for just over 8 miles as it changes name multiple times, finally ending at the trailhead for Harp Mountain (elevation 2360 feet). Trailhead parking is limited to a short stretch on

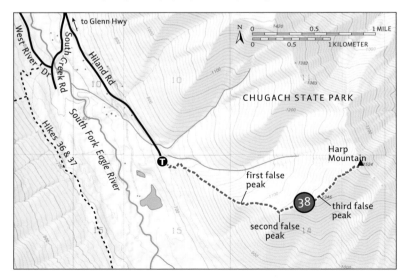

The final summit of Harp Mountain is equal parts foreboding and beautiful.

the left side of the road as you pull in. Do not park in the cul-de-sac or on private property.

ON THE TRAIL

The trail starts at the far end of the cul-de-sac, to the left of the last house; look for a faint, handwritten sign pointing the way to a clear footpath, which wastes no time in heading straight uphill. You have only about 0.1 mile to enjoy the fireweed, wild geraniums, monkshood, yarrow, and high-bush raspberries that come along with tree cover. There's cow parsnip too, so watch your bare skin.

By 0.25 mile (elevation 2680 feet) you're above the brushline, where you'll see the peak of Harp sitting like an emperor right in front of you, framed by ridges that fall away to either side. You're going to hike straight up the rightmost ridgeline, building toward the mountain in a series of three false summits.

The path is mostly loose dirt, climbing so steeply that even sure-footed hikers may want hiking poles for balance on the way down. At 0.5 mile it starts to get rocky, with dense clusters of Arctic sandwort and crowberry plants blooming in between the rocks, dotted with solitary harebells and proud king's crown.

At about 0.6 mile (elevation 3330 feet) you'll top the first of three major false peaks. At 1 mile (elevation 3920 feet) you'll reach the top of the second false peak, which is backed by a large, relatively flat area that makes the perfect spot for a picnic. Listen for the odd, chuckling coo of ptarmigan hidden in the rocks, and the buzz of grasshoppers on hot summer days. At about this point you'll also start getting great views of the round, deep blue Symphony Lake (Hike 36) in a distant valley to your right.

At 1.2 miles (elevation 4230 feet) the trail gets into rocky scree. It's a short, steep push up loose trail to the top of the third false peak at 1.3 miles (elevation 4390 feet). The trail starts to get patchier here; when in doubt, you can generally pick the defined trail back up on your left.

Although this trail is consistently steep from the start, the only place it's truly exposed comes in the next short, steep push at 1.6 miles (elevation 4720 feet), where the left side of the trail has eroded into almost nothing at the very edge of a steep drop. Avoid this section by hiking/scrambling around to the right. Once past that point it's a clear shot to the mountain's 5001-foot summit, a rocky, grassy knob that's just high enough to let you spy the waters of Cook Inlet over the endless washboard waves of mountain peaks around you.

39 Rendezvous Ski Loop

RATING/ DIFFICULTY	LOOP	ELEV GAIN/ HIGH POINT	SEASON
***/3	3.6 miles	1560 feet/ 4015 feet	May–Oct

Maps: USGS Anchorage A7 NW, USGS Anchorage B7 SW, National Geographic Chugach State Park, Imus Geographics Chugach State Park; **Contact:** Chugach State Park; **Notes:** Arctic Valley Ski Area parking pass required, or parking fee. Access gate closes at 10:00 PM and reopens at 6:00 AM. During winter, this becomes a fully functioning ski area; see the Arctic Valley website for season dates. Dogs permitted on leash at trailhead, under direct control in backcountry. Bear habitat; moose sightings are rare, but possible. Respect

boundaries of military land nearby; **GPS:** 61.2467°, –149.5356°

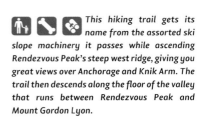 *This hiking trail gets its name from the assorted ski slope machinery it passes while ascending Rendezvous Peak's steep west ridge, giving you great views over Anchorage and Knik Arm. The trail then descends along the floor of the valley that runs between Rendezvous Peak and Mount Gordon Lyon.*

GETTING THERE
From Anchorage, drive northeast on the Glenn Highway. After about 7 miles, take the Arctic Valley exit. Turn right and continue straight ahead on Arctic Valley Road for another 7 miles, past a golf course, as the road transitions to washboard gravel and ends at Arctic Valley Ski Area. Park in the upper of the two parking areas (elevation 2620 feet). An access gate is closed from 10:00 PM to 6:00 AM, and on rare occasions the access road may be closed due to military exercises.

ON THE TRAIL
From the upper parking lot of the Arctic Valley Trailhead, walk back down the access road for 400 feet, looking for an old maintenance road striking out into the bushes on the left. You'll pass under two ski lifts as you ford a small creek and walk the old road through the thick, bushy alders that carpet the toe of this ridge. Just before 0.5 mile (elevation 2560 feet) you'll strike a four-way intersection; turn left and hike steeply uphill.

At 0.7 mile (elevation 2800 feet) the trees open enough to give you a splendid lookout over Anchorage and Knik Arm to the west.

Communications equipment atop one of the arms of Rendezvous Peak

By about 0.8 mile (elevation 3080 feet) your efforts are rewarded as you pop out above the treeline and the machinery at the top of one of Arctic Valley's ski lifts. Just before 1 mile (elevation 3300 feet) you'll pass another set of lift machinery.

At 1.3 miles (elevation 3600 feet) you'll pass the top of another ski lift. Stop and look around: you have incredible panoramic views over the mostly uninhabited valley to your right (east), while to the west you can see all the way to Fire Island, where a wind farm supplies a small portion of Anchorage's electricity. Once past the ski lifts, the trail converges to a narrow footpath and follows the obvious ridge.

Just before 1.9 miles (elevation 3900 feet) you'll pass a fourth ski lift and reach a small but broad saddle, with a creek running down a small gully. From here, you have a few choices: you can take a narrow, steep, and often muddy footpath down the gully to your left, eventually intersecting with one of several trails that leads back along the valley floor to the trailhead. You can make a sharp right, tracing Rendezvous Ridge (see Hike 41); or you can sidehill around the east flank of Rendezvous Peak instead of actually climbing it.

But you came here to climb a mountain, and you're almost there. Keep going on the obvious uphill footpath, passing clumps of sentinel-like boulders on a last push to the 4015-foot summit of Rendezvous Peak, just shy of 2 miles from the trailhead.

From the summit, you could return the way you came—but it saves you almost a half-mile of walking to complete the loop by

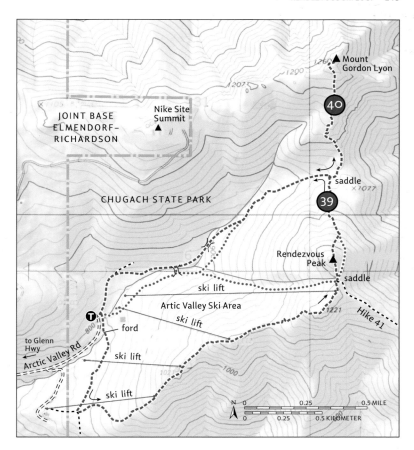

hiking down the far side of Rendezvous Peak (again, there are several trails to choose from). At about 2.4 miles from the trailhead (elevation 3500 feet) you'll reach the saddle between Rendezvous Peak and Mount Gordon Lyon (see Hike 40).

From there, a recently improved trail leads downvalley for the remaining 1.2 miles of the hike. On days with decent visibility,

you'll see some interesting white buildings atop the ridge to your north (on the right as you descend). Those are part of the Nike Site Summit, a retired missile defense emplacement on access-restricted military land. You can learn more about the site's very interesting history—and book a guided tour, which is currently the only way to visit—at the Friends of Nike Site Summit website.

④⓪ Mount Gordon Lyon

RATING/ DIFFICULTY	ROUNDTRIP	ELEV GAIN/ HIGH POINT	SEASON
***/3	3.8 miles	1500 feet/ 4105 feet	May–Oct

Maps: USGS Anchorage A7 NW, USGS Anchorage B7 SW, National Geographic Chugach State Park, Imus Geographics Chugach State Park; **Contact:** Chugach State Park; **Notes:** Arctic Valley Ski Area parking pass required, or parking fee. Access gate closes at 10:00 PM and reopens at 6:00 AM. During winter, this area becomes a fully functioning ski area; see Arctic Valley website for season dates. Dogs permitted on leash at trailhead, under direct control in backcountry. Bear and Dall sheep habitat; moose sightings are rare, but possible. Respect boundaries of military land nearby; **GPS:** 61.2467°, –149.5356°

 This straightforward trail goes up to a saddle between 4105-foot Mount Gordon Lyon and Rendezvous Peak, then veers left to climb up Gordon Lyon. While the mountain's rocky flanks look imposing from a distance, this is actually a reasonably easy hike, and it's a great family-friendly alternative to popular Rendezvous Peak.

GETTING THERE
From Anchorage, drive northeast on the Glenn Highway. After about 7 miles, take the Arctic Valley exit. Turn right and continue straight ahead on Arctic Valley Road for another 7 miles, past a golf course, as the road transitions to washboard gravel and ends at Arctic Valley Ski Area. Park in the upper of the two parking areas (elevation 2620 feet). An access gate is closed from 10:00 PM to 6:00 AM, and on rare occasions the access road may be closed due to military exercises.

ON THE TRAIL
There is a network of braided trails to explore in this valley, but the nicest is the recently improved gravel-over-dirt trail that starts to the left of the pay kiosk in the main parking lot. From here, the trail side-hills through brushy alders before climbing through wiry, waist-high willows along the left (north) side of the valley. At 0.2 mile (elevation 2730 feet) the trail forks; take the right fork, which starts easing back down the slope toward the creek that runs through the middle of this valley.

Although it's tempting to explore uphill from the trail, especially during berry-picking season, only do this if you have a good map that shows the poorly marked border between Chugach State Park and Joint Base Elmendorf-Richardson's military land. If you wander onto military land without a permit (available from Joint Base Elmendorf-Richardson at jber.isportsman .net), you can get an expensive ticket.

Just before 0.5 mile (elevation 2800 feet) you'll come to a bridge. If you were to cross and turn right you'd find yourself on an old, dirt trail back to the parking area; stay on the left side of the creek instead.

At about 0.6 mile (elevation 2900 feet) the trail meets the creek again. This time, cross the bridge and continue uphill on a recently improved trail that climbs steadily to the saddle between Mount Gordon Lyon (on your left) and Rendezvous Peak (to your right). Just before 1.4 miles (3500 feet) you'll reach the saddle. From here, look to your left (north) for a fairly steep footpath that leads up Mount Gordon Lyon.

Practice your Superman pose on one of Mount Gordon Lyon's twin summits.

Like most human trails established by sheer dint of foot traffic along old goat paths, the trail up Mount Gordon Lyon braids and rejoins itself, winding around short, rocky towers that periodically sprout out of an otherwise easy-to-navigate tundra slope. More military land is just to the west, but as long as you stay on the main trail to the summit, you'll be safely on Chugach State Park land. You'll reach the 4105-foot summit—two small rocky crags that offer views into South Fork Eagle River Valley to the east and over Anchorage and Knik Arm to the west—at 1.9 miles.

The buildings on the ridge to the west are relics of the Nike Site Summit, a retired missile defense emplacement on military land. You can learn more about the site's history—and book a guided tour, which is currently the only way to visit—at the Friends of Nike Site Summit website.

41 Rendezvous Ridge

RATING/ DIFFICULTY	ONE-WAY	ELEV GAIN/ HIGH POINT	SEASON
*****/4	7.9 miles	2860 feet/ 3910 feet	June–Oct

Maps: USGS Anchorage B7 SW, USGS Anchorage A7 NW, USGS Anchorage A7 NE, National Geographic Chugach State Park, Imus Geographics Chugach State Park; **Contact:** Chugach State Park; **Notes:** Arctic Valley Ski Area parking pass required for parking at Arctic Valley, or Alaska State Parks Pass for parking at South Fork Eagle River, or parking fee at either trailhead. Access gate closes at 10:00 PM and reopens at 6:00 AM. During winter, the area around the Arctic Valley Trailhead becomes a fully functioning ski area; see Arctic Valley website for season

dates. Dogs permitted on leash at trailhead, under direct control in backcountry. Bear and moose habitat. Respect boundaries of military land nearby; **GPS:** Arctic Valley: 61.2467°, –149.5356°; South Fork Eagle River: 61.2326°, –149.4562°

A long ridge walk that gives you bird's-eye views over two of the most popular hiking areas in Southcentral Alaska. It's especially lovely when the alpine tundra is ablaze with its best fall colors.

GETTING THERE
Arctic Valley Trailhead: From Anchorage, drive northeast on the Glenn Highway. After about 7 miles, take the Arctic Valley exit. Turn right and continue straight ahead on Arctic Valley Road for another 7 miles, past a golf course, as the road transitions to washboard gravel and ends at Arctic Valley Ski Area. Park in the upper of the two parking areas (elevation 2620 feet). An access gate is closed from 10:00 PM to 6:00 AM, and on rare occasions the access road may be closed due to military exercises.

South Fork Eagle River Trailhead: From Anchorage, drive northeast on the Glenn Highway. After about 11 miles, take the marked exit for Eagle River Loop Road/ Hiland Road, turn right, then turn right again onto Hiland Road. Stay on Hiland as it changes names multiple times; after about 7.5 miles turn right on South Creek Road, followed by a right onto West River Drive. The trailhead is on your left.

ON THE TRAIL
Although this trail is a wonderful walk starting from either trailhead, setting out from the Arctic Valley Trailhead saves you about

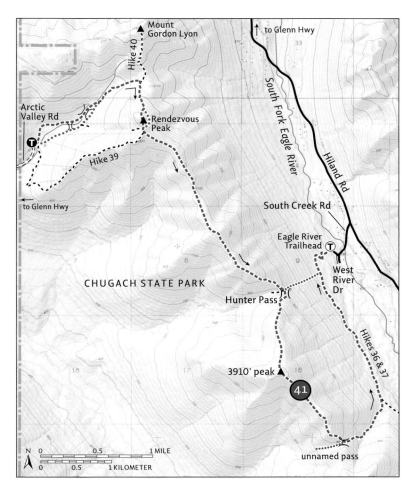

CHUGACH STATE PARK

N   0   0.5   1 MILE

0   0.5   1 KILOMETER

600 feet of elevation gain and treats you to early views of Eagle and Symphony lakes (Hike 36) as you walk along the ridge.

From the Arctic Valley Trailhead, follow any of the braided trails that lead straight up the valley to the saddle between Mount Gordon Lyon (Hike 40) and Rendezvous Peak (part of Hike 39). At about 1.25 miles (elevation 3400 feet) you'll see several side trails that crisscross their way to the 4015-foot summit of Rendezvous Peak. Pick the trail of your choice and hike up and over

One of two marked passes from the South Fork Eagle River Valley (Hike 36) up to Rendezvous Ridge

the back side of the peak, or save yourself a little elevation gain by taking a clear footpath that sidehills to the left (east) side of the peak.

Either way, once you reach the back side of Rendezvous Peak, look for a patchy footpath leading along the broad ridge to your left (southeast). At about 3 miles (elevation 3820 feet) look straight ahead (east) for views of Eagle and Symphony lakes in the distance.

At about 3.8 miles (elevation 2860 feet) you'll reach Hunter Pass, from which you could take a brutally steep shortcut down to the valley floor, then turn left to reach the South Fork Eagle River Trailhead. But I

would encourage you to explore the pass itself—there are lovely views off to the right—then keep going, making a 1080-foot ascent to the next peak in the ridge at about 4.6 miles (elevation 3910 feet).

From here, it's all downhill. You'll reach an unnamed pass at 5.6 miles (elevation 3130 feet); enjoy the valley views to the right, then go back and descend to the valley floor on a footpath that rejoins the main Eagle and Symphony Lakes Trail (Hikes 36 and 37) at 6.2 miles (elevation 2420 feet).

Turn left and follow the Eagle and Symphony Lakes Trail, gently losing another 450 feet in elevation until you reach the South Fork Eagle River Trailhead at 7.9 miles.

Opposite: The hikes clustered around Anchorage may be (relatively) easy to get to and (relatively) well traveled, but they still pack as much beauty and adventure as the rest of the state (Hike 49).

anchorage area

It may be tempting to write some of these off as "urban" trails; after all, they're right on the fringes of Alaska's largest city, Anchorage (population about 300,000). But Alaska's urban treks are any other state's wild adventures, and here you'll find a full serving of the scenery, wildlife, and relative solitude you'd hope for on any outing. If you really want to have the most popular trails to yourself, my favorite trick remains getting up early enough to watch the sun rise as I hike.

42 Lost Cabin Valley and Basher Loop

RATING/ DIFFICULTY	LOOP	ELEV GAIN/ HIGH POINT	SEASON
***/3	4.1 miles	860 feet/ 1330 feet	Year-round

Map: USGS Anchorage A8 NE; **Contact:** Chugach State Park; **Notes:** Alaska State Parks Pass or parking fee at Prospect

This hike can get brushy during the summer, but in winter it's a welcoming tromp through blankets of fresh snow.

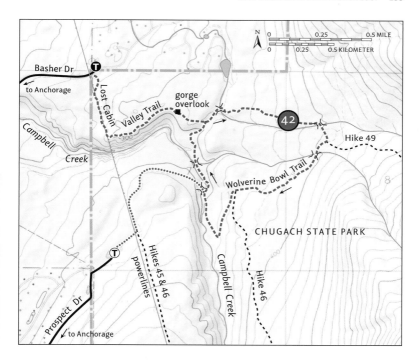

Heights; no fee at Basher as of 2018. From Basher, first part of trail is open to fat bikes November 15 through March 31. From Prospect, open to mountain bikes year-round. Dogs permitted on leash at trailhead, under direct control in backcountry. Bear and moose habitat; **GPS:** Basher Trailhead: 61.15158°, –149.71437°; Prospect Heights Trailhead: 61.13887°, –149.71135°

 I can't say I'm a big fan of this hike during its brushy summer phase, but it makes a great access trail to other hikes for those who live in east Anchorage—and it's a wonderful snowshoe or hiking outing in winter.

GETTING THERE

Basher Trailhead: From Tudor Road in Anchorage, turn south onto Campbell Airstrip Road, which after several miles becomes Basher Drive. Drive past the North Bivouac and South Bivouac trailheads, then look for the Basher Trailhead (elevation 825 feet) on your right, 3.1 miles from Tudor Road. If you reach the Stuckagain Heights neighborhood, you just missed the trailhead.

Prospect Heights Trailhead: From Anchorage, drive south on the New Seward Highway, take O'Malley Road east until it makes a sweeping curve to the left and becomes Hillside Drive. Make an immediate right onto Upper O'Malley Road, then turn left onto

Prospect Drive and stay on this road through a couple of name changes. The Prospect Heights Trailhead (elevation 1056 feet) will be on your right.

ON THE TRAIL

If you live on the south side of town, you can also hike this trail as a loop starting from the Prospect Heights Trailhead; but this description is for a hike starting from the Basher Trailhead in east Anchorage.

The trail starts as a couple of stiff but short hills alongside what will soon become one wall of Campbell Creek Gorge—but for now, it's just a sloping, brushy hillside with a trail along its crest. The path passes under a set of powerlines and then, at about 0.3 mile (elevation 940 feet), hooks a sharp left to trace the north wall of Campbell Creek Gorge. The trail climbs gently until a great overlook of the gorge at 0.75 mile (elevation 1030 feet).

Then at 0.9 mile the trail dips briefly to an intersection that is signed for Wolverine Bowl straight ahead and Prospect Heights to the right. Continue straight, crossing two footbridges and climbing a moderate slope that peaks in another intersection at 1.6 miles (elevation 1330 feet). Continuing straight would put you on the trail to Wolverine Peak (Hike 49). Instead turn right, staying in the forest and following signs for Prospect Heights, crossing one more footbridge along the way.

Most locals call this the Basher Loop but, technically speaking, up until this intersection you were traveling on the Lost Cabin Valley Trail, and from this point on you're on the Wolverine Bowl Trail.

Starting here, the trail descends a little more steeply than it had climbed. At 2.2 miles (elevation 1200 feet) you'll reach an intersection with the Middle Fork Loop Trail (Hike 46). Stay right.

Just before 2.5 miles the trail bends sharply back to the right, followed by one of your only close-up views of Campbell Creek. Take a right turn just before a small footbridge leads across the creek. The intersection does have a sign, but it's easy to miss; if you keep going straight you'll find yourself on a 0.9-mile access trail to the Prospect Heights Trailhead, with Campbell Creek Gorge between you and the Basher Trailhead.

Assuming you made the turn, you'll cross one more branch of Campbell Creek on a footbridge. At just before 3.2 miles watch for the sign indicating a left turn to the Basher Trailhead. This is where you started the loop and, again, it's easy to accidentally skate right past the sign on your first time through. Make that left turn and retrace the last 0.9 miles along the Lost Cabin Valley Trail back to the Basher Trailhead.

43 Flattop Mountain (front side)

RATING/ DIFFICULTY	ROUNDTRIP	ELEV GAIN/ HIGH POINT	SEASON
***/3	3.4 miles	1450 feet/ 3510 feet	May–Oct

Maps: USGS Anchorage A8 SE, National Geographic Chugach State Park, Imus Geographics Chugach State Park; **Contact:** Chugach State Park; **Notes:** Alaska State Parks pass or parking fee. Bikes allowed on very first part of access trail. Dogs permitted on leash in parking area, under direct control in backcountry, but dogs and some humans may struggle with rocky scramble at the top. Bear and moose habitat.

Flattop is one of many local peaks where you can see paragliders hiking up the mountain with their chutes packed in huge backpacks, then gliding back down.

Avalanche hazard in winter; **GPS:** 61.10349°, −149.68343°

🥾 *Easily the most hiked mountain in all of Alaska, Flattop is a rite of passage for any hiker in Southcentral, especially on the summer solstice. If you're used to Lower 48–style crowds, its popularity won't faze you— but locals have been known to deliberately hike early or late so they can have the mountain (mostly) to themselves.*

GETTING THERE

From Anchorage, drive south on the New Seward Highway; take O'Malley Road east (toward the mountains). After 3.6 miles turn right on Hillside Drive. After 1 mile turn left on Upper Huffman, and right onto Toilsome Hill Drive, which becomes Glen Alps Road.

After almost 2 miles, the large Glen Alps Trailhead (elevation 2180 feet) will be on your left. An overflow lot is available to the east of the main parking area. Be respectful of "No Parking" signs or you'll get a ticket.

ON THE TRAIL

Once upon a time, the Flattop Trail led up a set of wooden stairs to the right of the "iron ranger" pay kiosk in the southeast corner of the parking lot. But now it starts on the broad gravel maintenance road just to the left of the kiosk. For the most direct route, make an immediate right turn onto the marked Flattop Trail, which heads uphill at a moderate grade and is wide enough for three or four people to easily walk abreast.

If you want a gentler start, you can continue just over 0.2 mile down the

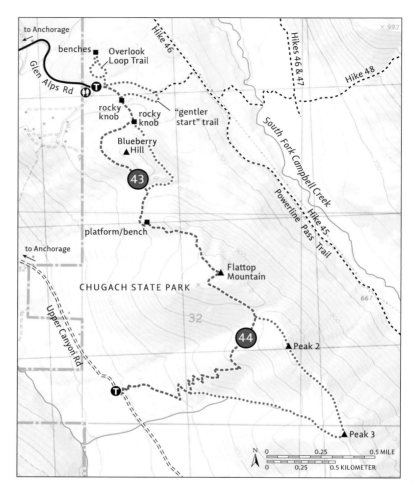

maintenance road to another right turn, which takes you up a much gentler grade but adds an extra 0.5 mile to the trip.

Assuming you take the first turn, the trail winds gently through a series of diminutive hemlock trees that have been wildly twisted and warped by the frequent high winds here. It emerges onto a bald, rocky knob after 0.1 mile; this is also where the gentler starting trail rejoins the main trail.

The trail continues more or less straight uphill until at 0.2 mile it reaches a steep, eroded dirt slope. Crest this and you'll be on top of another rocky knob. The trail splits around the big hill right in front of you, which is appropriately called Blueberry Hill. (It's full of blueberries in late summer.) I usually take the right fork, which showcases views over Anchorage, Cook Inlet, and Mount Susitna—also known as Sleeping Lady—in the distance. But you can also take the left fork for views of South Fork Campbell Creek valley and the Powerline Pass Trail (see Hike 45). Both forks end up in the same place, and both travel about the same distance.

The two forks rejoin on the far side of Blueberry Hill just before 1 mile from the trailhead (elevation 2550 feet). From there, the trail—still very broad and easy to walk—heads to the south, continuing uphill at a moderate grade. At 1.1 miles (elevation 2600 feet) you'll hit a wildly eroded set of stairs, followed by a big wooden platform that serves as a bench.

From here, the trail hooks sharply to the right and continues scaling more eroded stairs. Watch your step! At 1.4 miles (elevation 2960 feet) the trail enters an extremely rocky area. You'll see an obvious path leading straight up, eroded by the passage of many thousands of feet over the years; but it's much nicer to walk a switchback trail through the rocks. It's not very easy to spot from below, but if you keep an eye out for downward-bound hikers who are obviously zigzagging back and forth, you'll find it.

Even with the switchbacks, by 1.5 miles you'll be almost scrambling—using both hands and feet to progress through the harder spots—and by 1.6 miles you'll scramble in earnest to the top, following spray-painted blobs of color on the rock that are supposed to mark the easiest way. This rock is notoriously fragile, so be careful

which hand- and footholds you trust, keep an eye out for falling rocks, and take those "guide blobs" with a grain of salt. If you drop anything or kick loose rocks off at people below you, yell "Rock! Rock! Rock!" until whatever it was comes to a stop.

Some people are very understandably uncomfortable with that last scramble, especially when there are a lot of people on the trail. There's no shame in turning around, and you can always choose to hike up the scramble-free back side of Flattop (see Hike 44), which is much nicer and will eventually take over as the primary Flattop Trail. If you do choose to scramble, pay close attention to where you emerge onto Flattop's rocky summit plateau at 1.7 miles (3510 feet); that makes it much easier to find your way down.

If you're traveling with family members who don't want to hike the Flattop Trail, there's a pleasant, handicap-accessible 0.4-mile Overlook Loop Trail that starts on the north end of the parking lot. At the "top" of the overlook, a cluster of benches offers views over Anchorage, Cook Inlet, and Mount Susitna.

44 Flattop Mountain (back side)

RATING/ DIFFICULTY	ROUNDTRIP	ELEV GAIN/ HIGH POINT	SEASON
***/3	3.4 miles	1610 feet/ 3510 feet	May–Oct

Maps: USGS Anchorage A8 SE, National Geographic Chugach State Park, Imus Geographics Chugach State Park; **Contact:** Chugach State Park; **Notes:** Parking fee or Alaska State Parks parking pass. Rough access road, may be impassable in winter.

One of the beautiful new switchbacks on the back side of Flattop seems to take you straight into the sky.

Dogs permitted on leash at trailhead, under direct control in backcountry. Bear and moose habitat. Avalanche hazard in winter; **GPS:** 61.08184°, −149.68114°

  Once a steep, eroded corridor leading directly up the back of Flattop Mountain, this has been rehabilitated into a beautiful, broad trail with a lot of switchbacks. At some point the trailhead parking will be expanded and this will take over from Hike 43 as the primary trail up Flattop.

GETTING THERE
From Anchorage, drive south on the New Seward Highway; take DeArmoun Road east for 3.8 miles until it turns into Upper DeArmoun, then 0.6 mile later it becomes Canyon Road. Veer right at the next intersection to stay on Canyon Road, which then goes through several more name changes over the next 1.7 miles before becoming Upper Canyon Road and dead-ending at the small trailhead. The last part of the road is rough and rocky, but a carefully driven passenger vehicle can usually get you to within a short walk of the trailhead (elevation 1960 feet).

ON THE TRAIL
You can't miss the broad, hardened dirt trail that starts switchbacking uphill 1000 feet before the end of Canyon Road—but just in case, look for the small brown "Flattop Trail" sign bolted to a large rock. As you climb the lovely switchbacks, you might still see traces of the old trail starting at 0.25 mile, a horribly steep and eroded path that zipped straight up the mountainside.

Just past 0.5 mile (elevation 2380 feet) the trail forks; stay left to keep going up the back side of Flattop. The right fork goes up another mountain known as Peak 3, which you can also access by walking the ridge after you reach the peak of Flattop.

Just past 1.1 miles (elevation 3030 feet) the new trail rejoins the old straight-line trail of years past. This is a good opportunity to pause and enjoy the scenery around you: Flattop is the obvious rocky plateau to the left of the saddle. Peak 2 is the long pile of rocks to the right of the saddle, and Peak 3 is the more photogenic peak to the right of that, farther down the ridge.

They're all joined by a swath of rock-studded tundra that turns bright red and orange in the fall. In late summer and fall you'll see many people picking berries here, along with bears that are doing the same thing, grazing on the berries to fatten up for winter.

Continue straight up on the old trail. At 1.4 miles you'll reach the saddle (elevation 3240 feet). From here, turn left and continue hiking up a straight, even grade to the top of Flattop (elevation 3510 feet) at 1.7 miles. From there, you can retrace your route to the saddle and make somewhat scrambly but nontechnical extensions on a faint footpath that leads up the rocky "comb" of Peak 2 and along the ridge to Peak 3. These peaks are also popular with backcountry skiers, but regardless of your mode of travel, be aware of avalanche hazard on all three mountains in winter and spring.

45 Powerline Pass

RATING/ DIFFICULTY	ROUNDTRIP	ELEV GAIN/ HIGH POINT	SEASON
****/3	12.2 miles	1640 feet/ 3650 feet	May–Oct

Maps: USGS Anchorage A8 NE, USGS Anchorage A8 SE, USGS Anchorage A7 SW, USGS Seward D7 NW, National Geographic Chugach State Park, Imus Geographics

Chugach State Park; **Contact:** Chugach State Park; **Notes:** Alaska State Parks pass or parking fee. Open to mountain bikes, horses, and snowmachines when snow cover is sufficient. Popular for snowshoeing, skiing, fat biking in winter. Dogs permitted on leash at trailhead, under direct control in backcountry. Bear and moose habitat; **GPS:** 61.10349°, –149.68343°

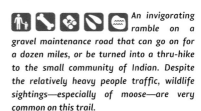 *An invigorating ramble on a gravel maintenance road that can go on for a dozen miles, or be turned into a thru-hike to the small community of Indian. Despite the relatively heavy people traffic, wildlife sightings—especially of moose—are very common on this trail.*

GETTING THERE

From Anchorage, drive south on the New Seward Highway; take O'Malley Road east (toward the mountains). After 3.6 miles turn right on Hillside Drive. After 1 mile turn left on Upper Huffman, and right onto Toilsome Hill Drive, which becomes Glen Alps Road. After almost 2 miles, the large Glen Alps Trailhead (elevation 2180 feet) will be on your left. An overflow lot is available to the east of the main parking area. Be respectful of "No Parking" signs or you'll get a ticket.

ON THE TRAIL

You can start this trail from the Prospect Heights Trailhead and hike toward the Glen Alps Trailhead, gaining 1170 feet of elevation over 3 miles. But this stretch of trail is quite unremarkable, whereas the rest of the trail is very interesting, with great views up the valley and the potential for seeing lots of wildlife (especially moose). So I recommend starting from the Glen Alps Trailhead. But

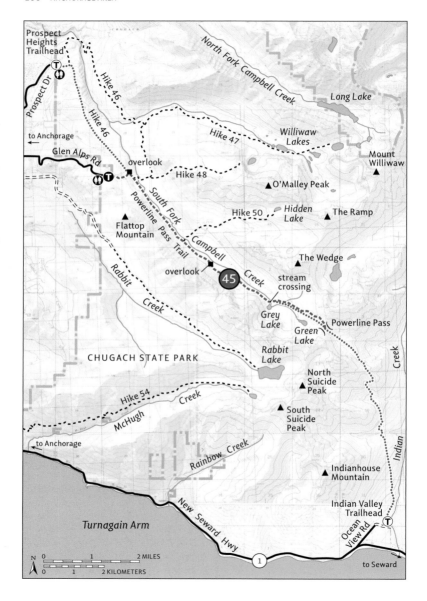

Prospect
Heights
Trailhead

Prospect Dr

North Fork Campbell Creek

Long Lake

Hike 46

Hike 46

to Anchorage

Glen Alps Rd

overlook

Hike 47

Williwaw
Lakes

Mount
Williwaw

South Fork

Hike 48

O'Malley Peak

Powerline Pass Trail

Hike 50

Hidden
Lake

The Ramp

Flattop
Mountain

Campbell

The Wedge

overlook

45

Creek

stream
crossing

Rabbit

Powerline Pass

Creek

Grey
Lake

Green
Lake

Creek

CHUGACH STATE PARK

Rabbit
Lake

North Suicide
Peak

Hike 54

Creek

McHugh

South
Suicide
Peak

to Anchorage

Rainbow Creek

Indianhouse
Mountain

Indian

Turnagain Arm

Indian Valley
Trailhead

New Seward Hwy

Ocean View Rd

N   0   1   2 MILES

1

0   1   2 KILOMETERS

to Seward

A winter stroll past one of two lakes near Powerline Pass. Beware of avalanche hazard in the pass.

before I describe that section of trail, one little tip: the Glen Alps to Prospect Heights section of the trail is fabulous for sledding in the winter, if you start at Glen Alps and set up a car shuttle from the Prospect Heights Trailhead (see Hike 46 for driving directions to Prospect Heights).

From the Glen Alps Trailhead, take the broad access trail that starts just left of the pay kiosk. Just past 0.3 mile (elevation 2220 feet) the access trail intersects with the Powerline Pass Trail—a wide gravel maintenance road—at a commanding overlook of South Fork Campbell Creek valley. The valley is enormous, so if you want to spot wild animals, bring binoculars or a spotting scope.

From that overlook, turn right and follow the Powerline Pass trail/road down a gentle hill. Expect to see a lot of bicyclers, runners,

and dog walkers here; during the winter, fat biking and skiing are popular, and when adequate snow cover is present, snowmachiners have the use of most of the valley from here to the south.

At 0.5 mile (elevation 2170 feet) the trail forks. Going left and down at this point would set you on the trail to Middle Fork Loop, Williwaw Lakes, or Little O'Malley (and "big" O'Malley) peaks (see Hikes 46, 47, and 48, respectively). Continue straight to stay on the Powerline Pass Trail, which continues more or less level, sidehilling along the valley's southwest wall.

The valley floor rises up toward you, which, combined with the more or less level trail, creates the illusion that you're hiking downhill—but you're not! By the time you hit the intersection for Hidden Lake (see Hike 50) at 2.25 miles (elevation 2260 feet) the valley floor has risen to nearly level with the trail, and the scrubby hemlocks and wiry willows of the first two miles are giving way to smaller alpine plants; look for wildflowers through summer and berries in late summer.

This intersection, plus an overlook at 2.6 miles (elevation 2350 feet), are both great spots for watching moose along the valley floor, especially during the fall rut. Sometimes the moose get very close to the trail. Remember to give these massive—and often cranky—animals plenty of space, and to never, ever get between a mother moose and her calf.

From here, the trail narrows and the uphill grade increases; some bike riders like to stash their ride in the boulders near mile 4.6 (elevation 2750 feet) and finish the rest of the steepening grade on foot. Waterproof boots or shoes come in handy for several shallow streams that run straight across or through the trail along this stretch, but unless the water is unusually high, it's easy to step or hop rocks across and keep your feet dry.

The one exception is a stream crossing at 5 miles (elevation 2920 feet), where South Fork Campbell Creek flows out of Grey Lake. You can either wade a shallow ford or poke around slightly upstream to find a place where you can hop across. Once you're across, follow the water upstream to see the lake, which makes a nice picnic or rest spot.

At about 5.1 miles, the trail forks; stay left for a slightly gentler, sidehilling ascent into the pass (6.1 miles, elevation 3650 feet). The pass and the last mile of trail before it can be much windier and colder than the valley floor, so bring an extra layer if you plan to spend much time here.

From the pass, I prefer to turn around and hike back the way I came, enjoying the

downhill grades that become much more obvious as you walk them. But some hikers and bikers like to turn this into a thru-hike to the Indian Valley Trailhead in the small Turnagain Arm community of Indian, where you'll need a car shuttle to get you back to the Glen Alps Trailhead. To reach the Indian Valley Trailhead, drive south from Anchorage on the New Seward Highway. At about mile marker 103, turn left onto Bore Tide Road and drive through the small community of Indian to arrive at the trailhead.

If you do this, add another 5.2 miles to your one-way distance, along with 420 additional feet of elevation gain and a whopping 3800 feet of elevation *loss*. You'll also have to be ready for thick brush, muddy wet trail, and a lot of mosquitoes, all of which are why I don't particularly like this extension. At least if there's a strong breeze going, it'll help keep the bugs off.

46 Middle Fork Loop

RATING/ DIFFICULTY	LOOP	ELEV GAIN/ HIGH POINT	SEASON
***/2	8.9 miles	1485 feet/ 2210 feet	Year-round

Maps: USGS Anchorage A8 NE, USGS Anchorage A8 SE, National Geographic Chugach State Park, Imus Geographics Chugach State Park; **Contact:** Chugach State Park; **Notes:** Alaska State Parks pass or parking fee. Open to horses. Mountain bikes allowed year-round except for along the east side of the valley, from past the Wolverine Trail until the Powerline Pass Trail; here, fat-tire bikes are allowed November 15 through March 31. Popular for skiing and snowshoeing during the winter. Dogs permitted on leash at trailhead, under direct

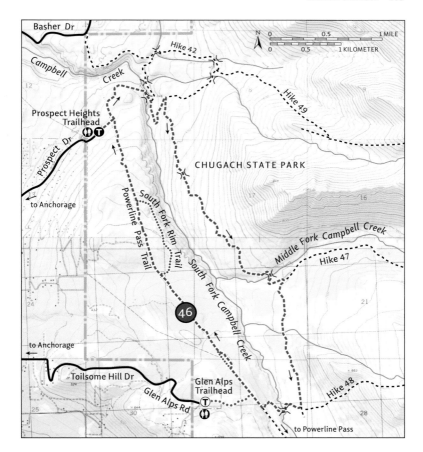

control in backcountry. Bear and moose habitat. Avalanche hazard in winter; **GPS:** 61.13887°, −149.71135°

   This "connector loop" knits together a number of popular trails in South Fork Campbell Creek valley, but it's also a pleasant, easy hike in its own right. The rolling terrain takes you through spruce forest, gnarled hemlock trees, and grassy meadows at the feet of familiar peaks in the Chugach front range.

GETTING THERE

From Anchorage, drive south on the New Seward Highway; take O'Malley Road east for 3.7 miles until it makes a sweeping curve to the left and becomes Hillside Drive. Make an immediate right onto Upper O'Malley Road. Continue for 0.5 mile, then turn left onto Prospect Drive and stay on this road for another 1 mile through a couple of name changes. The Prospect Heights Trailhead (elevation 965 feet) will be on your right.

ON THE TRAIL

From the Prospect Heights Trailhead, set out on the obvious, wide roadbed at the far end of the parking lot. This approximately 0.1-mile access trail links you to the north end of the Powerline Pass Trail (see Hike 45). If you were to turn right, it'd take you to the Glen Alps Trailhead and beyond.

Instead, turn left and follow this clear footpath as it cuts through a forest of spruce and birch trees, mixed in with pretty but dangerous cow parsnip, which can cause burns. The vast swath of forested land in the distance to your left is 4000-acre Far North Bicentennial Park.

Just before 0.9 mile you'll cross a big bridge over South Fork Campbell Creek, and at just past 1.4 miles (elevation 1130 feet) you'll reach a marked intersection with the Wolverine Bowl Trail. Going straight would take you up Wolverine Peak (see Hike 49). Instead, turn right to continue on the Middle Fork Loop, paralleling the edge of the surprisingly pretty gorge that holds Campbell Creek.

At about 2.1 miles you'll cross a small bridge, then transition into a stretch of hardened gravel trail, which gives way to elbow-high grass just before mile 2.5. Watch out for extremely muddy ground around mile 2.8, especially if it's been wet; things start to dry out and shift to tree roots in a dirt path around mile 3.25.

The Middle Fork Loop trail ushers you through a microcosm of small-scale landforms.

At 3.6 miles (elevation 1890 feet) there's a lovely new bridge over Middle Fork Campbell Creek—a tributary of the South Fork—followed by a signed intersection with the Williwaw Lakes Trail (Hike 47) at 3.9 miles; turn right to stay on the Middle Fork Loop Trail. This is one of my favorite sections of this trail. Notice how the biome shifts quickly to open, subalpine meadows, dotted with hemlock trees and a profusion of summer wildflowers.

Just past 5 miles (elevation 2100 feet) you'll hit a signed four-way intersection. Turning left takes you up a gully in the saddle to the right of Little O'Malley Peak (see Hike 48), and turning right keeps you on the Middle Fork Loop.

Next you'll strike a long boardwalk that leads down to another bridge over South Fork Campbell Creek, at 5.4 miles (elevation 2010 feet). From here it's a stiff little climb—about 200 feet—to where this trail rejoins the Powerline Pass Trail at mile 5.8 (elevation 2210 feet). You're now back on the same side of the valley that you started on.

Turn right to follow the Powerline Pass Trail back to the Prospect Heights Trailhead or, if you've staged a car shuttle at Glen Alps, you can reach that trailhead with a marked left turn at 5.8 miles.

At 6.2 miles this portion of the Powerline Pass Trail splits briefly, with the segments rejoining 0.1 mile later. Just before 7.3 miles (elevation 1740 feet) you'll see a marked right turn for the short but pretty South Fork Rim Trail, which rejoins the trail at 8 miles—a good example of the short but surprisingly picturesque trails that wind along this hillside region. At 8.7 miles, make a left turn back onto the broad, unmistakable access trail that delivers you back to the Prospect Heights Trailhead after a total of 8.9 miles of walking.

47 Williwaw Lakes

RATING/ DIFFICULTY	ROUNDTRIP	ELEV GAIN/ HIGH POINT	SEASON
****/3	14.4 miles	1460 feet/ 3300 feet	June–Oct

Maps: USGS Anchorage A8 SE, USGS Anchorage A7 SW, National Geographic Chugach State Park, Imus Geographics Chugach State Park; **Contact:** Chugach State Park; **Notes:** Alaska State Parks pass or parking fee. Popular backpacking destination. Open to horses. Mountain bikes allowed on the first part of the trail. Crosses snowmachine travel corridor in winter. Dogs permitted on leash at trailhead, under direct control in backcountry. Bear and moose habitat; **GPS:** 61.10349°, –149.68343°

 *This all-day stroll takes you through the most popular valley in Southcentral Alaska, around the toe of a long ridge, and back into the relative solitude of a valley dotted with vibrant, blue-green lakes and subalpine versions of your favorite flowers.*

GETTING THERE
From Anchorage, drive south on the New Seward Highway; take O'Malley Road east (toward the mountains). After 3.6 miles turn right on Hillside Drive. After 1 mile turn left on Upper Huffman, and right onto Toilsome Hill Drive, which becomes Glen Alps Road. After almost 2 miles, the large Glen Alps Trailhead (elevation 2180 feet) will be on your left.

ON THE TRAIL
From the Glen Alps Trailhead, take the broad access trail located just to the left of

Keep going! A clear, rambling footpath beckons you into the Williwaw Lakes valley.

the pay kiosk. At 0.3 mile it intersects with the Powerline Pass Trail (Hike 45); the intersection also marks a wonderful overlook over the valley in front of you, which often holds dozens of moose—and a true blaze of fall colors—during the autumn rut.

Turn right and follow the Powerline Trail—at this point, a gravel access road—until a marked left turn for Williwaw Lakes at 0.5 mile. Make that turn, following the hard-packed dirt trail down to a bridge over South Fork Campbell Creek, 0.75 mile from the trailhead (elevation 2000 feet). Just after the bridge the trail veers left and uphill, climbing out of the valley. Just before 1 mile you'll reach a four-way intersection

with trails that lead up Little O'Malley Peak (Hike 48).

Turn left, following the signs for Williwaw Lakes; this section of trail also coincides with part of the Middle Fork Loop (Hike 46). There may be a few patches of mud, but extensive work has gone into hardening this trail over the last few years. At 1.25 miles you'll start to encounter patches of grass that can sometimes grow to elbow-high by late summer.

At 1.75 miles, cross a large footbridge over one of many tributaries to South Fork Campbell Creek, which runs through the middle of the valley you're leaving behind. The trail stays relatively flat until you pass a signed

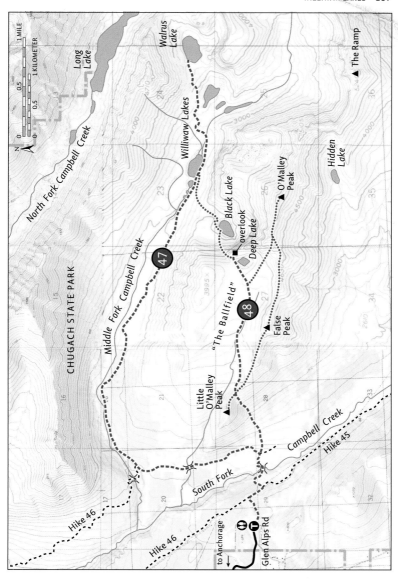

N

0   0.5   1 KILOMETER

0   0.5   1 MILE

Long
Lake

Walrus
Lake

The Ramp ▲

North Fork Campbell Creek

Williwaw Lakes

Hidden
Lake

O'Malley
Peak ▲

CHUGACH STATE PARK

Black Lake

overlook ■

Deep Lake

Middle Fork Campbell Creek

47

3995

"The Ballfield"

48

False
Peak ▲

Little
O'Malley
Peak ▲

Campbell Creek

Hike 45

South Fork

Hike 46

Hike 46

to Anchorage

Glen Alps Rd

intersection with the Middle Fork Loop Trail, just before mile 2.5. Here, the Williwaw Lakes Trail turns east and roughly parallels Middle Fork Campbell Creek, starting a steady, gradual climb into another valley.

You'll find summer wildflowers dotted all over the front range of the Chugach Mountains, but this valley outdoes itself with profusions of monkshood, wild geranium, fireweed, and Sitka burnet, among many others.

The next two miles of trail are unremarkable, except that you'll be leaving behind ready access to water for a couple of miles as you sidehill around the toe of a ridge that leads to Little O'Malley Peak and beyond it, "Big" O'Malley Peak (see Hike 48). Most of this stretch passes through dense stands of mountain hemlock trees and a few patchy stands of grass, but by 4.75 miles (elevation 2500 feet) the trees have opened up and start giving way to tundra meadows.

At 5.5 miles you're once again close to Middle Fork Campbell Creek, which at this point is a gentle stream flowing from the first of the Williwaw Lakes. You'll reach the lakeside, which has a series of broad, flat rocks jutting into the water, by 5.9 miles.

If you'd like to keep going from here, you have two options. To continue the recommended hike, continue on the trail as it works across the valley floor and climbs up to Walrus Lake (7.2 miles, elevation 3300 feet).

Or you can backtrack and, about 0.2 mile from that first lake, look for a side trail to the southwest (left) that leads uphill beside an obvious scree gully. This trail crests out in a large, flat expanse known as the Ballfield, and can be turned into a 9.7-mile loop hike, using the Little O'Malley Trail (Hike 48) to bring you back to the Glen Alps Trailhead.

48 Little O'Malley Peak and O'Malley Peak

Little O'Malley Peak and Black Lake Overlook

RATING/ DIFFICULTY	ROUNDTRIP	ELEV GAIN/ HIGH POINT	SEASON
****/4	6.6 miles	2180 feet/ 3823 feet	May–Oct

O'Malley Peak

RATING/ DIFFICULTY	ROUNDTRIP	ELEV GAIN/ HIGH POINT	SEASON
****/5	8.2 miles	4140 feet/ 5192 feet	June–Oct

Maps: USGS Anchorage A8 SE, USGS Anchorage A7 SW, National Geographic Chugach State Park, Imus Geographics Chugach State Park; **Contact:** Chugach State Park; **Notes:** Alaska State Parks pass or parking fee. First part of trail open to mountain bikes and horses. When adequate snow cover is present, a snowmachine-use corridor passes through the first part of the trail. Dogs permitted on leash at trailhead, under direct control on trails. Bear and moose habitat; **GPS:** 61.10349°, −149.68343°

 The first of these peaks, Little O'Malley, is a short, steep, but fun hike that's perfect for families or a quick day outing. The second one, "big" O'Malley, is a much steeper rock scramble or scree slog but has become very popular for its wonderful views over the Chugach front range.

GETTING THERE

From Anchorage, drive south on the New Seward Highway; take O'Malley Road east (toward the mountains). After 3.6 miles turn right on Hillside Drive. After 1 mile turn left

Taking the long view toward "big" O'Malley Peak, an unmistakably spikey peak that can be seen from Anchorage (Photo by Eric Lopez)

on Upper Huffman, and right onto Toilsome Hill Drive, which becomes Glen Alps Road. After almost 2 miles, the large Glen Alps Trailhead (elevation 2180 feet) will be on your left.

ON THE TRAIL

Regardless of whether you're ascending Little O'Malley Peak or going all the way to "big" O'Malley Peak, the first part of this trail coincides with part of Middle Fork Loop (Hike 46) and Williwaw Lakes (Hike 47).

Starting from the Glen Alps Trailhead, take the broad access trail that begins just left of the pay kiosk. At 0.3 mile (elevation 2220 feet) this trail intersects with the Powerline Pass Trail (Hike 45), a wide gravel maintenance road that offers commanding views over South Fork Campbell Creek valley. Turn right and descend a short hill; at 0.5 mile take a left turn that's marked for Williwaw Lakes and follow the hard-packed dirt trail down to a bridge over South Fork

Campbell Creek, 0.75 mile from the trailhead (elevation 2000 feet).

Just after the bridge the trail veers left and uphill, climbing out of the valley. Just before 1 mile (elevation 2100 feet) you'll reach a four-way intersection. The most straightforward path to the top (no pun intended) is to continue straight, following the sign for O'Malley Gully, which leads up a steep and massively eroded gully to the saddle between Little O'Malley Peak and the west ridge of O'Malley Peak.

This trail can be sandy on dry days, muddy on wet days, and grit-in-your-eyes miserable on windy days, but it gets you to the saddle quickly, at 1.75 miles (elevation 3180 feet). It also comes with an unexpected wealth of summer wildflowers, including Sitka burnet, fireweed, tiny wild roses, even tinier orchids, gentian, and harebells. Once you reach the saddle, it's a quick side trip to the west to tag the summit of Little O'Malley Peak at 1.9 miles (elevation 3200 feet).

Many people turn around here and head back after tagging Little O'Malley. However, from the saddle, you also have the first of two reasonably easy options for summiting "big" O'Malley Peak: scramble straight up the ridge to the east, sidehilling around several false peaks (including a prominent false peak that's named—wait for it—False Peak) on your way to the top of O'Malley Peak at mile 3.9, elevation 5192 feet.

As long as you choose your way carefully and don't mind all those false summits, this is a nontechnical route, although there is some exposure. The rule for anything like this is to never climb up something you wouldn't be comfortable coming back down, and keep in mind that rock in these mountains is notoriously loose and crumbly—so think twice before you trust anything to hold your weight.

Even if you don't care to summit O'Malley Peak, it's worth continuing on a slender footpath through the wide, almost-flat expanse behind Little O'Malley Peak. This broad area is known variously as the Ballfield, the Football Field, and so on. Once the snow has melted off, it offers easy walking through wildflower-studded tundra.

Just before 2.9 miles (elevation 3780 feet) you'll reach your second opportunity to summit O'Malley Peak via a route known as the northwest gully (not to be confused with the northwest ridge). We'll get to that in a minute, but first, here's how the main trail finishes: at 3 miles (elevation 3823 feet) you'll pass an alien-looking series of boulders poking out of the tundra, followed shortly by views down into appropriately named Deep Lake, which is set deep in a tundra bowl. When the sun hits it at just the right angle, the water glitters like black diamonds.

Bear right after the lake, and at 3.3 miles the trail will lead you to a wonderful overlook over the Williwaw Lakes valley and, in the near distance, Black Lake, which is actually colored a deep blue. Distances given for Little O'Malley and Black Lake Overlook take you to this point. If you have the time and energy, you can retrace your steps to Deep Lake and this time bear slightly left, scramble down a steep path alongside a scree and boulder slope, then stop by the shores of Black Lake before you hike back out along the mostly level Williwaw Lakes Trail (Hike 47).

Now, back to your summit opportunity at mile 2.9. As long as you don't mind steep scree, this route is ultimately easier and faster than scrambling up the west ridge. Turn right before you reach Deep Lake and hike up the obvious scree gully with a northwest aspect (you should be able to see the "path"—really just tracks made by other people—in the scree). Once you reach the top of the gully, turn left and carefully scramble the rest of the way to the top of O'Malley Peak (4.1 miles from the trailhead, elevation 5192 feet).

49 Wolverine Peak

RATING/ DIFFICULTY	ROUNDTRIP	ELEV GAIN/ HIGH POINT	SEASON
****/4	10.6 miles	3625 feet/ 4491 feet	May–Oct

Maps: USGS Anchorage A8 NE, USGS Anchorage A7 NW, National Geographic Chugach State Park, Imus Geographics Chugach State Park; **Contact:** Chugach State Park; **Notes:** Alaska State Parks pass or parking fee. First part of trail open to mountain bikes and horses. Lower trails are

The final push to Wolverine Peak, a true prize of the Chugach front range

popular for cross-country skiing. Dogs permitted on leash at trailhead, under direct control on trail. Bear and moose habitat; **GPS:** 61.13887°, –149.71135°

![icons] *A strenuous but wonderfully rewarding hike to one of the highest peaks in the Chugach front range offers stunning views over the North and Middle Fork Campbell Creek valleys. On a clear day, you can see all the way to the Alaska Range.*

GETTING THERE

From Anchorage, drive south on the New Seward Highway; take O'Malley Road east for 3.7 miles until it makes a sweeping curve to the left and becomes Hillside Drive. Make an immediate right onto Upper O'Malley Road. Continue for 0.5 mile, then turn left onto Prospect Drive and stay on this road for another mile through a couple of name changes. The Prospect Heights Trailhead (elevation 965 feet) will be on your right.

ON THE TRAIL

The trek up 4491-foot Wolverine Peak is challenging, but it's almost a pilgrimage for beginner and intermediate hikers who've built a good base of fitness, or seasoned hikers who just can't get enough of Wolverine's sweeping views of the Alaska Range, the Talkeetnas, and Mount Susitna across the water.

The trek begins on an arrow-straight access trail from the popular Prospect Heights Trailhead. At 0.1 mile, turn left onto the marked Powerline Pass Trail, an extended part of Hike 45. Stay on this broad dirt trail as it makes a sweeping curve out and right around the hillside's edge. Just under 1 mile it crosses South Fork Campbell Creek on a bridge then briefly continues alongside the creek, giving you nice views into its petite gorge, a highlight of the rolling and furrowed land in this valley.

At 1.2 miles the trail turns sharply back to the left; at 1.5 miles (elevation 1130 feet) it passes a signed intersection with the Middle

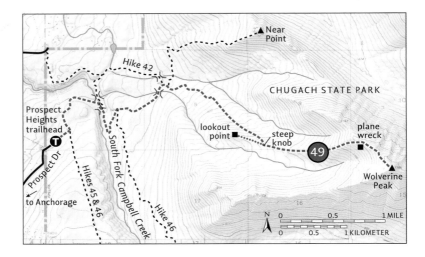

Fork Trail (Hike 46). This web of trails is still heavily wooded, but the trails are well marked; continue straight past the intersection, following signs for the Wolverine/Wolverine Bowl trails.

At 2.1 miles you'll cross a second bridge. This is your last chance for water before beginning the strenuous trek up the mountain, which can be fiercely exposed to both sun and wind. At 2.4 miles (elevation 1500 feet) the trail passes a signed turnoff to the left for Near Point. Take the right fork, signed for Wolverine. Now the broad, flat trail you'd been following fades to a footpath and settles in for some sustained elevation gain, ascending just over 3000 feet in the next 2.7 miles.

At 3.5 miles (elevation 2700 feet) you gain the top of a steep knob, well clear of brushline. Now you can finally see your objective, an obvious spine leading up and to the left to the summit ridge. There's also a short side trail to the west, marked by an enormous

cairn, that leads to a lookout point with views into South Fork Campbell Creek valley, which is where you started.

Watch your footing as you head back up the spine to the summit ridge. Although the views are spectacular, the trail is steep and full of loose dirt and gravel that can act like ball bearings underfoot.

At about 4.5 miles (elevation 3850 feet), just shy of the ridge crest, keep an eye out to the right for a sad little pile of rusting, twisted metal. This wreck is all that's left of a light plane that became lost in heavy fog in 1956, crashing here and killing all aboard.

The last 0.8-mile push to the summit (elevation 4491 feet) gains another 650 feet in elevation, but the views are so exhilarating that the mountain practically draws you right up to its peak. Once there, you can perch atop a short, rocky pillar and survey the rich views around you: Long Lake to the east (straight ahead), Williwaw Lakes to the southeast, or peek behind you for the surest perspective on what you've earned, as other hikers look like tiny ants crawling up the spine toward the ridge.

50 Hidden Lake

RATING/ DIFFICULTY	ROUNDTRIP	ELEV GAIN/ HIGH POINT	SEASON
***/3	10.4 miles	1955 feet/ 3710 feet	May–Oct

Maps: USGS Anchorage A8 SE, USGS Anchorage A7 SW, National Geographic Chugach State Park, Imus Geographics Chugach State Park; **Contact:** Chugach State Park; **Notes:** Alaska State Parks pass or parking fee. Popular backpacking destination. Open to horses. Open to mountain bikes for first 2.6 miles. Parts of trail are open to snowmachines during the winter. Dogs permitted on leash at trailhead, under direct control in backcountry. Bear and moose habitat; **GPS:** 61.10349°, –149.68343°

    *Discover a delightful—and very popular—wander over rolling tundra to a well-concealed, rock-studded lakeshore. Despite its name, this trail is no secret. I prefer to hike it in the early morning hours, before most other hikers are up.*

GETTING THERE

From Anchorage, drive south on the New Seward Highway; take O'Malley Road east (toward the mountains). After 3.6 miles turn right on Hillside Drive. After 1 mile turn left on Upper Huffman, and right onto Toilsome Hill Drive, which becomes Glen Alps Road. After almost 2 miles, the large Glen Alps Trailhead (elevation 2180 feet) will be on your left. An overflow lot is available to the

east of the main parking area. Be respectful of "No Parking" signs or you'll get a ticket.

ON THE TRAIL

From the Glen Alps Trailhead, take the broad access trail that starts just left of the pay kiosk. At 0.3 mile this trail intersects with a gravel maintenance road, also known as the Powerline Pass Trail (Hike 45). If you have binoculars with you, this juncture is also a great vantage for spotting moose and sometimes grizzly bears in the valley below.

Turn right and follow the gravel road along mostly flat terrain until a marked intersection with the Hidden Lake Trail at 2.5 miles (elevation 2250 feet). Make the left turn onto the Hidden Lake Trail and, at just past 2.6 miles, cross a bridge across South Fork Campbell Creek. You can still see the shallow, easy ford people used before the bridge was built. Bikes are not allowed past this point, but there's a bike rack where you can stow your ride.

After the bridge, the trail climbs up a moderate slope on the far side of the valley. Just past 3.3 miles (elevation 2600 feet) it levels out briefly, until you cross a small creek at 3.8 miles—no wading required. From here the trail starts another slow, rolling climb toward Hidden Lake.

This valley often harbors patchy snow cover into early summer, which can make it a challenge to find the right footpath through the tundra. But as long as visibility is decent, you can still find your way—just aim for the northeast corner of the valley, picking up threads of trail whenever you can. When in doubt, trend left; if you veer too far right, you'll end up at Ship Lake Pass instead.

You'll more or less parallel Hidden Creek (to your left) until at 5 miles (elevation 3710

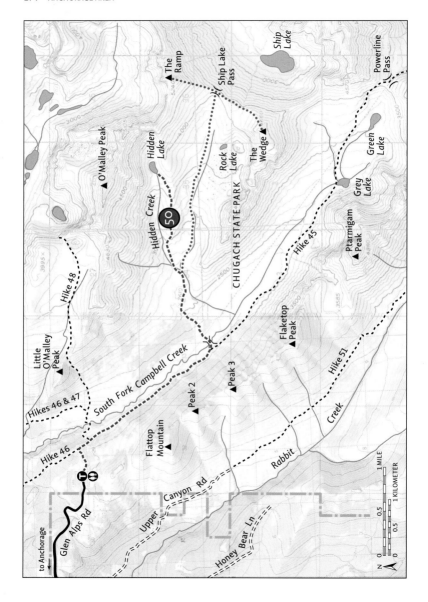

Burbling Hidden Creek is never far from the trail, but it can be hard to spot in the rolling tundra topography.

feet) you'll cross a final swell and in another 0.2 mile arrive at Hidden Lake in its sunken bowl, surrounded by a Mars-like scene of rock and scree that's tumbled down the flanks of 5192-foot O'Malley Peak, which crowns the rocky ridgeline to your left. In summer, keep an eye out for tundra wildflowers and the strange, cooing cackle of ptarmigan nesting among the rocks.

The lake's water level has been much lower than usual over the last few years, exposing a previously hidden rocky shoreline, but there's still plenty of soft tundra beyond the rocks for picnicking or camping. Despite the area's popularity, the persistent, glacier-sculpted swells in the tundra make it easy to feel like you have a tiny pocket of the world all to yourself.

Some hikers enjoy an optional side trip from this hike: at about 3.8 miles, keep an eye out for another small footpath that veers slightly to the right. This side trail skips Hidden Lake, takes you past tiny Rock Lake that is often hidden beneath a shelf of snow or ice well into the summer, and then leads you up to Ship Lake Pass (elevation 4080 feet).

From the pass, you can hang a left to walk up the Ramp (elevation 5240 feet) or a right to walk up the Wedge (elevation 4660). There are roped, technical climbs on both peaks, so make sure you stick to the primitive trails and manageable terrain.

RATING/ DIFFICULTY	ROUNDTRIP	ELEV GAIN/ HIGH POINT	SEASON
***/2	10.2 miles	1615 feet/ 3215 feet	May–Oct

Maps: USGS Anchorage A8 SE, USGS Anchorage A7 SW, National Geographic Chugach State Park, Imus Geographics Chugach State Park; **Contact:** Chugach State Park; **Notes:** Alaska State Parks pass or parking fee. Rough access road, may be impassable in winter. Dogs permitted on leash in parking area, under direct control on trail. Bear and moose habitat. Fishing for rainbow trout; **GPS:** 61.08189°, –149.68520°

 *A family-friendly hike through a brushy corridor into tundra, this trail offers very gradual elevation gain and a beautiful, sapphire-blue lake at the end. It's a perfect beginner or lazy-day hike that also links in to a number of other popular trails.*

GETTING THERE

From Anchorage, drive south on the New Seward Highway; take DeArmoun Road east for 3.8 miles until it turns into Upper DeArmoun, then 0.6 mile later it becomes Canyon Road. Veer right at the next intersection to stay on Canyon Road, which then goes through several more name changes over the next 1.7 miles before becoming Upper

North and South Suicide peaks punctuate the valley that contains Rabbit Lake, hidden just over the rise in front of you.

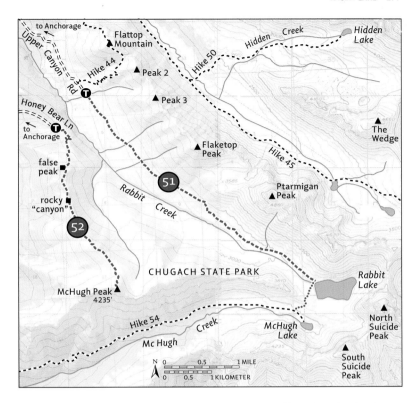

Canyon Road and dead-ending at the small trailhead. The last part of the road is rough and rocky, but a carefully driven passenger vehicle can usually get you to within a short walk of the trailhead (elevation 1960 feet).

ON THE TRAIL

This easy, family-friendly hike follows an old roadbed through a line of brush that parallels the ridge behind Flattop Mountain. In fact, you can hike a recently improved trail up the back side of Flattop (see Hike 44) from the same trailhead.

To reach Rabbit Lake, take the obvious broad, rocky roadbed that is a continuation of Upper Canyon Road. Except for the alders on either side of the trail, you have good visibility here; during the fall, it's common to see black or brown bears grazing for berries on the slopes above, fattening themselves up before the long winter.

At 0.6 mile the trail enters a particularly brushy corridor—this is a good place to practice being bear- (and moose-) aware by making noise so they can hear you coming and get out of the way. You can still see the mountain peaks in the ridge to your left: after Flattop's characteristic broad summit, you have Peak Two, Peak Three, Flaketop Peak, and Ptarmigan Peak, with McHugh Peak (see Hike 52) presiding over the far side of the valley.

The trail escapes the brushline at 2 miles in, then crests a small rise at 2.6 miles (elevation 2900 feet). From there to mile 4.8 (elevation 3190 feet) the elevation gain is so gradual you don't even notice it until at just past 5 miles you top a small hill and find yourself staring down at the glittering sapphire water of Rabbit Lake, with the North and South Suicide peaks standing like twin sentinels at the head of the valley.

This is a popular spot for picnics and camping, or bring a fishing pole and try for rainbow trout. And to the right, the outlet of Rabbit Creek makes a great place for skipping stones. The trail ends here, but if you thought ahead and set up a car shuttle, you could also wade across the mouth of Rabbit Creek and pick up the McHugh Lake Trail, which runs 6.6 miles down to the McHugh Creek Trailhead (see Hike 54). Heads up: because of this valley's openness and the surrounding topography, it's prone to high winds and sudden weather changes, so come prepared with warm clothing.

52 McHugh Peak

RATING/ DIFFICULTY	ROUNDTRIP	ELEV GAIN/ HIGH POINT	SEASON
****/4	6 miles	2455 feet/ 4235 feet	May–Oct

Map: USGS Anchorage A8 SE; **Contact:** Chugach State Park; **Notes:** Very limited parking. No parking from 11:00 PM to 6:00 AM. Dogs permitted on leash at trailhead,

under direct control on trail. Moose and bear habitat. Respect private property and do not block fire lanes/emergency vehicle access; **GPS:** 61.07235°, –149.68869°

By far the easiest approach to imposing McHugh Peak, this trail takes you huffing and puffing straight uphill from a tiny neighborhood trailhead, then on an almost pastoral stroll along a broad alpine ridge.

GETTING THERE
This trailhead is variously known as Bear Valley, Honey Bear, and Golden View. From Anchorage, drive south on the New Seward Highway, take the Rabbit Creek exit, and turn east (toward the mountains). When Rabbit Creek veers to the left after 2.6 miles, turn right on Clarks Road. Follow Clarks Road for 2 miles then veer right onto Kings Way Drive, turn left onto Snow Bear Drive, turn right on Black Bear Drive, then turn left on Honey Bear Lane and park in the designated (and very limited) spots at the end of the road (elevation 2090 feet).

ON THE TRAIL
This is the shortest, easiest (and by far the most pleasant) approach to McHugh Peak, starting just below treeline on the north ridge. The trailhead accommodates only four to six cars, and parking out of place blocks access for emergency vehicles and residents—so if the trailhead is full, do another hike instead of trying to cram your car in and risking a ticket or angering nearby residents.

The first part of the trail is brutally steep on loose dirt, gaining more than 200 feet in just 0.25 mile (elevation 2280 feet). That's enough for you to break out of the alders

This unmistakable crown of rocks marks the final approach to forbidding McHugh Peak.

and grass and into the open, with nice views of the Canyon Road Trailhead and the trail to Rabbit Lake (Hike 51) on the far side of the valley to your left. The McHugh Peak Trail also forks here; take a hard right to go up and across the bluff in front of you, instead of continuing straight and downhill.

There are a couple of switchbacks in the barest, rockiest part of the slope at 0.3 mile, but otherwise it's just you, your quads, and the burn as you gain more than 1000 feet by mile 0.9. That gets you to a false peak with a rocky windbreak on it, and you're high enough to get majestic views over Turnagain Arm to your right.

From here the trail becomes an easy stroll along a broad ridge, although you're not done with the false summits yet: there are three more, each more convincing than the last. That's made up for by the amazing views of Rabbit Creek valley, Rabbit Lake, and the Suicides, all on your left, where other hikers look small enough to be ants.

At 1.4 miles (elevation 3235 feet) the trail enters a small, rocky "canyon": going down, it's all loose dirt and rocks, while the "up" on the other side is friendly tundra. By about 2.1 miles the trail peters out in a broad shelf of rocky, barren tundra at 3785 feet of elevation.

At this point, you can finally see the real McHugh Peak: an enormous, remote-looking hill on the ridge, topped by a spikey, crownlike pile of rock. The footpath you're on fades out to almost nothing, but you can follow Leave No Trace etiquette by walking on rocky ground when you can, and piecing together a few scraps of trail on the left side of the hill that leads up to the rocky summit.

Most people will stop at the base of the crown of rocks. But if you work your way around to the left (north) side of the rocks, some very easy scrambling gets you up to a fun "window" in the rocks that looks out over Turnagain Arm to the west, 3 miles from the trailhead. The little window feels almost like looking through an arrow slot in medieval fortifications. If you want to get to the very tippy top (elevation 4235 feet), you'll have to pull a couple of extremely exposed class 5 moves on very sketchy rock.

This is a great example of where height estimates for mountains in the Chugach Range vary: one map says McHugh Peak is 4298 feet high, another says 4301, and yet another says 4311. But having done that last scramble, my GPS measured only 4235 feet; so I'll let that measurement stand.

Opposite: *The hikes just south of Anchorage are exposed to the elements, especially to fierce, high winds that can kick up with little notice—but they make up for it with the views (Hike 57).*

south of anchorage

Just one road leads south of Anchorage: the New Seward Highway, with the Chugach Mountains looming to one side and the fast-moving waters of Turnagain Arm on the other. Most of the trailheads for these hikes are strung along the highway like so many beads on a string, but a few do require a short drive off the highway or, in two cases, a train ride that parallels the road. Either way, these little detours are worth it to see glaciers, cascading creeks, and views of Turnagain Arm from mountain slopes.

53 Turnagain Arm Trail

RATING/ DIFFICULTY	ONE-WAY	ELEV GAIN/ HIGH POINT	SEASON
***/3	10.4 miles	2325 feet/ 880 feet	May–Oct

Maps: USGS Anchorage A8 SE, USGS Seward D8 NE, USGS Seward D7 NW, National Geographic Chugach State Park, Imus Geographics Chugach State Park; **Contact:** Chugach State Park; **Notes:** Alaska State Parks pass or parking fee at Potter and McHugh trailheads. Limited winter parking at Potter and McHugh; the Potter to McHugh section is popular for year-round use, including snowshoeing. Dogs permitted on leash in parking areas, under direct control on trail. Bear and moose habitat; bear encounters especially common near Potter and McHugh Creek. Requires crossing a very mild ford; **GPS:** Potter: 61.0477°; –149.7914°; McHugh: 61.0220°, –149.7378°; Rainbow: 61.00002°, –149.64053°; Windy: 60.9848°, –149.6047°

One of the better early season hikes, this often underestimated thru-hike showcases a very different biome in each of its three sections, plus sweeping views over Turnagain Arm along the length of the trail. A total of four trailheads within 10 miles of each other make it easy to customize the length of your hike.

Spring is a great season to walk this stretch of trail, between the Rainbow and McHugh Creek trailheads.

GETTING THERE

From Anchorage, drive south on the New Seward Highway. The first trailhead, Potter—not to be confused with the wetlands and boardwalk of Potter Marsh, which you've already passed—is on the left at mile marker 115. In order, the other trailheads are McHugh Creek (mile 112); Rainbow (mile 108); and Windy Corner (mile 106).

ON THE TRAIL

One of the most enjoyable things about this trail is the way each section displays its own unique character. The stretch from Potter to McHugh has the thickest tree cover—although the trail itself is plenty wide and clear—and is a popular snowshoeing destination in the winter. This part of the trail passes through a typical boreal forest, full of spruce and birch trees that cluster thickly together.

Begin the trail from the uppermost of Potter's two parking lots, cresting a small hill by 0.9 mile for pretty views over Turnagain Arm. Once the trees leaf out, the best views will be from a lookout knoll and bench, set off to the right of the trail at that 0.9-mile mark.

From here, the trail continues through the forest, more or less level, with only a few small hills, until it intersects the turnoff point for McHugh Lake (Hike 54) at mile 3.4 (elevation 300 feet). From here, the trail traces a very gentle downward slope until at 3.8 miles (elevation 200 feet) it reaches the uppermost of three parking areas at the McHugh Creek Trailhead.

Keep an eye out for mountain goat nannies and their kids on the grassy ramps overlooking this trailhead. Bear sightings also tend to be very common on the stretch of trail between the Potter and McHugh trailheads. In fact that holds true for the entire McHugh Creek area in general, so mind your bear manners.

From the McHugh Creek Trailhead, follow signs indicating "Rainbow," cutting briefly uphill before you resume your sidehilling progress, more or less parallel to the highway. This stretch of trail takes you through a forest of tall, ghostly cottonwood trees and across stretches of wildflower-laden trail. At 5.6 miles you'll start up the only sizable hill on this trail, stepping across a small creek at mile 6.4 (elevation 610 feet). As long as you have good balance, there should be no need to get your feet wet.

At 7.1 miles (elevation 880 feet) you'll hit the high point of this hike; just before the trail descends the back side of the hill, look for a scree trail heading straight uphill on the left. This is the lead-in for Rainbow Knob (see Hike 55). For the Turnagain Arm Trail, however, continue straight as the trail switchbacks downhill through a forest of stately birch trees. This is one of my favorite parts of this hike during the spring, when the trees are just leafing out in fresh, minty green.

The trail crosses a small residential road at 7.9 miles (elevation 270 feet), with a bridged stream crossing before and another crossing (also bridged) after. Then, at 8.4 miles, you reach the Rainbow Trailhead (elevation 65 feet).

To continue, walk to the opposite end of the Rainbow Trailhead's long parking area and follow the trail to Windy Corner as it heads up a gradual slope. The next stretch of trail is one of the brushiest you'll encounter near town.

By about mile 8.7 the brush thins out, and the remainder of the walk to Windy Corner—also known simply as "Windy"—is

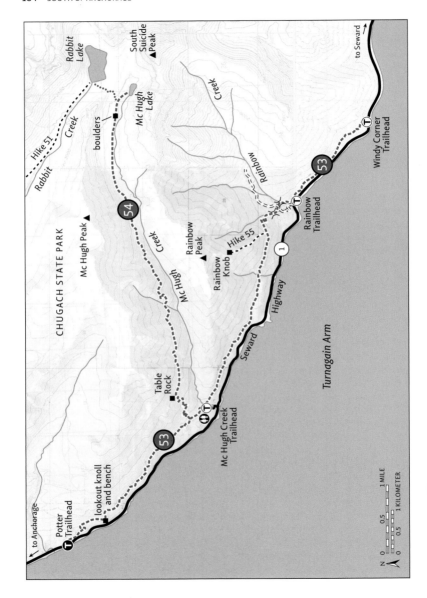

Rabbit Lake

South Suicide Peak ▲

Hike 51

Rabbit Creek

boulders

Mc Hugh Lake

Creek

53

Windy Corner Trailhead

to Seward

CHUGACH STATE PARK

Mc Hugh Peak ▲

54

Creek

Mc Hugh

Rainbow

Rainbow Peak ▲

Rainbow Knob ■

Hike 55

T

Rainbow Trailhead

1

53

Table Rock ■

T

Mc Hugh Creek Trailhead

Seward

Highway

Turnagain Arm

Potter Trailhead

to Anchorage

lookout knoll and bench

N

0   0.5   1 MILE

0   0.5   1 KILOMETER

another one of my favorite stretches, full of lofty-feeling vantage points over the water and a lot of early summer wildflowers blooming among the rocks. As you near the Windy Corner Trailhead at 10.4 miles, keep an eye out for mountain goats and Dall sheep in the rocky bluffs to your left. Falling rocks are also a hazard here but, happily, quite rare. If you find the trail running out in a precipitous scree slope, you just missed your turnoff to get down to the trailhead.

54 McHugh Lake

RATING/ DIFFICULTY	ROUNDTRIP	ELEV GAIN/ HIGH POINT	SEASON
*****/3	13.2 miles	3400 feet/ 3040 feet	May–Sept

Maps: USGS Anchorage A8 SE, USGS Anchorage A7 SW, National Geographic Chugach State Park, Imus Geographics Chugach State Park; **Contact:** Chugach State Park; **Notes:** Alaska State Parks pass or parking fee. Lower parking area is open year-round, but gate to upper area closes once ice and snow set in. Dogs permitted on leash at trailhead, under direct control in backcountry. Bear and moose habitat, bear encounters are common here. Look for mountain goats and Dall sheep in rocky cliffs; **GPS:** 61.01829°, –149.73318°

 Although it packs a fair bit of elevation gain, this hike also offers almost anything you could want: great views over Turnagain Arm, good chances of seeing Dall sheep, hiking through a stretch of remote alpine tundra that doesn't see much foot traffic, and your choice of two picturesque lakes at the end.

GETTING THERE
From Anchorage, drive south on the New Seward Highway to the McHugh Creek Trailhead, which will be on your left near mile marker 112. Drive or walk to the upper lot (elevation 190 feet), where the hike begins.

ON THE TRAIL
The first part of this hike coincides with the Turnagain Arm Trail, as if you were hiking west toward the Potter Trailhead (see Hike 53). Keep your eyes out for a signpost that, just before mile 0.4 (elevation 300 feet), marks your right turn for the McHugh Lake Trail.

From here the trail switchbacks uphill through slender young aspen trees and tall, gnarled cottonwoods. At 1.1 miles (elevation 915 feet) look for the broad, flat Table Rock off to your left; it's a popular picnic spot and hiking destination for families with kids.

At about 1.5 miles (elevation 1150 feet) you'll start encountering dead trees—a lot of them. This "tree graveyard" and the somewhat denuded mountain slopes around it are one of several aftereffects from a 2016 wildfire, caused by an unextinguished campfire that was whipped back to life by high winds.

The trail is often muddy through this stretch, and you'll have to step across a number of unbridged creeks trickling down the mountainside. There should never be any need to wade, but the short, steep descent to each creek, then the ascent after, presents more of a slippery, muddy obstacle than the water itself. When you can, spare an eye for the rocky cliffs above you; Dall sheep are commonly sighted here, whereas shaggy mountain goats are more common near the coast.

McHugh Creek starts its downhill journey from its headwaters, McHugh Lake.

By 2.75 miles (elevation 1775 feet) the trail gets grassy, to the point that you sometimes can't see rocks or tree roots waiting to trip you. By 3.75 miles the trail is still climbing steadily through alternating bands of alders and grass, and switchbacks are nothing but a fond memory. By 4.1 miles the vegetation starts trending toward the alpine, with small hemlock trees and scrubby willow shrubs.

At 5.4 miles (elevation 2800 feet), as you exit the brushline and enter a paradise of alpine tundra, there are a few spots where the trail becomes a little patchy. Just take your time and look ahead: the trail runs steadily to the left of the creek, so as long as visibility is decent it's not hard to spot places where the trail picks up again.

There's a little boulder hopping at about mile 6.1 (elevation 2950 feet)—nothing extreme, just some uneven footing—and you can already see small McHugh Lake tucked in a valley to your right; the creek trickling out of it through a small gully makes for one of the prettiest sights you'll ever see in the mountains.

At 6.4 miles (elevation 3040 feet) you have to make a choice. You can pick your way down and right to McHugh Lake at 6.6 miles (elevation 2990 feet). Or you can keep going another 0.6 mile north and east, around the toe of the obvious ridge to larger Rabbit Lake, which is the endpoint for Hike 51.

In fact, you can combine the McHugh Lake and Rabbit Lake trails to make a picture-perfect thru-hike of about 12 miles. But if you're going to do that, start from the Rabbit Lake side. That spares you a couple thousand feet of elevation gain, and also gives you great views over Turnagain Arm as you descend toward the McHugh Creek Trailhead.

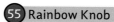

55 Rainbow Knob

RATING/ DIFFICULTY	ROUNDTRIP	ELEV GAIN/ HIGH POINT	SEASON
***/5	4 miles	2080 feet/ 2080 feet	May–Oct

Maps: USGS Anchorage A8 SE, National Geographic Chugach State Park, Imus Geographics Chugach State Park; **Contact:** Chugach State Park; **Notes:** Dogs permitted on leash at trailhead, under direct control in backcountry, but because of the scrambling leave Fido at home. Bear and moose habitat; **GPS:** 61.00002°, –149.64053°

Nothing encapsulates the unique, DIY nature of hiking in Alaska like Rainbow Peak. For most people, a prominent knob reached two-thirds of the way up is the ideal turnaround point. The rest of the way is a free-for-all scramble past cliffs and steep scree slopes, with no marked trail at all.

GETTING THERE
From Anchorage, drive south on the New Seward Highway. The Rainbow Trailhead (elevation 50 feet) is on your left at about mile marker 108, just as the road bends sharply to the right. It's easy to drive past by mistake.

ON THE TRAIL
This trail starts as a wide, gravelly roadbed that briefly parallels Rainbow Creek, then crosses it on a bridge at just past 0.2 mile (elevation 140 feet). The trail then crosses a small residential road, followed by a bridged crossing over another picturesque stream.

From here, the trail winds fairly steeply through a forest of tall, slender birches; this is one of my favorite stretches of trail in the spring, when the leaves are just budding out. The trail levels out at 1.25 miles (elevation 875 feet), at which point you can spot a steep trail of loose gravel that cuts sharply up and to the right. If you start heading back downhill on the main trail you missed your turnoff, which is just opposite an obvious lookout point on the left.

This is where things get interesting. This section of trail is steep, sometimes brutally so, on loose footing that genuinely feels like one step forward, two steps back. There are occasions where you might find yourself needing both hands and feet to make forward progress—the most basic definition of a scramble.

Continue gutting it out uphill until at 2 miles (elevation 2080 feet) the trail seems to end in a prominent knob on Rainbow Peak's southeast ridge. By now, you can clearly see the peak above you, but the rest of the way up is a steep, rocky riddle—so most people are happy to collect the sweeping views over Cook Inlet from this point and call it good.

If you do go on, be aware that the rest of the hike requires excellent routefinding and scrambling skills, and a very healthy dose of common sense. It's not *quite* a technical climb, but the mountain is riddled with cliffs and loose rock, and even those who are familiar with the trail can easily stray off-route and find themselves verging

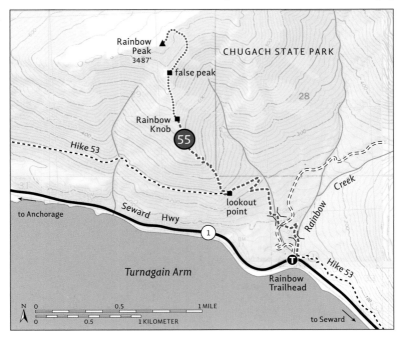

The Rainbow Knob Trail may not come easy, but beautiful views over Turnagain Arm help soothe the burn in your calf muscles and quads.

on technical terrain or just a nasty, loose scramble.

So, leave yourself plenty of daylight for routefinding and be very attentive to the number one rule of scrambling: never go up something that you're not comfortable coming down backward, because that's exactly what you'll have to do on the way back.

From Rainbow Knob, the generally agreed "best" route is to eschew the goat trail that cuts off into the horribly steep tundra on the right (one star, would not hike again), and instead scramble straight up the shoulder of the ridge until you reach a prominent false peak (about 2.3 miles from the trailhead, elevation 2850 feet).

Look for a clear, walkable goat trail leading off into the rocks on your right, along the base of the cliffs. The trail takes you to a steep, southeast-facing gully, where you have your pick of several steep, miserable scree slopes for gaining the summit ridge. Once you're on the ridge, double back to the left (southwest) to reach the summit and its breathtaking views.

The stats at the beginning of this hike are written on the assumption that you turn back where most people do, at the knob before the serious scrambling begins. If you do the entire hike, it's about 5.2 miles roundtrip, with 3500 feet of elevation gain to a 3487-foot high point.

56 Falls Creek

RATING/ DIFFICULTY	ROUNDTRIP	ELEV GAIN/ HIGH POINT	SEASON
****/5	7.4 miles	3080 feet/ 3010 feet	June–Oct

Maps: USGS Seward D7 NW, USGS Anchorage A7 SW, National Geographic Chugach State Park, Imus Geographics Chugach State Park; **Contact:** Chugach State Park; **Notes:** No parking fee. Limited parking off a busy highway. No bikes allowed. Dogs permitted on leash in parking area, under direct control on trail. Bear and moose habitat. One ford required. Area subject to trapping in winter months; **GPS:** 60.98432°, –149.576°

Falls Creek is one long cascade tumbling down from its headwaters, far above the sea level trailhead where you started.

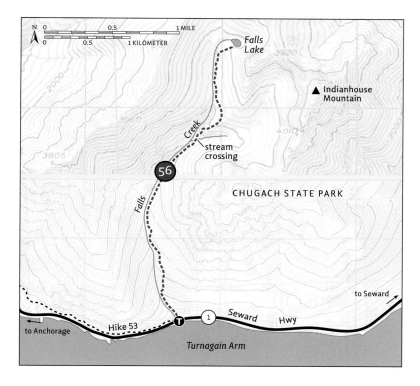

N 0   0.5   1 MILE
0   0.5   1 KILOMETER

Falls
Lake

Indianhouse
Mountain

Creek

stream
crossing

56

CHUGACH STATE PARK

Falls

to Seward

Hike 53   Seward   Hwy   1

to Anchorage

Turnagain Arm

Try one of the steepest hikes in Southcentral and also one of the prettiest: a fairyland of moss and sun-dappled forest with an enchanting creek cascading down the mountain.

GETTING THERE

From Anchorage, drive south on the New Seward Highway. The trailhead (elevation 75 feet) is on your left at mile 105.6, about 25 miles out of town. It's a tiny pullout on the mountain side of the road, marked only by blue "hike" signs on the highway and by the creek itself, which cascades into a culvert that routes it under the roadway and out into Turnagain Arm.

ON THE TRAIL

There are two parts to this trail: a wonderland ramble through mossy forest, followed by easy tundra walking to an isolated, icy tarn—the headwaters of Falls Creek. As you're standing in the parking area and facing the creek itself, the trail starts on the right, zooming straight up a steep incline. Get used to it, because until you hit the tundra, this trail is nothing but nonstop steep—but at least there are a lot of pretty cascades to look at during rest stops.

At 0.4 mile (elevation 390 feet) the trail takes a quick, sharp jog to the right, then heads back uphill, veering away from the creekside for a while. Be on the lookout for very poisonous baneberry on these lower stretches of trail, along with burn-inducing cow parsnip and spiky devil's club.

At almost 0.8 mile (elevation 920 feet) the trail veers back toward the creek. From here it's straightforward—albeit steep, and sometimes overgrown—walking until about 1.8 miles (elevation 1790 feet), when the trail passes through a particularly grassy section. The left side of the trail has been undercut and almost crumbles into the creek, so watch your footing.

The grass and rushing water are also a perfect recipe for surprise wildlife encounters, so this is a good place to practice being bear aware (e.g., making plenty of noise so they hear you coming and have time to get out of the way).

Shortly after this the trail opens out into the tundra, heading up a lush, green-walled valley carved by the stream. (The shape of the valley tells you how it was made; the sort of V-shaped valley you'll see here was carved by running water, whereas broader U-shaped valleys were ground out by the passage of glaciers.)

At 2.3 miles (elevation 2100 feet) you'll encounter the only notable stream crossing on this hike. You should be able to step across the tributary to Falls Creek on boulders, but if the water is running high be ready to get your feet wet. At 2.6 miles (elevation 2570 feet) the slope starts to ease off.

You'll leave the maintained trail behind as you continue into the broad, glacier-carved

valley (note its U shape), but from here it's easy to follow the narrow footpath as it ascends to the left of the prominent tundra knob in front of you, following Falls Creek—now little more than a stream—to its headwaters in Falls Lake. At 3.6 miles you'll reach the lake itself, a pretty but frigid tarn that, in a normal year, harbors an underwater sheet of ice that often lasts well into summer.

57 Bird Ridge

RATING/ DIFFICULTY	ROUNDTRIP	ELEV GAIN/ HIGH POINT	SEASON
****/5	5.2 miles	3350 feet/ 3505 feet	May–Oct

Maps: USGS Seward D7 NW, USGS Anchorage A7 NW, USGS Anchorage A7 SE, National Geographic Chugach State Park, Imus Geographics Chugach State Park; **Contact:** Chugach State Park; **Notes:** Chugach State Parks pass or parking fee. Popular with mountain runners. Dogs permitted on leash at trailhead, under direct control on trail. Moose and bear habitat. Cornicing and avalanche hazard in winter; **GPS:** 60.97476°, –149.47438°

One of the Anchorage area's steepest hikes, Bird Ridge's southern exposure means it is one of the first trails to start melting out of the snow come spring. Even if you hike only partway up, there's no better place for lofty views over the constantly changing waters of Turnagain Arm.

GETTING THERE
From Anchorage, drive south on the New Seward Highway for about 26 miles. The best parking is at the massive Bird Creek turnout at mile 100, but you can also park

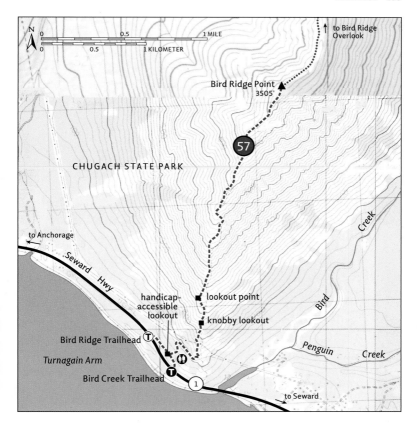

at the much smaller Bird Ridge Trailhead at mile 101.

ON THE TRAIL

From the large Bird Creek parking area, take the obvious large path on the west (toward Anchorage) end of the lot. Within 0.1 mile this paved multiuse trail passes a small juncture with a couple of pit toilets. If you started at the small Bird Ridge Trailhead, this is where the two access trails meet.

A short spur trail leads to a handicap-accessible lookout over the water—just a taste of the views that await you up on the ridge. When you're ready, take the obvious uphill trail as it snakes through a hemlock forest paved with fallen needles. At 0.6 mile there's a knobby little lookout that makes a great rest stop.

As you continue uphill from this point, the trail starts braiding, splitting, and then rejoining itself any time it meets an obstacle

Views, views, views: once you start gaining altitude on Bird Ridge, you can see for miles along the waters of Turnagain Arm.

such as a tree or a big rock. For the path of least resistance, take the most obviously traveled forks.

At 1 mile (elevation 1450 feet) a short side trail leads to another great lookout point with stunning views over the water. From here the trail gets rockier, with occasional short scrambles over rocky slabs in the trail. At 1.2 miles the trail splits briefly as it passes through an especially rocky area. Both forks require some very mild scrambling; the left trail is easier to see, but the right trail is easier to traverse if you don't mind a little exposure.

Marmots love this sort of rocky terrain, so keep an ear out for their sharp, shrieking whistles. By 1.3 miles the trail is back to easy dirt with a little loose gravel. The grassy false peak you see in front of you is a favorite place for a picnic spot, but it's not the top—yet. At 1.5 miles the trail leads you to an easy scramble over a few more rocky spots, then plows through a thick stretch of

bushes, a jumble of mountain ash, cow parsnip, fireweed, yarrow, and tall grass.

At 1.6 miles the trail opens up for easier walking—a rock-studded dirt path through the tundra—and picking crowberries is a great way to stay occupied during rest breaks. If the winds that often scour this ridge didn't hit you as soon as you emerged from the trees, they'll wallop you now.

At 1.9 miles you've gained the obvious ridgeline and are in the home stretch, although you still need to cope with a few false peaks. Check out the amazing views of uber-brushy Bird Creek Valley below you on the right.

Just before 2.6 miles you'll hit a series of three "peaks" that you can't really tell apart in terms of height. The middle one, with a survey/summit marker at the very top, is 3505-foot Bird Ridge Point, the high point for this hike. That said, if you've packed enough water and clothing layers and don't mind a little exposure, you can walk a whopping 3.5 miles farther along the ridgeline before gaining the 4625-foot Bird Ridge Overlook, deep in the Chugach Range. That makes for a total round-trip of 12.2 miles and elevation gain of 4500 feet, roughly on par—in both beauty and effort—with hiking Pioneer Peak (see Hike 23).

58 North Face

RATING/ DIFFICULTY	ROUNDTRIP	ELEV GAIN/ HIGH POINT	SEASON
***/4	5 miles	2075 feet/ 2250 feet	June–Oct

Maps: USGS Seward D6 NW, National Geographic Chugach State Park; **Contact:** Alyeska Resort; **Notes:** Trail opening/closure is dependent on snow conditions; contact

Alyeska Resort for current conditions. Dogs permitted under direct control. Dogs cannot ride the aerial tram up, but if you hike up they can ride the tram down. Bear and moose habitat; **GPS:** 60.96994°, –149.09387°

By winter, this is North America's longest continuous double black diamond ski run. During the summer it transforms into a fun, sweat-inducing summer hike that, at its peak, offers a panoramic view of seven different glaciers in the distance.

GETTING THERE
From Anchorage, drive south on the New Seward Highway for about 33 miles. At mile marker 90, just before the Tesoro gas

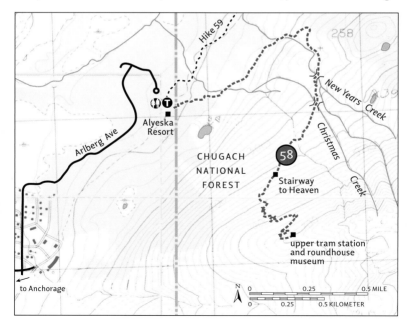

station, turn left onto the Alyeska Highway. Follow this road for about 3 miles until it ends in a T intersection. Turn left onto Arlberg Avenue. Stay on Arlberg Avenue for 1 mile until you reach Alyeska Resort, then follow signs for parking (elevation 340 feet).

ON THE TRAIL

The North Face Trail starts just behind the Alyeska Resort's aerial tram building, the anchor for 0.75 mile of cables that stretch to the upper tram terminal that also happens to be the endpoint of this hike. Dogs can't ride the tram at all when it's going up. But if you hike to the upper tram station, you (and your dog) can ride the tram down for free.

The first 0.6 mile of the North Face Trail is on an easy, broad maintenance road. During the summer you'll see a lot of happy tourists here, but don't worry—soon after the trail starts heading more steeply uphill at the 0.6-mile mark, the crowds thin out.

After 0.75 mile, the trail turns to relatively steep, sometimes muddy footing. At 1 mile (elevation 870 feet) the alders open up and you enter a pretty subalpine meadow with a stretch of boardwalk. At 1.1 miles you'll cross a bridge over New Years Creek, and at 1.25 miles (elevation 1060 feet) you'll cross Christmas Creek.

The vegetation here is an interesting mix of bushy ferns, which you'd more typically

Summer green wages a losing war against the onset of fall colors in the tundra, near the summit of the North Face Trail.

see in the forest, along with bushy alders, fireweed, and berry bushes. Speaking of berries, Girdwood is basically black bear central—so even though this trail is well traveled, remember to be bear aware.

At 1.7 miles (elevation 1440 feet) you'll pass the very aptly named Stairway to Heaven, a series of rocky stairs that deliver you to a series of steep switchbacks that ping back and forth across the mountain's steep face. Kids will enjoy counting the dozen or so switchbacks, each of which is clearly labeled with a number. The switchbacks continue all the way to the upper tram station at 2.5 miles (elevation 2250 feet). There's also a small roundhouse museum that showcases slices of local history.

The aerial trams arrive every few minutes; to claim your ride down, just walk up to any open tram as it's loading. But first, see if you can count all seven glaciers that should be visible from this point on the mountain. And if you want to make this hike even more rewarding, consider joining the annual Alyeska Climbathon, a September event in which people run or hike laps up the North Face Trail in a fundraising event for fighting women's cancers.

59 Winner Creek

RATING/ DIFFICULTY	ROUNDTRIP	ELEV GAIN/ HIGH POINT	SEASON
****/2	7 miles	1435 feet/ 730 feet	July–Sept

Maps: USGS Seward D6 NW, USGS Seward D6 NE; **Contact:** Chugach National Forest, Glacier Ranger District, Girdwood; Alyeska Resort for information about the hand tram; **Notes:** Hand tram is closed during the winter season and occasionally during summer for maintenance; hand tram status is usually posted at the Alyeska Resort Trailhead. Dogs permitted on leash. Bear and moose habitat, especially black bears; **GPS:** Alyeska Resort: 60.9697°, –149.0952°; Crow Creek Mine Road: 60.99533°, –149.09297°

A beautiful and popular stroll through a lush, temperate rainforest is punctuated by views of Glacier Creek, Winner Creek, and a thrilling hand tram.

GETTING THERE

Alyeska Resort Trailhead: From Anchorage, drive south on the New Seward Highway for about 33 miles. At mile marker 90, just before the Tesoro gas station, turn left onto the Alyeska Highway in Girdwood. Follow this road for about three miles until it ends in a T intersection. Turn left onto Arlberg Avenue. Stay on Arlberg Avenue for 1 mile until you reach Alyeska Resort, then follow signs for parking (elevation 340 feet).

Crow Creek Road Trailhead: From Anchorage, drive south on the New Seward Highway for about 33 miles and, at mile marker 90, just before the big Tesoro gas station, turn left onto the Alyeska Highway. After 1.9 miles, turn left onto unpaved Crow Creek Road. The signed trailhead is on your right at mile 2.9 of Crow Creek Road. If you reach the turnoff for the Crow Creek Mine, you went about a half mile too far.

ON THE TRAIL

Like the North Face Trail (Hike 58), this trail begins behind the base of Alyeska Resort's aerial tram. I'm writing this as an out-and-back hike starting from Alyeska Resort, but you can also do it as a thru-hike in either direction, and, of course, you can start from the Crow Creek Road Trailhead too.

Looking across the gap on the Winner Creek hand tram

Trails don't come any nicer than this in Alaska. The first 0.7 mile is wide, well-maintained boardwalk, followed by a level, well-packed dirt path. Keep an eye out for spiky devil's club and a profusion of high-bush blueberries buried in the lush vegetation on either side of the trail. Every August, Alyeska Resort celebrates the latter with a two-day Blueberry Festival.

At about 1.6 miles the trail hits a T intersection. To the right, Upper Winner Creek is a very rough trail that leads 9 miles over Berry Pass, almost to Twentymile River. This branch is not a day hike; if you're going to backpack it, be ready to deal with very primitive and sometimes brushy conditions.

The main trail continues to the left until you pass an enormous, somewhat broken-down Sno-Cat bridge on the right at 2.25 miles. I like taking a snack break on this bridge, swinging my legs over the rushing waters of Winner Creek, but don't bother exploring the muddy trail remnants on the far side of the bridge.

Once you're back on the main trail, it winds gently downhill to another bridge.

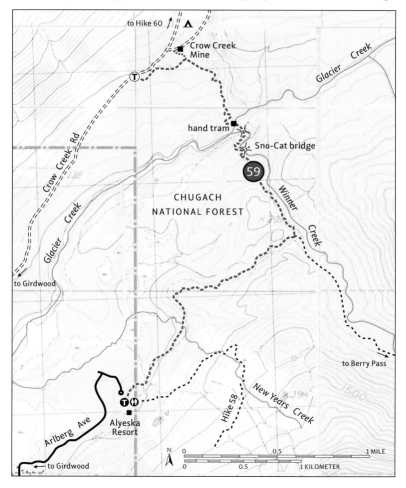

This one takes you all the way across roiling, milky blue Winner Creek and is one of the prettiest spots on the trail.

The next highlight—literally—is the hand tram across Glacier Creek, 2.5 miles from the trailhead. It's open only during the summer, and is taken offline on rare occasions for maintenance. If you want to go across, check Alyeska Resort's summer mountain report on their website to make sure the tram is open. Bring light gloves to protect your hands from the rough rope.

Once across the tram, the trail narrows to a moderate grade until its modest high point at about 3.1 miles (elevation 730 feet). The trail forks here; turn left to reach the Crow Creek Road Trailhead, a total distance of 3.5 miles. If you turn right you'll end up at Crow Creek Mine, a private property that charges an admission fee.

60 Raven Glacier

RATING/ DIFFICULTY	ROUNDTRIP	ELEV GAIN/ HIGH POINT	SEASON
*****/4	7.4 miles	2420 feet/ 3600 feet	June–Oct

Maps: USGS Anchorage A6 SW, National Geographic Chugach State Park, Imus Geographics Chugach State Park; **Contact:** Chugach National Forest, Glacier Ranger District, Girdwood; **Notes:** Dogs permitted on leash at trailhead, under direct control in backcountry. Bear and moose habitat; bear sightings are extremely common here. Extreme avalanche hazard in winter and spring; **GPS:** 61.02819°, –149.11617°

 *This hike presents the prettiest and steepest part of the famous 24-mile Crow Pass hike. It takes you past mine ruins to a crystal-clear lake and, just beyond the pass, overlooks of Raven Glacier.*

GETTING THERE

From Anchorage, drive south on the New Seward Highway for about 33 miles. At mile marker 90, just before the big Tesoro gas station, turn left onto the Alyeska Highway. After 1.9 miles, turn left onto unpaved Crow Creek Mine Road, which runs another five miles into the mountains, becoming narrow and sometimes very rough. The trailhead (elevation 1550 feet) is at the end of the road.

ON THE TRAIL

When people rave about how beautiful the 24-mile Crow Pass Trail is, they're usually talking about these first four miles leading into the pass. Even the trailhead itself is beautiful, with foamy Milk Creek cascading down a boulder-filled gully just before you reach the trailhead, and lush mountainsides opening up all around you.

You'll get a taste of that lushness straight out of the trailhead, as the well-maintained path dives right into dense alders and a profusion of grass, false hellebore, and the burn-inducing cow parsnip. By 0.75 mile (elevation 2060 feet) the alders shrink back down to shrub size, giving you better visibility as you climb an extremely rocky trail up the east side of an alpine valley.

By 1.5 miles (elevation 2500 feet) you're just about out of the bushes entirely, and you also have a decision to make. Most hikers will want to turn right at this point, taking the maintained (and relatively gentle) trail to the top of the pass. The very fit and fearless, however, may prefer a more direct and exciting route: going straight ahead, past the

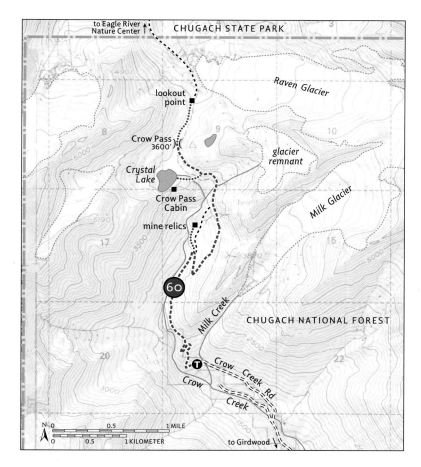

relics from an old mine, then scrambling up a steep, slippery footpath beside the rocky stream gorge.

Assuming you stick to the maintained trail, it makes a sustained, moderate climb up a couple of big switchbacks, then heads left (north) on a slope of packed-down rock. At mile 2.5 (elevation 3120 feet) the

alternate, scrambling route rejoins the main trail, and at mile 2.7 (elevation 3275 feet) you cross the first of several wide but shallow streams that flow across the trail. Sometimes you can hop rocks across, sometimes you have to wade. The water isn't deep, but because it flows from the remnants of a glacier, it is . . . very brisk.

The approach to Crystal Lake, just before Crow Pass: winter lasts longer up here, with snowbanks lingering long into summer.

At the 3-mile mark, you'll be able to see gorgeous, milky blue Crystal Lake in front of you and the dark wood of the Crow Pass Cabin perched on its shore. You can reserve the use of this cabin, for a fee, at recreation.gov.

This trail is so busy that the people using the cabin don't get much privacy—but there's plenty of room for you to picnic around Crystal Lake without bothering them. Reach its shores by wading through the lake's gentle outflow to the left of the trail at mile 3.1 (elevation 3480 feet).

When you continue on the main trail, you can look forward to an almost level walk, although the trail can be extremely wet at 3.5 miles. At 3.7 miles (elevation 3600 feet) you'll reach the sign marking Crow Pass itself. Just a few hundred feet farther down the trail is a great lookout over Raven Glacier, a massive sheet of ice creeping its way down the flanks of Summit Mountain to your right.

From here, the Crow Pass Trail continues another 20 miles to the Eagle River Nature Center. If you're thinking of doing the whole hike, do your research and come prepared—it includes many miles of brushy, overgrown trail through bear country and a major ford of Eagle River. And as many people who've done the entire trail will tell you, you've walked the prettiest part of it already.

61 Trail of Blue Ice

RATING/ DIFFICULTY	ROUNDTRIP	ELEV GAIN/ HIGH POINT	SEASON
****/2	9.7 miles	415 feet/ 270 feet	May–Oct

Maps: USGS Seward D5 SW, USGS Seward D6 SE, National Geographic Kenai National Wildlife Refuge; **Contact:** Chugach National Forest, Glacier Ranger District, Girdwood; **Notes:** Handicap accessible. Open to bikes. Dogs permitted on leash in parking areas, "restrained" on trails. Bear and moose habitat. Can be buggy in summer. Known avalanche hazard between miles 3 and 4; **GPS:** Moose Flats end: 60.81150°, -148.94196°; Portage Lake end: 60.78291°, -148.84129°

   This wide, mostly level path isn't exactly a hardcore hike—but it's the perfect stroll from any of Portage Valley's developed recreation sites, and it showcases so many glaciers draped over nearby mountaintops, that even the most jaded of hikers will marvel at its beauty.

GETTING THERE

From Anchorage, drive south on the New Seward Highway. At mile marker 79, about 50 miles out of town, turn left onto Portage Glacier Road. The first access point to this trail, Moose Flats, is located at mile 1 of Portage Glacier Road. The other access points are Explorer Glacier Pullout at mile 2.5, Five Fingers Campground at mile 3, and the Williwaw Campground at mile 4; the trail ends at the Begich, Boggs Visitor Center, which is located at mile 5 of Portage Glacier Road.

ON THE TRAIL

As you can see, this trail has many access points. For the sake of keeping it simple, I'll describe it as a roundtrip hike (or a fabulous bike trip) from Moose Flats to the Begich, Boggs Visitor Center, then back again. If you're here during the winter, be aware that the trail crosses several known avalanche runouts, especially between miles 3 and 4.

From the Moose Flats day use area, the trail starts just behind a US Forest Service marker on the east side of the parking lot. At 0.6 mile it crosses Portage Glacier Road—look out for drivers distracted by all the pretty views—and continues along the south side of the road, surrounded by slender trees.

At 1.2 miles, the trail passes between the Explorer Glacier Pullout on the left and a placid, tree-lined pond to the right. A small gravel beach makes a great place to sit and watch the water—if the bugs aren't too bad. Take a minute to look up to the right: the big chunk of blue ice atop the mountains is Explorer Glacier.

You'll pass another access point at 2.1 miles: the Five Fingers Campground. At 2.5 miles the trail crosses a bridge with a lovely, arcing superstructure, then passes over a long boardwalk until it tucks right up against the Williwaw Campground at mile 3.3.

There's a nice, 1.25-mile side trip here: backtrack through the campground to the Williwaw fish viewing platform and, during mid- to late summer, watch salmon spawning in the water below. Then hike the Williwaw Nature Trail, which passes under Portage Glacier Road, around a couple of ponds (give moose plenty of space if you see them), and back across the highway to rejoin the Trail of Blue Ice at 3.9 miles from the trailhead.

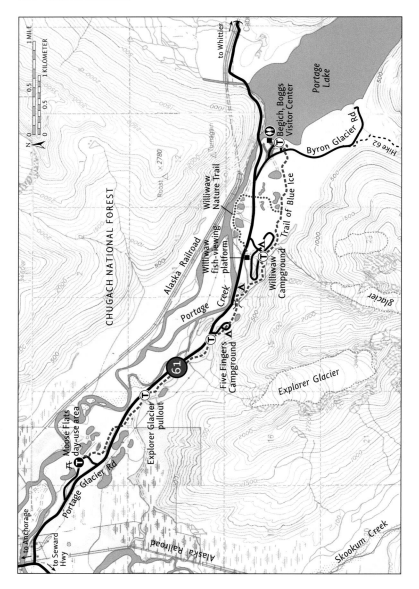

One of several graceful bridges along the Trail of Blue Ice

If you stay on the Trail of Blue Ice, at 3.8 miles it's actually paved for a short stretch. Then, shortly after the intersection with the Williwaw Nature Trail, it passes one of the best viewpoints on the entire trail: a beautiful, rock-studded pond on the left, full of vibrant blue-green water, with a massive hanging glacier draped over the mountains straight ahead.

At 4.6 miles the trail crosses Byron Glacier Road, an access point for Hike 62; watch for cars. It then climbs over a short hill that slightly exceeds the grades allowed for handicap access before arriving at the shores of Portage Lake and the Begich, Boggs Visitor Center, a total distance of just over 4.8 miles. A short bypass to the left allows wheelchair users to shortcut around the hill. Leave yourself some time to explore the shore of the lake and the visitor center, which is typically open from Memorial Day to mid-September, before you head back.

62 Byron Glacier

This short, easy hike rewards you with glorious valley views and glimpses of rapidly receding Byron Glacier. Perfect for tourists, families with kids, and anyone looking for some windy solitude in the moraine—a huge pile of boulders left behind by the glacier in its retreat.

RATING/ DIFFICULTY	ROUNDTRIP	ELEV GAIN/ HIGH POINT	SEASON
****/2	2.3 miles	395 feet/ 475 feet	June–Oct

Maps: USGS Seward C5 NW, USGS Seward D5 SW, National Geographic Kenai National Wildlife Refuge; **Contact:** Chugach National Forest, Glacier Ranger District, Girdwood; **Notes:** Dogs permitted on leash. Bear and moose habitat. Extreme avalanche hazard in winter and spring; **GPS:** 60.77371°, -148.84382°

GETTING THERE

From Anchorage, drive south on the New Seward Highway. At mile marker 79, about 50 miles out of town, take a clearly marked left turn onto Portage Glacier Road. Continue 5 miles, then bear right on Byron Glacier Road and look for the trailhead sign at the

A first glimpse of rapidly receding Byron Glacier in the distance

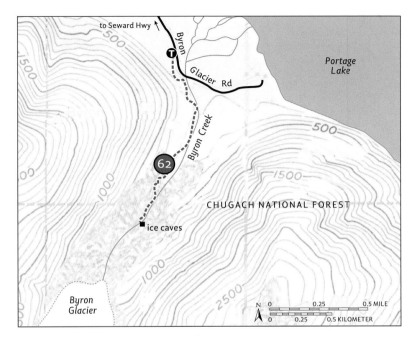

head of a large parking lot on your right (elevation 175 feet).

ON THE TRAIL

The Byron Glacier Trail starts on a broad trail of hardened gravel, lined with alders, small cottonwoods, and ferns.

There's a short, stiff elevation gain of about 100 feet as you leave the parking lot, but other than that the trail is mostly flat and is well suited to families with kids or elders. At 0.25 mile in you get great trailside access to silty Byron Creek, with a particularly good creek overlook just before the 0.5-mile mark.

At 0.7 mile the trail departs the creekside, curving up and right through stands of thick alders. It returns to the creek at 1 mile. Within the next 0.2 mile it peters to an end in Byron Glacier's broad floodplain. The glacier itself is a distant blue gem on the rocky valley wall, receding farther every year. In a typical year you'll see Byron Creek at its broadest and gentlest here, flowing out from a tunnel of snow and ice just to your left.

Although the walls of the ice tunnel look blue, it isn't a part of the glacier. Instead, it's carved from the remnants of the avalanches that thunder down from above every winter and spring, making this trail a very poor choice for winter travel. In spring there can still be avalanche danger from above, even when the trail itself is clear. The ice caves usually linger throughout the year and, although they're beautiful, they're also potentially deadly: they can collapse or shed pieces of ice at any moment, and falling ice can (and has) injured eager hikers who trek into the caves for pictures. In 2018 there was a fatality in the ice caves; please take this risk seriously.

The glacier moraine—an obvious pile of rocky debris left by the melting glacier—makes a fine place to scramble around for better views of the glacier. If you scramble all the way to the far side of it—about a quarter of a mile—there's a pretty gravel beach that makes the perfect place for a quiet picnic on this relatively crowded trail.

Some people cross the creek and scramble as close as they can to the glacier's receding toe, hunting for more ice caves. But be aware: the rock faces here are full of technical roped climbs, and it's easy to find yourself accidentally scrambling up something you can't easily get back down.

63 Spencer Overlook

Interpretive Pavilion

RATING/ DIFFICULTY	ROUNDTRIP	ELEV GAIN/ HIGH POINT	SEASON
*****/2	3 miles	40 feet/ 165 feet	May–Sept

Glacier Overlook

RATING/ DIFFICULTY	ROUNDTRIP	ELEV GAIN/ HIGH POINT	SEASON
*****/2	7 miles	555 feet/ 650 feet	May–Sept

Maps: USGS Seward C6 NE, National Geographic Kenai National Wildlife Refuge; **Contact:** Chugach National Forest, Glacier Ranger District, Girdwood; **Notes:** Access only via the Alaska Railroad's Glacier Discovery train, which runs late May to mid-September; see the Alaska Railroad website. The first 1.5 miles of this trail are handicap accessible. Dogs are permitted on leash at trailhead, under direct control on trails, but while on the train must stay in an airline-approved kennel in the baggage car. Bear and moose habitat; **GPS:** 60.70586°, –149.05383°

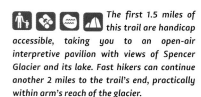 *The first 1.5 miles of this trail are handicap accessible, taking you to an open-air interpretive pavilion with views of Spencer Glacier and its lake. Fast hikers can continue another 2 miles to the trail's end, practically within arm's reach of the glacier.*

GETTING THERE
This trail starts from the Spencer Glacier Whistle Stop (elevation 125 feet), accessible only via the Alaska Railroad's Glacier Discovery train, which runs from late May to mid-September; see the Alaska Railroad website (alaskarailroad.com). Don't miss your ride back! The train typically arrives at the Spencer Glacier Whistle Stop between 1:45 PM and 2:00 PM, and you must be back at the trailhead by no later than 4:30 PM to catch it on the return trip.

ON THE TRAIL
From the trailhead, take the obvious broad, gravel path to the south. At 0.6 mile the trail passes a beautiful, arched bridge over the Placer River. The trail does extend on the far side but doesn't actually connect to anything else—yet. One day, it'll be connected to other whistle stops along the line. Just past the bridge, a bench makes the perfect place to sit and watch the roiling water—and sometimes, happy rafters or kayakers—passing by.

The trail grade picks up slightly after you pass the fully accessible glacier-viewing pavilion.

From here, the trail roughly parallels the Placer River until mile 1, at which point it jigs briefly away from the water. At about 1.3 miles you'll pass a set of group campsites on the left; they must be reserved in advance. There's also an outhouse to the right.

Continue straight past a gravel administrative road and at 1.5 miles you'll reach an open-air interpretive pavilion that looks out over Spencer Lake and the glacier beyond. You can also walk straight down to the lakeshore. The trail up to this point is accessible to the adventurous handicapped, gaining less than 50 feet total from the trailhead.

Remember, it's absolutely imperative that you be back at the trailhead by 4:30 PM in order to catch your train on its only return trip back to town. So, for slower hikers, this is a good turnaround point. Speedy hikers can continue around the lake to the left on what remains a broad gravel path. At 1.8 miles you'll pass a gentle beach to the south, an ideal put-in spot for kayakers and rafters.

The trail incline steepens just a bit here, and at 2 miles (elevation 200 feet) you'll pass another bench overlooking Spencer Lake from a slight rise, then another, right at the lakeshore, at 2.5 miles (elevation

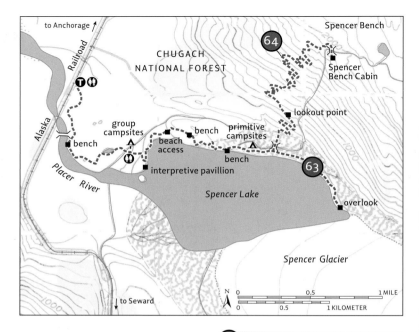

310 feet). At about 2.6 miles you'll pass a set of nine primitive campsites with tent pads; these are first come, first served.

At 2.75 miles (elevation 400 feet) the trail to Spencer Bench and the public use Spencer Bench Cabin shoots off to the left (see Hike 64). The overlook trail climbs another 250 feet and ends at a wide, barren overlook 3.5 miles from the trailhead (elevation 650 feet) surrounded by rocky piles deposited during the glacier's retreat. If the glacier calves, which it does with some frequency, you'll have a front-row seat.

I can't think of a better picnic spot, but, again, make sure you leave plenty of time to make the 3.5-mile hike back to the trailhead before 4:30 PM—all in all, a very brisk round-trip for most hikers.

64 Spencer Bench

RATING/ DIFFICULTY	ROUNDTRIP	ELEV GAIN/ HIGH POINT	SEASON
*****/4	11.8 miles	2080 feet/ 1920 feet	May–Sept

Maps: USGS Seward C6 NE, National Geographic Kenai National Wildlife Refuge; **Contact:** Chugach National Forest, Glacier Ranger District, Girdwood; **Notes:** Access only via the Alaska Railroad's Glacier Discovery train, which runs late May to mid-September; see the Alaska Railroad website. Dogs permitted on leash at trailhead, under direct control on trails, but while on the train must stay in an airline-approved kennel in the baggage car.

Chocolate lilies above, Spencer Glacier below: exploring the tundra "bench" past the Spencer Bench public use cabin

Bear and moose habitat; **GPS:** 60.70586°, −149.05383°

 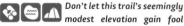 *Don't let this trail's seemingly modest elevation gain fool you—all the uphill happens in a mad rush at the end. You'll miss your train back if you try to do the whole thing, but trail runners and speedy hikers can enjoy the views from partway up, and overnight campers can do it as a long day hike.*

GETTING THERE

This trail starts from the Spencer Glacier Whistle Stop (elevation 125 feet), accessible only via the Alaska Railroad's Glacier Discovery train, which runs from late May to mid-September; see the Alaska Railroad website (alaskarailroad.com). Don't miss your ride back! The train typically arrives at the Spencer Glacier Whistle Stop between 1:45 PM and 2:00 PM, and you must be back at the trailhead by no later than 4:30 PM to catch its single return trip for the day.

ON THE TRAIL

This challenging 11.8-mile hike is much too long to complete in the limited time before the train returns. But it makes a stunning day hike for campers who are already planning to stay overnight, and strong, speedy hikers (or runners) can snag great views from a lookout point partway up the trail. Keep a close eye on the time—if you miss the train back, you'll be spending the night.

The first 2.75 miles of this trail coincides with the Spencer Glacier Overlook Trail (see Hike 63). At mile 0.6, you'll pass a beautiful, arched bridge over the Placer River that doesn't really go anywhere—yet. At mile 1.5 you'll find an interpretive pavilion overlooking Spencer Lake and the glacier beyond; at mile 1.8 there's a good beach access where kayakers and rafters put their watercraft in the water, and at about 2.6 miles you'll pass a set of nine primitive first-come, first-served campsites.

Then at 2.75 miles (elevation 400 feet) you bid farewell to the overlook trail's gentle grades and wide, gravel trail, turning left to follow the trail to Spencer Bench into a dip, across a bridge, and then straight up the mountainside.

By 3 miles the trail goes up a series of steep switchbacks, and at 3.5 miles (elevation 500 feet) you gain a lookout point over the glacier and lake. The only way to best these views is by going all the way to the top of Spencer Bench.

If you're a trail runner or a very speedy hiker, you might be able to make it here and back in time to catch the return train. Only continue past this point if you're committed to staying the night, or starting an early day hike after camping down by the water.

If you do go on, the trail never lets up its steep grade, passing through thick brush as it switchbacks all the way to the top of Spencer Bench at 5.75 miles (elevation 1840 feet). The trail is well-made and frequently maintained, but you'll have to deal with rocky footing, loose gravel, and sporadic thick grass, even while the ridge above you is still topped by lingering snowpack.

Once you top out on the bench, follow the trail as it bears east, then south, and crosses a rushing creek on a damaged bridge. If at any point the bridge becomes impassable, there are several reasonable ford spots nearby.

At this point the Spencer Bench Cabin, which must be reserved through the Alaska Railroad during the summer months, is just a short walk away, 5.9 miles from the trailhead (elevation 1920 feet). Be respectful of people using the cabin and, if you haven't reserved it, seize the opportunity to explore off-trail on the naturally terraced bench above the cabin, taking in bird's-eye overlooks of Spencer Glacier down below.

There is no established trail beyond the cabin, so practice your best Leave No Trace principles, and take care to note where you descend to regain the trail for your return trip. I like to tie a brightly colored bandana to a tree as a marker.

Opposite: *Don't be misled by blue skies: even a short pass like Portage Pass, seen here, can pack surprisingly harsh weather if it's in the mood (Hike 66).*

whittier area

Whittier packs a lot of history and personality in one place—not bad for a town of about two hundred people! Once a World War II–era port town, it's now a fishing town, cruise port, and popular destination for waterborne outdoor recreation. It has some really interesting hiking trails too, with Portage Pass as the standout attraction.

65 Horsetail Falls

RATING/ DIFFICULTY	ROUNDTRIP	ELEV GAIN/ HIGH POINT	SEASON
***/2	2 miles	570 feet/ 644 feet	May–Sept

Map: USGS Seward D5 SE; **Contact:** City of Whittier; **Notes:** Mostly boardwalk. Toll required for tunnel. Dogs permitted on leash in parking area, "restrained" on trail. Moose habitat. Prime bear habitat; **GPS:** 60.77440°, -148.67270°

Enjoy a pleasant walk through a rainforest to a small wooden platform that offers views over Passage Canal, the town harbor, and many waterfalls skipping down nearby mountain slopes.

GETTING THERE

From Anchorage, drive about 50 miles south on the New Seward Highway. At mile marker 79, follow signs for the Whittier access road and queue up to go through the single-lane Anton Anderson Memorial Tunnel, the longest combined vehicle/railroad tunnel in North America. Traffic alternates directions every half hour, with occasional delays to let the train through. There is a toll. Check the

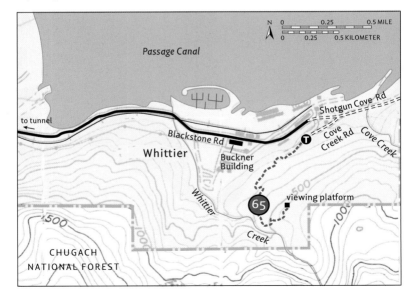

Even when the waterfalls aren't running strong with spring snowmelt, Horsetail Falls Trail offers stunning views of Whittier and Passage Canal.

tunnel schedule with the Alaska Department of Transportation and Public Facilities (see Resources). After exiting the Anton Anderson Memorial Tunnel into Whittier, continue straight on West Camp Road, the only road into town. Turn right on Whittier Street, then continue straight onto Blackstone Road at an awkward four-way intersection. Drive past the Buckner Building—an abandoned cement barracks—then veer right onto unpaved Shotgun Cove Road. Take the first right onto Cove Creek Road and park in a spacious but somewhat uneven gravel pullout at the end of the road.

ON THE TRAIL

The Horsetail Falls Trail starts just past a rusty gate at the far end of your parking pullout, climbing slowly but steadily toward its modest high point of 644 feet. The first 0.2 mile of trail is on an old gravel roadbed, bordered by coastal rainforest with a dense, lush layer of undergrowth. Look for high-bush blueberry and salmonberry bushes alongside the trail, and listen for songbirds, including the burbling, liquid call of the hermit thrush, a plump little bird with a white body, brown spots on its chest, and brown head, wings, and tail.

At 0.2 mile a series of boardwalks begins; they'll take you all the way to a viewing platform at the end of the trail. Be aware that the boardwalks get slippery when wet—and things in Whittier are usually wet. There are also a few broken (or about to break) planks, so watch your step.

At 0.6 mile you'll go up a set of stairs in a patch of salmonberry bushes so thick you practically have to wade through them. Salmonberries look like orange-colored raspberries and are a favorite of both humans and bears, so always use your best "bear aware" manners when moving through thick vegetation like this.

At 0.7 mile the boardwalk narrows down to a single board and stays that way, wandering through wildflower-dotted meadows. And just before you reach the 1-mile mark you'll arrive at a very "Alaskan" viewing platform, some wooden decking sitting at an angle on the hillside.

Despite its ramshackle condition, the platform has lovely views of Passage Canal and many waterfalls skipping down the nearby mountainsides; look for the distinctive arcing plume of Horsetail Falls during spring and early summer, when melting snow gives all the waterfalls a serious boost.

66 Portage Pass

RATING/ DIFFICULTY	ROUNDTRIP	ELEV GAIN/ HIGH POINT	SEASON
*****/3	5.2 miles	935 feet/ 800 feet	June–Oct

Map: USGS Seward D5 SW; **Contact:** Chugach National Forest, Seward Ranger District, Seward; **Notes:** Limited space for parking. Toll required for tunnel. Dogs permitted on leash in parking area, and under direct control on trail. Bear and moose habitat; **GPS:** 60.77537°, -148.73058

Simply one of the most gobsmacking trails in Alaska, this short walk takes you to a broad beach with the only

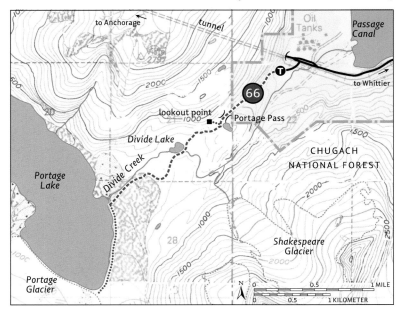

The trail makes a sandy descent to a flat, beach-like floodplain across the lake from Portage Glacier.

land-based views to be had of Portage Glacier, which has long since receded out of view of the visitor center that was built to showcase it.

GETTING THERE

From Anchorage, drive about 50 miles south on the New Seward Highway. At mile marker 79, follow signs for the Whittier access road and queue up to go through the single-lane Anton Anderson Memorial Tunnel, the longest combined vehicle/railroad tunnel in North America. Traffic alternates directions every half hour, with occasional delays to let the train through. There is a toll. Check the tunnel schedule with the Alaska Department of Transportation and Public Facilities (see Resources). Once in Whittier, take the first right turn across the railroad tracks (marked with a small brown sign for "Forest Access") and follow posted signs for the small trailhead (elevation 85 feet).

ON THE TRAIL

The trail follows a rocky old jeep road up a stiff, constant grade; by 0.8 mile you've gained 800-foot Portage Pass. Despite its low altitude, the pass is notorious for violent winds, quickly changing weather, and rain in all seasons, so always check the forecast and take a peek at FAA Aviation Weather Cameras (http://avcams.faa.gov/sitelist.php) for Whittier before you go.

On a clear day, you can see all the way to the glacier itself, glittering in the distance to the southwest, while the bright blue waters of Passage Canal beckons from behind you. There's a sizable pond on the far side of the pass; skirt it to either side.

Once you're past the pond, the trail forks. The very short right spur takes you to a lookout point that offers the full panoramic view of the glacier and the waterfall-draped mountains around you. The main trail continues left, past a small unnamed lake, then descends into the trees.

Just before 1.4 miles (elevation 600 feet) you'll pass to the left of shallow, reedy Divide Lake. At 1.5 miles, just past the lake, the trail forks again. The spur trail to the right leads to the banks of the creek that flows out of Divide Lake, but you'll have a chance to see it from the main trail later on.

Continue left on the marked trail for Portage Lake. The trail continues more or less level until, just before 2.3 miles (elevation 620 feet), it passes right next to bubbling Divide Creek and emerges from the alders atop a short, sandy hill that leads down to a wonderfully broad beach of sand, mud, and cobbles.

From here the trail dips down to the beach beside the lake, which is now the only thing that separates you from Portage Glacier. Look behind you: a small sign at the brushline and a series of enormous, white-topped cairns make it easy to find your way back to the trail.

At 2.6 miles you reach the beach—a great place for a picnic, or you can walk almost a mile around the lake to the left for closer views of the glacier, until you come up against another rushing creek. While some do ford the creek and continue right up to the glacier, it's not a crossing to be taken lightly. Nor is an approach to the glacier, which, although it's not as active as some, can and does calve ice into the water—or onto land—at any time, and is riddled with the same crevasses, moulins, and other typical dangers you'd find on any glacier.

During your visit, you might see a blocky ship on the water: that is the MV *Ptarmigan*, the only motorized craft allowed on Portage Lake. It sails five times a day from May through September; see Portage Glacier Cruises (portageglaciercruises.com) for details. You can also paddle a canoe or kayak along the nonmotorized boat corridor that hugs the mountainous shoreline.

67 Emerald Cove

RATING/ DIFFICULTY	ROUNDTRIP	ELEV GAIN/ HIGH POINT	SEASON
***/3	4.3 miles	650 feet/ 100 feet	June–Oct

Map: USGS Seward D5 SE; **Contact:** City of Whittier; **Notes:** Toll required for tunnel. Bear habitat, especially during summer salmon runs and fall berry season. Requires fords. Extremely muddy and slippery, especially in the fall. Ongoing trail improvements likely; **GPS:** 60.78675°, -148.62706°

Stroll through temperate rainforest to a pretty waterfall. Beyond this, the trail offers gorgeous views over seaside coves—if you're willing to venture onto a muddy, slippery, and over-grown trail.

GETTING THERE

From Anchorage, drive about 50 miles south on the New Seward Highway. At mile marker 79, follow signs for the Whittier access road and queue up to go through the single-lane Anton Anderson Memorial Tunnel, the longest combined vehicle/railroad tunnel in North America. Traffic alternates directions every half hour, with occasional delays to let the train through. There is a toll. Check the tunnel schedule with the Alaska Department of Transportation and Public Facilities (see Resources). After exiting the Anton Anderson Memorial Tunnel into Whittier, continue straight on West Camp Road. Turn right on Whittier Street, then continue

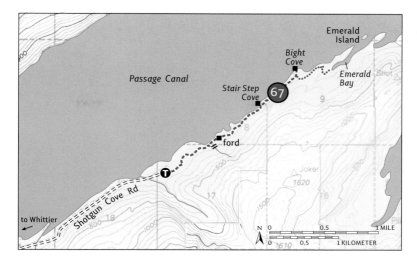

straight onto Blackstone Road at an awkward four-way intersection. Drive past the Buckner Building—an abandoned cement barracks—then veer right onto unpaved Shotgun Cove Road. Stay on Shotgun Cove Road until the road ends in an enormous, rough gravel parking area.

ON THE TRAIL

A couple of years ago, you had to ford a couple of rushing streams to get to where the trail starts now. Those streams are now bridged, just one of the improvements the city of Whittier has recently made to this trail.

Your walk starts as a narrow gravel roadbed, pushing through the alders at one end of the gravel parking area. By 0.1 mile the trail starts getting muddy. Sporadic boardwalks and a lot of gravel, first laid by volunteer workers in 2017, help keep the trail walkable. At 0.7 mile (elevation 85 feet) you reach a pretty, unnamed waterfall off to your right.

If you'd like to keep going, the trail turns left and leads to a pair of very pretty seaside coves—but you'll have to brave a muddy, often slippery hike to get there. Take my advice and plan your hike during a stretch of nice weather; it'll help cut down on the mud. Also, be aware that salmon do run up these creeks, and the dense overgrowth creates perfect conditions for a surprise wildlife encounter—so mind your bear manners.

As you continue hiking, you'll face a series of small streams that are easy to simply step across—no need to wade—but still notable because of the particularly muddy, slippery footing they offer.

At 0.8 mile (elevation 40 feet) you'll have gorgeous views down over the water to your left, followed by a small ford that, in normal water conditions, is never more than knee-deep. Take note of where you cross, because on the way back it's easy to accidentally pop out too far downstream on the opposite bank. You're also close enough

Pending further trail improvements, idyllic Bight Cove is (for now) the ideal ending spot for the Emerald Cove trail.

to the sea that the creek's water levels are tidally affected, which can cause some confusion.

The trail continues weaving through the trees, berry bushes, and spiny devil's club, occasionally passing through small, sunny meadows. This isn't the place for exploring off-trail; thick tree cover impedes GPS coverage somewhat (my original tracks look like they were drawn on an Etch A Sketch) and if you wander off the path, it's almost impossible to find again.

At 1.5 miles (elevation 70 feet) you'll pass a small cove to your left; locals call this Stair Step Cove.

Just past 2 miles, the trail splits. I very strongly recommend that you take the left fork, which heads steeply down toward a second cove that isn't named on the map; I've heard it called Bight Cove. Its sunny slate beach and shallow lagoon are the perfect place to lounge and watch the boat and kayak traffic passing by.

If you do continue via the right fork, trail builders have put heroic effort into many boardwalks and bridges to make this stretch passable—and at some point in the near future, they hope to make more improvements. But for now, it's so slippery, muddy, and difficult to follow that even very strong hikers are lucky to average 1 mile per hour and avoid injury. There's especially high risk of a dangerous surprise bear encounter in this stretch of trail too. So until further trail improvements are made, the real recreational hike ends at Bight Cove.

Opposite: *The area around Hope has only a few hikes, but they're some of the most scenic—and memorable—in the state (Hike 69).*

hope area

This quiet little community of almost two hundred people is known for having some of the best live music and cafés you'll find in a Southcentral Alaska summer, along with a gorgeous public campground overlooking the water. There are three "official" trails here; Gull Rock and Hope Point are old favorites in any local's list, while the Palmer Creek Lakes Trail has (quite rightly) emerged from obscurity in the last few years.

Maps: USGS Seward D7 SW, National Geographic Kenai National Wildlife Refuge; **Contact:** Chugach National Forest, Seward Ranger District, Seward; **Notes:** Unmarked trailhead. Access road is rough and narrow. Dogs permitted on leash in parking areas, under direct control on trail. Bear and moose habitat. One optional ford; **GPS:** 60.79283°, –149.54788°

Some adventurous driving gets you to one of Southcentral's dreamiest short hikes above the treeline: an old mining road and clear-cut footpath take you to a pretty cascade out of the twin lakes, and the valley is big and isolated enough that it's easy to feel like you're completely on your own.

68 Palmer Creek Lakes

RATING/ DIFFICULTY	ROUNDTRIP	ELEV GAIN/ HIGH POINT	SEASON
*****/3	2.6 miles	935 feet/ 2840 feet	June–Oct

Can you see me now? A hiker dials in the perfect shot, looking back toward the trailhead.

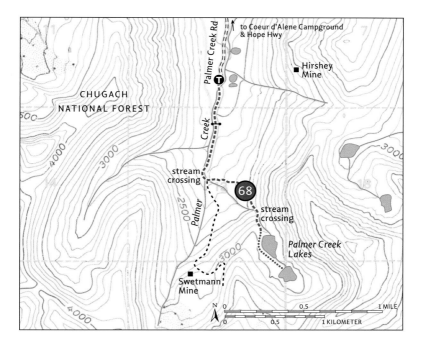

GETTING THERE

From Anchorage, drive south on the New Seward Highway. At mile marker 56.5, turn right (west) onto the Hope Highway. After 16.2 miles, turn left onto unpaved Resurrection Creek Road for 0.5 mile. Turn left onto Palmer Creek Road, passing through a gate that is typically closed by October for the winter season, and drive 6.7 miles to the Coeur d'Alene Campground. Continue through the campground on Palmer Creek Road for another 4.1 miles. Those last few miles are quite rough single-lane road with a shallow stream crossing, but some passenger cars with decent clearance can get through in dry weather if carefully driven. Park at a rough pullout at the end of the road.

ON THE TRAIL

I've heard this trail called both Palmer Lakes and Twin Lakes, and it appears as Palmer Creek Lakes in 55 *Ways to the Wilderness in Southcentral Alaska* (by Helen Nienhueser and John Wolfe, Jr., published by Mountaineers Books). From the trailhead (elevation 1900 feet) continue on a wide gravel roadbed that leads into an expansive valley studded with spruce and hemlock trees. Pretty, brush-lined Palmer Creek gurgles to your right. At 0.3 mile the trail passes through a gate and narrows to a rocky, wet footpath.

At 0.6 mile a small but clear footpath leads up and to the left. That's your trail, but it's very easy to miss. (If you reach a wide but shallow creek, you went just a little too far—and now you have a choice to make. You could wade across the creek and follow the old road as it zigzags to a lookout point near the Swetmann Mine, 1.4 miles from the trailhead. But you'll get better views if you either backtrack to the turn you missed or take the faint, muddy track to the left just before that creek crossing. That track rejoins the main trail—the turnoff you missed—at about 0.8 mile from the trailhead.)

The trail then cuts right (east) along the hillside in front of you, zeroing in on the pretty waterfall of Palmer Creek spilling out of the alpine bowl that holds its twin headwaters. This is the steepest part of the trail, gaining 400 feet in just 0.3 mile, but that clear, straight path makes it feel easy. At 1.1 miles the trail fades out, but it's easy to find your way up the grassy tundra, keeping to the left side of the creek and bringing you level with the first Palmer Creek lake. If you decide to scramble down to the edge of the cascade, be very careful—it's steeper and more slippery than it looks.

At 1.2 miles you'll find an easy spot to cross the creek where it splits into two channels; you'll see bits of worn trail to help you find the right place. At 1.3 miles you'll be right on the shore of the first lake, and any remaining fragments of trail are long gone.

A scree slope keeps you from going around the left side of the lake, but you can walk across tundra on the right side to reach the second lake. This is exactly the sort of delicate terrain you hear about in Leave No Trace discussions. So if you do walk around the lake, take care to step on the most durable (rocky) surfaces available to you, and if you see a trail emerging, stick to that trail in order to minimize damage to other parts of the tundra.

69 Gull Rock

RATING/ DIFFICULTY	ROUNDTRIP	ELEV GAIN/ HIGH POINT	SEASON
*****/3	11.6 miles	2430 feet/ 350 feet	May–Oct

Maps: USGS Seward D8 NE, National Geographic Chugach State Park, Imus Geographics Chugach State Park; **Contact:** Chugach National Forest, Seward Ranger District, Seward; Kenai National Wildlife Refuge; **Notes:** No parking fee. Popular backpacking destination. Very popular with mountain bikers. Closed to pack/saddle stock April 1–June 30. Dogs permitted on leash or "restrained." Bear and moose habitat. Avalanche hazard in winter; **GPS:** 60.9267°, –149.6631°

  Take advantage of one of the rare flat—well okay, "flattish"—hikes that you'll find in Southcentral Alaska. Don't be scared off by the elevation gain; it's stretched out over the length of a lovely walk that offers spectacular views over the water to a seemingly limitless horizon.

GETTING THERE
From Anchorage, drive south on the New Seward Highway. At mile marker 56.5, about 73 miles out of town, turn right (west) onto the Hope Highway. After 17.8 miles, look for the marked Chugach National Forest Trailhead (elevation 160 feet) on your left. If you reach the Porcupine Campground at the end of the road, you went about 500 feet too far.

ON THE TRAIL
Right out of the trailhead, the trail crosses a small footbridge—take the signed turn to the

Looking out at an endless horizon from a perch atop Gull Rock

left—then starts up a short, stiff hill. This is as steep as anything gets on this trail, gaining about 150 feet in 0.25 mile. Despite the brief incline, this part of the trail is a broad, pleasant avenue of soft dirt or fallen birch leaves, depending on the season. Near the peak of the hill, you'll pass a signed intersection for the Hope Point Trail (Hike 70) on the left.

The Gull Rock Trail continues straight and then bends sharply right, dipping downhill as steeply as it had climbed, heading for another intersection at 0.9 mile. Here, a sharp right turn would take you to the Porcupine Campground, which used to serve as the trailhead for this hike. Instead, veer left as the trail undulates along the coast, never cresting past 350 feet in elevation.

The trail's character stays pretty consistent for the next few miles: mostly tree roots buried in fallen hemlock needles, varying in severity from "Hey, I'm a cute little root!" to "The unwary among ye shall trip and die." Those roots might be one of the reasons that Chugach National Forest lists this trail as not

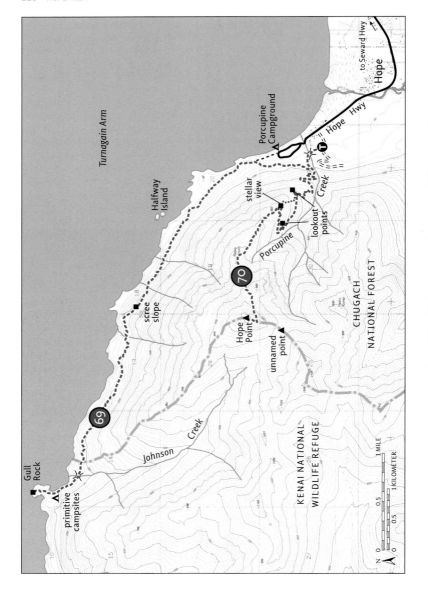

Turnagain Arm

Halfway Island

to Seward Hwy

Hope

Porcupine Campground

Hope Hwy

stellar view

Porcupine Creek

lookout points

Porcupine

70

CHUGACH NATIONAL FOREST

scree slope

Hope Point

unnamed point

69

Johnson Creek

KENAI NATIONAL WILDLIFE REFUGE

Gull Rock

primitive campsites

N

1 MILE

1 KILOMETER

0   0.5

0   0.5   1

recommended for horses or bicycles, but it remains enormously popular with mountain bikers anyway.

There's also one short scree slope shortly after mile 3 that some people find unnerving, but it's really not bad. If you struggle with vertigo or stability, try using a pair of hiking poles for extra balance.

At 4.6 miles the trail takes a brief jog inland, winding along a forested hill that slowly gives way to brush. Look for mountain ash plus spots of devil's club and cow parsnip, both of which belong firmly in the "you'll be sorry if you touch me" category.

Just past 5 miles your views over the water really open up. Look for a small, weathered sign telling you that you've left Chugach National Forest lands and entered the Kenai National Wildlife Refuge. At 5.25 miles there's a nice little bridge over Johnson Creek—your last and best source of water on the trail.

At 5.4 miles you'll start seeing great views over small coves to your right, and at 5.6 miles you'll hit a set of primitive campsites tucked around a clearing among wind-warped hemlock trees. Note how the trees' branches are shorter on one side than the other, thanks to the overwhelming force of the high winds that are common in this area.

It's tempting to think the trek ends here, and you can get great views over seaside coves in either direction. But the trail continues on the far side of the clearing, leading you up onto the prominent overlook that is Gull Rock (elevation 350 feet), 5.8 miles from the trailhead. A seemingly endless, water-filled horizon sits to the west. Listen for the soaring, shrieking gulls that give this place its name, and guard your shiny objects; clever, cheeky Steller's jays will gladly snatch anything that looks interesting or tasty.

There are no established trails down into the coves, but some daring hikers choose to pick their way down anyway. If you do this, keep in mind that Turnagain Arm has one of the most extreme tidal fluctuations in the world, and the innocent-looking tidal flats turn to quicksand as the tide comes rushing in. So, stay off the flats and don't scramble down anything you're not sure you can climb back up.

This trail is usually free of snow by May, but be aware of what's above you: this hike crosses a couple of known avalanche chutes. Even when you're walking on dry trail, there can still be enough snow above you to slide.

70 Hope Point

RATING/ DIFFICULTY	ROUNDTRIP	ELEV GAIN/ HIGH POINT	SEASON
*****/4	8.1 miles	3545 feet/ 3643 feet	May–Oct

Maps: USGS Seward D8 NE, National Geographic Chugach State Park, Imus Geographics Chugach State Park; **Contact:** Chugach National Forest, Seward Ranger District, Seward; **Notes:** No parking fee. Dogs permitted on leash or "restrained." Bear and moose habitat. No access to water on most of trail. Avalanche hazard in winter. Usually decent cell service for most of the hike; **GPS:** 60.9267°, –149.6631°

Hope Point is often praised as one of the prettiest hikes in the Chugach. If you hear horror stories about how steep this trail is, don't worry; new switchbacks render it an enjoyable, if somewhat long, hike that almost anybody can do.

GETTING THERE

From Anchorage, drive south on the New Seward Highway. At mile marker 56.5, about 73 miles out of town, turn right (west) onto the Hope Highway. After 17.8 miles, look for the marked Chugach National Forest Trailhead (elevation 160 feet) on your left. If you reach the Porcupine Campground at the end of the road, you went about 500 feet too far.

Follow this goat trail to a rocky ridge.

ON THE TRAIL

Not long ago, the Hope Point Trail started from the roadside, on the north side of Porcupine Creek, and ran so straight up the mountain that it could have doubled as an elevator shaft. A few years ago, the US Forest Service added a lovely trailhead and switchbacks that, although they basically double the length of the hike, also make it

Some of the most magical views—and photos—to be had in Southcentral come from here, along the ridge leading up to Hope Point.

into a pleasant—if long—walk that almost anybody can manage.

After 0.1 mile of clear, easy trail, the trail crosses Porcupine Creek on a bridge and turns left. At 0.25 mile, take a marked left turn to stay on the Hope Point Trail; the right fork would take you off on the Gull Rock Trail, which skirts along the lower flanks of Hope Point on its way to a rocky promontory overlooking the water (see Hike 69).

At about 0.3 mile (elevation 400 feet) the trail starts a series of long, lazy switchbacks through a forest of peeling birch, peppered with grass, cow parsnip, devil's club, and ferns. The grade on the new trail is fairly sustained here, gaining about 800 feet in the first mile, but easily managed if you take

your time and carry plenty of water (there is no more access after crossing Porcupine Creek).

At 1.3 miles (elevation 1100 feet) there's a lovely lookout point overlooking the water and the mountains, just before the trail winds sharply back to the left again, carving a gentle inroad along the toe of Hope Point. You'll have grand views of the mountains ahead of you and stunning lookouts over the water behind you. Keep an eye out for a well-worn footpath heading straight up the mountain to your right. This is a remnant of the old, near-vertical trail, which will intersect with the new path later on.

Stay on the broad switchback trail as it eases up the mountainside, by 2 miles (elevation 1500 feet) to top another lookout point that showcases your goal, Hope Point itself, looming above you to the northwest.

Just before 2.4 miles (elevation 1700 feet) the aforementioned old trail and the new trail you're on rejoin each other atop a prominent knob, which has truly stellar views over the tiny seaside town of Hope, Turnagain Arm, and the New Seward Highway on the opposite side of the Arm. The old trail drops so steeply off to the right from here that it can be hard to spot, unless you happen to see weary hikers groveling up it.

From here, the joined trails wind and climb along the grassy toe of the ridge above you, passing through clumps of short hemlock trees before emerging on a rocky spine at 3.2 miles (elevation 2400 feet). There

used to be a radio tower here, but there's no trace of it now.

From here, follow a goat trail along the rocky ridgeline until at 4 miles (elevation 3500 feet) you reach the saddle between Hope Point on the right and a small, unnamed point to the left. The walking on the ridge is easy, with just a little exposure on either side.

Turn right and keep hiking the less than 0.1 mile that remains to Hope Point's rocky peak. Most sure-footed hikers will have no problem with the short scramble required to reach the actual summit marker (elevation 3643 feet), and the views out across the water are truly breathtaking. Throw in a little late-afternoon light slanting across the inlet, and every photo taken here is magic.

Opposite: *Everything south of Moose Pass has to do with water, somehow. Here, a full moon shines over the ruined pier at North Beach (Hike 80).*

moose pass to seward

You'll find a little bit of everything on the hikes that stretch along this leg of the New Seward Highway, from the small roadside community of Moose Pass (population about 220) to the 2800-person port town of Seward, a popular destination for locals and cruise ship passengers alike. Where else can you explore World War II–era fortifications, watch breaching whales as you stroll a cobbled beach, or hike to spectacular lookouts over a massive icefield or the waters of Resurrection Bay?

71 Carter Lake

RATING/ DIFFICULTY	ROUNDTRIP	ELEV GAIN/ HIGH POINT	SEASON
****/3	6.6 miles	1260 feet/ 1515 feet	Year-round

Maps: USGS Seward B7 NW, National Geographic Kenai National Wildlife Refuge; **Contact:** Chugach National Forest, Seward Ranger District, Seward; **Notes:** Bikes and horses allowed after June 30, but not recommended. Possible motorized openings December through April. Dogs permitted on leash at trailhead, under direct control on trail. Bear and moose habitat. Shallow fords required. Grayling and trout fishing. Avalanche hazard in winter; **GPS:** 60.50718°, –149.44519°

Your reward for a few miles of sweat and muddy footing? A series of subalpine meadows so full of birdsong and wildflowers, they'll make almost anybody burst into spontaneous song. Oh, and there are a couple of beautiful lakes too.

GETTING THERE
From Seward, drive north on the New Seward Highway. The marked trailhead will be on your left at mile marker 33 (which is also 33 miles out of Seward).

ON THE TRAIL
The Carter Lake Trail climbs straight uphill at a moderate grade through hemlock, alder, and spruce forest, gaining most of its elevation—900 feet—in the first 1.4 miles. The trail itself is an old jeep road, which makes for easy walking, but it also tends to be wet, and you'll have to step across a number of small rivulets that cross the trail and, every so often, try to take it over.

There are three notable stream crossings to be aware of. The first is at 0.6 mile (elevation 880 feet), where you rock-hop across a medium-size creek. And at 1.2 miles (elevation 1355 feet) you might need to wade to get across another shallow creek. This is also where you start to get your first peeks of the wide valley you're ascending into.

At 1.4 miles you'll find the third and largest crossing: either wade the shallow creek or find a place upstream that's narrow enough to jump across. Soon after this the trail levels out and turns to broad, grassy meadows that are filled with birdsong and, in summer, a profusion of wildflowers. From here the trail is a solid, narrow footpath with only occasional muddy spots.

At 1.6 miles you'll see an unusual profusion of false hellebore (poisonous, don't eat) and fiddleheads (delicious if picked at the right time) and leave the last of the tall brush behind, although there are still patches of tough, wiry willow, alders, and hemlocks scattered across the valley.

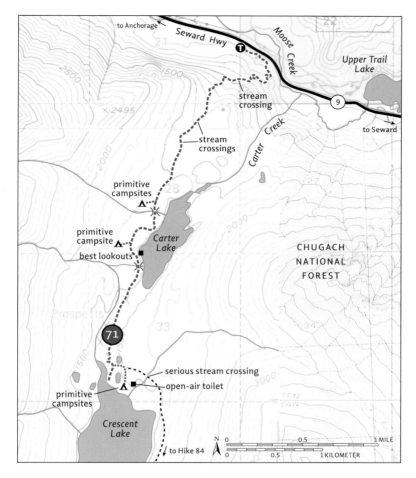

For the most part the trail winds between those patches, stopping at mile 1.9 for a marked turnoff to primitive campsites, and at 2 miles for a bridge over a creek that feeds into Carter Lake. Although you can see the lake itself from here, the best lookouts are farther down the trail.

At 2.3 miles there's a turnoff for more primitive campsites on the right, then the trail punches through a copse of alders

This bridge was probably damaged by the weight of deep snow—a common problem on some Southcentral trails.

before hitting the best lookouts over Carter Lake, followed by a bridge over another tributary. The bridge is broken—probably by heavy snowfall—but still walkable. Although Carter Lake is pretty, Crescent Lake is far prettier, and you've already gotten the hardest part of the hike out of the way.

At 3.2 miles you'll hit a signed intersection. Your options: Make a sharp left for the primitive trail that skirts the edge of Crescent Lake, connecting to the Crescent Saddle Cabin after a total of 7 miles and the Crescent Creek Trailhead (Hike 84) after a total of 17.7 miles, with a fairly serious stream crossing just 0.3 mile from this

sign. Or go slightly left for another series of primitive campsites with an open-air toilet overlooking Crescent Lake. Or go straight, and by 3.3 miles you can take your choice of footpaths down to several rock-cobbled beaches on the shore of Crescent Lake.

Although this trail does see year-round use, snow, ice, and meltwater can make the first portion difficult, and there is avalanche hazard in winter. If you're here for the fishing, Carter Lake has grayling and trout, and rumor is that Crescent Lake grows enormous, trophy-size grayling—if you can find a way to cast around the plentiful alders on the bank.

72 Ptarmigan Creek and Lake

RATING/ DIFFICULTY	ROUNDTRIP	ELEV GAIN/ HIGH POINT	SEASON
****/3	7.2 miles	1310 feet/ 940 feet	May–Oct

Maps: USGS Seward B7 NE, USGS Seward B6 NW, National Geographic Kenai National Wildlife Refuge; **Contact:** Chugach National Forest, Seward Ranger District, Seward; **Notes:** Bicycles, horses, and snowmachines permitted but not recommended. Closed to pack/saddle stock April 1 through June 30. Closed to motorized vehicles May 1 through November 30. Dogs permitted on leash at trailhead, under direct control on trail. Bear and moose habitat. Be especially bear-vigilant when salmon are running in mid- to late summer. Fishing for Dolly Varden and rainbow trout. Avalanche hazard in winter and spring; **GPS:** 60.40548°, –149.36224°

 *Not to be confused with Ptarmigan Valley (Hike 30), this trail takes you through a beautiful stretch of Seward's temperate rainforest. Rushing Ptarmigan Creek is a frequent companion along the way, and the lovely aquamarine waters of Ptarmigan Lake await at trail's end.*

GETTING THERE

From Seward, drive north on the New Seward Highway for about 23 miles. At mile 23.2, take the marked right turn into Ptarmigan Creek Campground, followed by a right turn to the marked Ptarmigan Creek Trailhead.

ON THE TRAIL

The first 0.5 mile of this trail is an easy forest walk past the slim, straight trunks of birch trees. For this stretch—and really, most of the trail—you'll be walking a mix of hardened gravel, boardwalks, and firm dirt, with

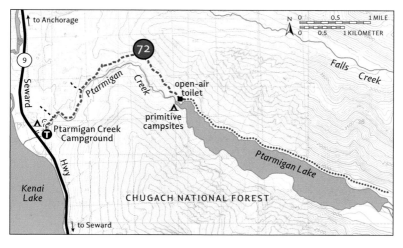

A peaceful woodland stroll near the "peak" of the Ptarmigan Lake trail, shortly before it descends back to the lake's aquamarine waters

occasional patches of mud. There are also a couple of points where the creek runs right beside the trail in that first 0.5 mile, which can lead to surprise encounters with bears who come here to fish for spawning salmon in mid- to late summer.

At 0.5 mile the trail bends to the right, peeling away from a series of rocky bluffs and sticking close to the creek as it winds through a forest of spruce and hemlock, carpeted with moss. At 0.8 mile there's a marked side trail that crosses over to the left; take the right fork to continue on the path to Ptarmigan Lake.

From this point on the trail starts feeling brushier although still well-maintained, following a series of rolling, sometimes steep hills that gradually pull you up and away from the water. The slopes sometimes have

muddy footing, and in a few cases the trail has crumbled to the point that there's mild exposure. But it's still a fairly easy walk, and from 2 miles onward you'll have great views through the trees to Mother Goose Glacier on a distant mountain perch.

Just before 2.5 miles there's another marked crossover trail to the left for the Falls Creek Mining Road. If you turn to look behind you, you'll also be treated to great views of Ptarmigan Creek coursing through the valley below.

Just before 3 miles you'll hit the high point of your forest walk, a modest 940 feet. The trail rambles along atop a fairly level bluff before at mile 3 it starts a long, gradual descent to the lakeshore. At 3.5 miles, it's like somebody flips a switch: as you pass some invisible barrier of humidity around the lake, the vegetation makes an abrupt transition from brushy hillside to mossy coastal rainforest, and you'll catch your first sight of Ptarmigan Lake's striking aquamarine waters through the trees. By 3.6 miles you'll reach the lakeshore (elevation 770 feet).

Depending on water levels, the lake's shore can be grassy or brushy, but the water is still one of the prettiest, most vibrant shades of blue-green I've ever seen in Alaska. For the intrepid, an overgrown, totally unmaintained primitive trail continues another 3.5 miles around the left side of the lake. But for most people, this lakeshore is the perfect place to picnic, camp, or skip stones before heading back.

You can also fish for Dolly Varden and rainbow trout in Ptarmigan Lake, and you'll find designated primitive campsites here, along with a charming open-air toilet (BYOTP), although the view from the throne's current location is not so great—you can barely see the lake.

73 Victor Creek

RATING/ DIFFICULTY	ROUNDTRIP	ELEV GAIN/ HIGH POINT	SEASON
****/3	5 miles	1515 feet/ 1240 feet	May–Sept

Maps: USGS Seward B7 SE, National Geographic Kenai National Wildlife Refuge; **Contact:** Chugach National Forest, Seward Ranger District, Seward; **Notes:** Very limited parking. Dogs permitted on leash at trailhead, under direct control in backcountry. Bear and moose habitat. Possible shallow ford. Avalanche hazard in winter and spring; **GPS:** 60.35758°, –149.35117°

If you're looking for a getaway in hushed rainforest that opens up to a dramatic valley headed up by a barely visible glacier, this is the hike for you. Just don't wait until late in the summer, because by the time August rolls around, the grass is easily head-high.

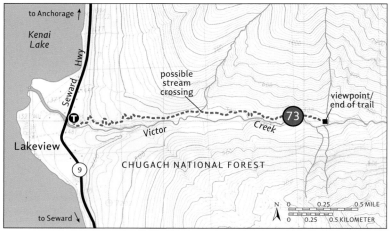

Hikers tackle the Victor Creek Trail in late spring, before the brush completely takes over later portions of the trail.

GETTING THERE

From Seward, drive north on the New Seward Highway for just under 20 miles. The trailhead (elevation 480 feet) is on the right (east) side of the road at mile 19.7. Getting into the trailhead requires a very sharp turn, and parking is limited; if you have more than one vehicle, park them close to each other to leave room for others. If a highway improvement plan goes through, this parking lot may be expanded.

ON THE TRAIL

Although the US Forest Service advertises the early part of this trail as a stiff elevation gain, I think it's pretty gentle. You gain only about 400 feet in the first mile as the trail winds through a few switchbacks in misty, temperate rainforest, working along one side of the valley carved by Victor Creek. If you turn and look back within the first 0.5 mile, you can also catch glimpses of blue-green Kenai Lake behind you.

Those misty, damp conditions and occasional mud patches will persist—hey, you're in a rainforest—but the trail usually offers good footing, as long as you don't mind a bunch of tree roots and small rivulets of water in the trail.

At 1.3 miles (elevation 960 feet) the trail levels out, and the trees open up just enough to give you enticing views up and down the valley before you dive into a very grassy stretch. In fact, this trail is so grassy that the rangers recommend hiking it in late May or June, because by late summer the grass can easily get head-high. There's a lot of cow parsnip and some spiny devil's club here too.

At 1.4 miles, you'll encounter a broad, shallow, and unbridged creek. Usually you can hop stones across it, but if the water's running high, you might have to wade. Then, from 1.5 miles on, thick clumps of alders start to intersperse with the grass.

Just past 1.8 miles (elevation 1040 feet) the trail zigs sharply back toward the creek and the dramatic gorge it occupies. You might feel the cool breeze flowing downvalley from the Mother Goose Glacier, which is just barely visible at the head of the valley.

Just before 2 miles the trail goes down a short, steep slope, then levels out in the grass. It stays grassy and brushy until just before 2.5 miles (elevation 1240 feet), when the alders fall away and you have great views of the valley, including the tip of the glacier and several waterfalls cascading down the far valley wall.

The trail ends abruptly at this point, in an avalanche gully that can harbor snow well into June. The far side of the gully is a dense wall of alders, and what's left of the trail quickly peters out into faint, hard-to-follow animal paths.

74 Lost Lake

RATING/ DIFFICULTY	ONE-WAY	ELEV GAIN/ HIGH POINT	SEASON
*****/3	15.6 miles	2340 feet/ 2210 feet	July–Oct

Maps: USGS Seward B7 SE, USGS Seward A7 NE (also USGS Seward B7 SW and USGS Seward A7 NW if you want maps of what's to the west of the trail), National Geographic Kenai National Wildlife Refuge; **Contact:** Chugach National Forest, Seward Ranger District, Seward; **Notes:** Popular backpacking destination. Open to mountain bikes and horses, but closed to pack/saddle stock April 1 through June 30. Motorized use allowed December 1 through April 30 when snow cover is sufficient; miners with permits

Backpackers set up a quiet camp along an offshoot of Lost Lake.

may use motorized vehicles year-round. Dogs permitted on leash at trailhead, under direct control in backcountry. Bear and moose habitat. Fishing for rainbow trout at outlet from Lost Lake; **GPS:** Primrose: 60.33983°, –149.37343°; Lost Lake: 60.17245°, –149.41101°

   One of the best backpacking trips in Southcentral, but some ambitious hikers traverse this entire trail in one day. Start from the Primrose Trailhead for relatively quick, steep access to lake-pocked high country, and pretty views over Resurrection Bay at the trail's relatively gentle end.

GETTING THERE

Primrose Trailhead: From Seward, drive north on the New Seward Highway for 17 miles. At mile marker 17, turn left (west). After 1 more mile you'll reach the Primrose Campground. Park in the large lot before entering the campground proper, and look for the trailhead (elevation 315 feet) at the far end of the campground road.

Lost Lake Trailhead: From Seward, drive north on the New Seward Highway for 5 miles. At mile 5, turn left (west) onto Scott Way and follow signs for the trailhead (elevation 280 feet).

ON THE TRAIL

It's typical for the entire trail—from Primrose Trailhead to Lost Lake Trailhead, or vice versa—to be referred to as simply "Lost Lake." But in actuality there are two trails here: the Primrose Trail and the Lost Lake Trail, which meet in the middle at—you guessed it—Lost Lake.

Because an out-and-back from either trailhead to the lake is about as long as the entire hike, I'm writing this as a thru-hike from the Primrose Trailhead to the Lost Lake Trailhead. This way you get to go up the relatively short, steep grade at Primrose, then down the gentler path toward the Lost Lake Trailhead. Also, if you don't want to set up a car shuttle, it's easier to get a taxi from the Lost Lake Trailhead to the Primrose Trailhead than doing it the other way around.

So, from Primrose, follow the trail as it climbs moderately through the temperate rainforest of hemlock, spruce, and an understory of berry bushes. At 0.5 mile the trail forks. The Primrose Trail continues to the right. The left fork follows the Meridian Lakes Trail, a forested walk that runs 4.2 miles until the intersection between Meridian and Grayling lakes (see Hike 75).

At 2 miles (elevation 890 feet) look for an unmarked spur trail leading off to the right. This steep 0.1-mile detour takes you to a pretty viewpoint for Primrose Falls, which tumbles down the far side of the gorge. You can usually hear the falls from the main trail; watch your footing on the spur trail, which can be quite slippery.

Continuing on the main trail, you'll pass the small Primrose Mine at 3.7 miles (elevation 1350 feet). Any items associated with it—including buildings, mining equipment, and ATVs, which can be brought on the trail only by miners with a special access permit—are private property and in place for active mining, not as tourist attractions; so please be respectful.

At 4.6 miles (elevation 1700 feet) the trail makes a last steep push to emerge above the treeline, giving you dramatic views of alpine tundra studded with small hemlock trees and a number of glacier-made tarns. You'll

get your first glimpse of Lost Lake in the near distance at 5.7 miles (elevation 2175 feet), and the wonderland of wildflower-filled tundra, vibrant blue lakes, and gently rolling trail continues until the Primrose Trail's technical end at 7.7 miles (elevation 1920 feet).

The endpoint is marked by a bridge over Lost Creek, and there's supposed to be decent rainbow trout fishing near the lake's outlet. As you continue on the far side of the bridge, the trail is officially named "Lost Lake" (i.e., the half of the trail that leads to the Lost Lake Trailhead).

At 8.4 miles (elevation 2020 feet) the trail forks. The 0.3-mile spur trail on the right leads straight to the south shore of Lost Lake; take the time to visit it. When you're ready, return to the fork and go straight ahead (or, if you didn't explore the side trail, turn left) to continue on the main trail. In a good snow year, you might find lingering banks of snow here until July.

At 11.5 miles (elevation 1690 feet) the trail forks again; the left fork runs 1.4 miles to the Dale Clemens Cabin, a public use shelter that must be reserved in advance at recreation.gov. This side trail then continues south as the steep, often muddy "winter trail," running down a ridgeline until it intersects the Lost Lake Trail some 3.25 miles after the initial fork.

If you continue on the main trail from here, you'll pass through wildflower-filled subalpine meadows, enjoying views of glittering Resurrection Bay ahead of you, until you dip back down into the hemlock trees at about mile 13.25 (elevation 1000 feet).

Once you're back in the forest, you'll descend gradually through a quiet, mossy rainforest on a well-maintained trail cut into the wall of a small canyon. At about 14.9 miles (elevation 360 feet) you'll find the intersection of the summer trail (which you're on) and the winter trail. If you started from the Lost Lake Trailhead, the sign here can be confusing; go right for the public use cabin but *left* for a summer thru-hike.

If you started from the Primrose side that's a total nonissue, as the trail ends at the Lost Lake Trailhead at 15.6 miles.

75 Meridian Lakes

Grayling Lake

RATING/ DIFFICULTY	ROUNDTRIP	ELEV GAIN/ HIGH POINT	SEASON
**/2	3 miles	610 feet/ 960 feet	Year-round

Meridian Lake

RATING/ DIFFICULTY	ROUNDTRIP	ELEV GAIN/ HIGH POINT	SEASON
**/2	2.6 miles	560 feet/ 890 feet	Year-round

Maps: USGS Seward B7 SE, National Geographic Kenai National Wildlife Refuge; **Contact:** Chugach National Forest, Seward Ranger District, Seward; **Notes:** Open to mountain bikes. Popular for cross-country skiing and snowshoeing. Open to pack and saddle stock July 1–March 31. Dogs permitted on leash at trailhead, under direct control in backcountry. Bear and moose habitat. Fish for grayling in Grayling Lake; fish for rainbow trout in Meridian Lake, Leech Lake, and Long Lake; **GPS:** Grayling Lake Trailhead: 60.2755°, –149.3467°; Divide Trailhead: 60.2541°, –149.3530°; Primrose Trailhead: 60.33983°, –149.37343°

 *These short trails are best for their access to fishing in Grayling and Meridian lakes,* *although you can also string them together for a long walk under forest canopy, made interesting by the rolling, glacier-carved topography.*

GETTING THERE

Meridian Lakes Trailhead: From Seward, drive north on the New Seward Highway for 13 miles. Just past mile marker 13, turn left (west) into the Meridian Lakes Trailhead (elevation 500 feet).

Divide Trailhead: From Seward, drive north on the New Seward Highway for a little more than 11 miles. Look for the Divide Trailhead (elevation 700 feet) on the left (west) at about mile 11.5.

Primrose Trailhead: From Seward, drive north on the New Seward Highway for about 17 miles. At mile marker 17, turn left (west); 1 mile later, you'll reach the Primrose Campground. Park in the large lot before entering the campground proper, and look for the trailhead (elevation 315 feet) at the far end of the campground road.

ON THE TRAIL

Although you can access this trail from any of three trailheads, its high point is a visit to Grayling and Meridian lakes, which are best reached from the Meridian Lakes Trailhead. This description covers an out-and-back trip to each of the lakes, with optional side trips to the Primrose and Divide trailheads.

The trail starts out between dense walls of alders. At 0.1 mile it crosses a set of railroad tracks before plunging back into the brush, and by 0.25 mile (elevation 625 feet) it transitions to the mossy, temperate rainforest that's so characteristic of the Seward area, dense with spruce and hemlock trees and high-bush blueberries and cranberries.

Fish on? A chance to fish for the eponymous grayling is the chief attraction at Grayling Lake, along the Meridian Lakes trail.

No matter which way you go, it'll stay that way—traversing rolling terrain and the occasional open muskeg meadow—for the entirety of the hike.

The trail forks at the 0.25-mile mark; follow the "Trail" sign along the right fork. Watch for muddy spots and numerous small streams—which you can rock-hop across without having to wade—as the trail climbs gradually to another intersection at 1 mile (elevation 860 feet). Here, you turn left for Grayling Lake or right for Meridian Lake.

If you turn left for Grayling Lake, the trail winds through a couple of boggy meadows before reaching the lakeshore at 1.5 miles. As you might expect, you can fish for grayling here.

If you want to continue farther, the trail parallels the eastern lakeshore until 1.7 miles, then cuts off to the left toward small Leech Lake (2.3 miles from the trailhead), where you can fish for rainbow trout. Keep going, and at mile 3.7 you'll reach the Divide Trailhead on the New Seward Highway.

If, from the intersection at 1 mile, you were to turn right for Meridian Lake instead, at 1.25 miles you'd reach another fork. The right spur takes you straight down to the shore of Meridian Lake itself, which has fishing for rainbow trout. Or, if you want more pretty hiking on singletrack through the forest, you can go left to continue on the Meridian Lakes Trail, which takes you over a series of small, sometimes steep, hills to Long Lake (3.6 miles from the trailhead), where you can also fish for rainbow trout.

If you keep going from here, the Meridian Lakes Trail continues until at mile 5.2 it intersects the Primrose Trail (part of Hike 74). Turn right here, and by mile 5.7 you'll reach the Primrose Trailhead. This entire network (including the Meridian Lakes Trail and the Lost Lake and Primrose trails) is part of the original and Historic Iditarod Trail, a

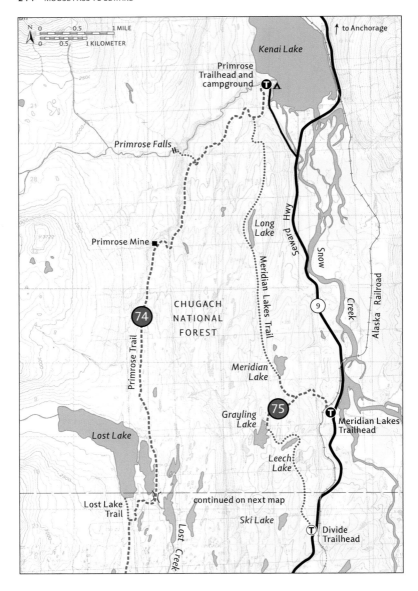

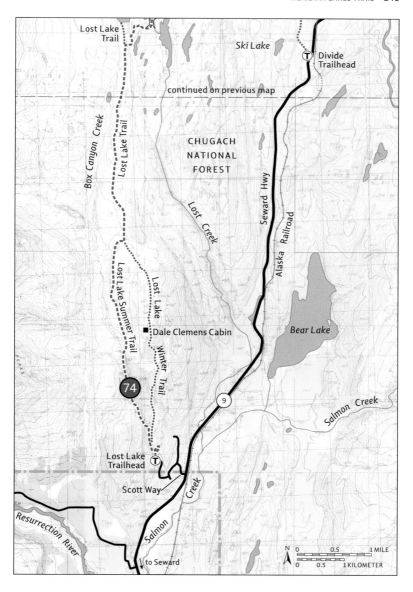

Lost Lake Trail

Ski Lake

T Divide Trailhead

continued on previous map

Box Canyon Creek

Lost Lake Trail

CHUGACH NATIONAL FOREST

Lost Creek

Seward Hwy

Alaska Railroad

Lost Lake Summer Trail

Lost Lake Winter Trail

■ Dale Clemens Cabin

Bear Lake

74

9

Salmon Creek

Lost Lake Trailhead **T**

Scott Way

Salmon Creek

Resurrection River

Salmon

to Seward

N

0   0.5   1 MILE

0   0.5   1 KILOMETER

National Historic Trail that is gradually being transformed into a series of hiking trails. This may come as a surprise because many people believe the life-saving serum run that's commemorated by the Iditarod Sled Dog Race began in Anchorage, but in fact it began in Seward.

 ## 76 Exit Glacier

Glacier View

RATING/ DIFFICULTY	LOOP	ELEV GAIN/ HIGH POINT	SEASON
****/1	2.1 miles	270 feet/ 620 feet	May–Sept

Outwash Plain Loop

RATING/ DIFFICULTY	LOOP	ELEV GAIN/ HIGH POINT	SEASON
****/1	1 mile	65 feet/ 410 feet	May–Sept

Map: USGS Seward A8 NE; **Contact:** Kenai Fjords National Park; **Notes:** Park is open year-round, but visitor center is closed mid-September through mid-May and access road is closed during winter. Motorized use, skiing, and other winter sports allowed on access road during winter. No dogs on this trail. Bear and moose habitat; **GPS:** 60.18819°, –149.63155°

These flat, stable trails trace a series of loops between the Exit Glacier Nature Center and the floodplains of the glacier, culminating in a viewing platform near the toe of the glacier itself.

GETTING THERE
From Seward, drive north on Third Avenue, which becomes the New Seward Highway. At mile 3, just as you leave town, turn left onto Herman Leirer Road, which your GPS might think is Exit Glacier Road. Follow this road for 8.4 miles until it ends at a parking lot just a short walk from the Exit Glacier Nature Center.

ON THE TRAIL
Starting from the Exit Glacier Nature Center, this loop hike starts on a wide, compacted trail. When it forks just outside the nature center, turn left, following signs for the glacier view/outwash plain. There's room for several people to walk side by side here, down the broad trail corridor lined with slim birch trees, bushy alders, ferns, moss, spiky devil's club, and a variety of berry bushes.

At 0.2 mile, you'll pass a sturdy bench. At 0.3 mile there's another bench, perfectly situated for views out over the outwash plain—basically, a floodplain created by meltwater flowing from Exit Glacier. While nobody will stop you from exploring the outwash plain, use common sense: this area isn't maintained for walkers, the streams can be cold and swift-moving, and the silt makes it almost impossible to tell how deep they are. Although it's extremely rare, ice dams can block up the flow of water from the glacier, then release it suddenly in a flash flood.

From here the main trail bends to the right, briefly paralleling the outwash plain before popping back out at 0.4 mile for a nice viewpoint looking toward the glacier, followed by another bench and a pair of pedestal-mounted binoculars.

Just before 0.7 mile you reach a key intersection: Turning right completes what I'll call the outwash plain loop, taking you back to the visitor center for a total hike distance of 1 mile. Turning left departs that original loop and takes you past the marked offshoot of the Harding Icefield Trail (Hike 77)

Did you know glaciers give birth to rivers? Here, Exit Glacier's ever-changing outflow winds its way along the glacier floodplain.

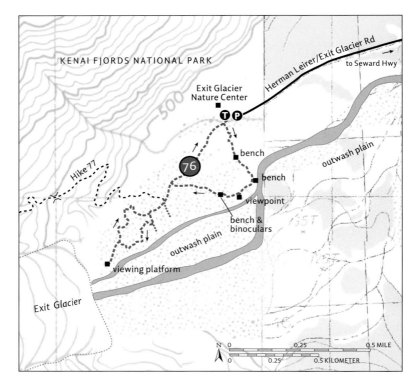

toward the toe of the glacier. The rest of this description is written on the assumption that you've turned left toward the glacier.

At 0.75 mile you reach another intersection: turn left for another look at the outwash plain, or continue straight for the toe of the glacier. Less than 0.1 mile after this, you'll hit another intersection declaring the outwash plain to the left and the glacier to the right.

Go ahead and turn left, then right again at the next intersection, climbing on a rocky, uneven path until at 1.2 miles you reach a roped-off viewing platform. There is a constant risk of icefall at the toe of the glacier, so pay attention to signs warning where it is and isn't safe to stand.

From here you can return the way you came or continue around the loop you started, descending a series of low stone steps. Once you reach the next intersection, continue straight to return to the visitor center along a more direct woodland route for a total loop distance of 2.1 miles. Along the way, take note of the small signs with dates on them. These indicate how far the glacier's leading edge extended during the years given.

77 Harding Icefield

RATING/ DIFFICULTY	ROUNDTRIP	ELEV GAIN/ HIGH POINT	SEASON
*****/5	9.2 miles	3250 feet/ 3525 feet	July–Sept

Map: USGS Seward A8 NE; **Contact:** Kenai Fjords National Park; **Notes:** Park is open year-round, but visitor center is closed mid-September through mid-May and access road is closed during winter. Motorized use, cross-country skiing, and other winter sports allowed on access road during winter. Winter hiking not recommended; this becomes a technical mountaineering route. No dogs on this trail. Bear and moose habitat; black bear sightings are especially common here. Usually does not require fords; **GPS:** 60.18819°, –149.63155°

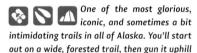 *One of the most glorious, iconic, and sometimes a bit intimidating trails in all of Alaska. You'll start out on a wide, forested trail, then gun it uphill for awe-inspiring views of Harding Icefield, a massive sheet of snow and ice that extends for miles past the horizon and spawns some forty glaciers. It's a true rite of passage for hikers.*

GETTING THERE
From Seward, drive north on Third Avenue, which becomes the New Seward Highway. At mile 3, just as you leave town, look for the left turn onto Herman Leirer Road, which your GPS might think is Exit Glacier Road. Follow this road for 8.4 miles until it ends at the Exit Glacier Nature Center (elevation 400 feet), which doubles as trailhead parking.

ON THE TRAIL
The first 0.4 mile of this trail coincides with the wide, mostly flat walk to Exit Glacier. From the Exit Glacier Nature Center (which doubles as the trailhead), take the right-hand fork and enjoy the easy stroll past cryptic signs that mark how far Exit Glacier extended in years past.

Don't let that civilized start fool you: once the Harding Icefield Trail veers off to

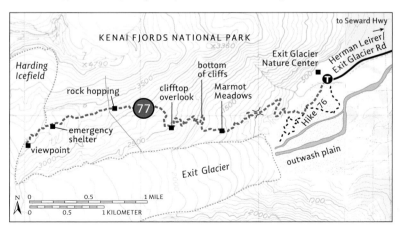

Exit Glacier spills from Harding Icefield, which is just visible on the horizon.

the right at 0.4 mile, it's a different beast entirely. (Continuing straight would keep you on the Exit Glacier Trail (Hike 76).) A long, sidehilling switchback makes this trail much easier than it used to be, but it's still a sustained climb through moist, mossy forest full of spruce trees, alders, ferns, and spiny devil's club.

At about 0.8 mile (elevation 690 feet) the trail gets very rocky and opens up for great lookouts over the silty floodplain that sits at the toe of Exit Glacier. At mile 1.25 (elevation 925 feet) the trail crosses a skinny little bridge—most useful as a distance marker—then keeps chugging along uphill until at 1.7 miles (elevation 1475 feet) you hit an open area with even better lookouts.

This is Marmot Meadows, a great turn-around point for anyone who isn't up to

finishing the whole hike. From here, you can see the icy blue fringe of Harding Icefield spilling over the mountains to your left, and great views of Exit Glacier, the tumbling cascade of blue ice to the left of the icefield.

From here the trail ascends a few short switchbacks, with every step earning an even better view of the ice to your left. Keep an eye out for a rocky outcropping, just before 2 miles (elevation 1710 feet), that makes a wonderful photo op.

Just after this, at about mile 2.1, the trail reaches a point that Park Service maps list as the "bottom of cliffs." Don't worry—you won't actually be climbing the cliffs, which overlook the glacier and icefield on your left, but instead hiking a series of short switchbacks up their gentler north side. At 2.75 miles (elevation 2450 feet) you'll emerge at a clifftop overlook, having left the brushline well behind, with a series of fantastic overlooks over the ice to your left (south).

The trail now becomes a very steep, rocky path. In places it feels as if rocks were put through a blender, then peppered with trail flagging to help you find your way. But the stumbling doesn't last long. By about mile 3.1 (elevation 2850 feet) you emerge onto a lovely hardened gravel trail with streams flowing across it at intervals.

You might not be able to avoid getting your feet wet during the rush of early summer snowmelt, but most of the time you can step or jump across without much trouble. At about 3.6 miles (elevation 3290 feet) you can hop rocks across a slightly bigger creek.

Once past that creek, you'll enter a fantastical, desolate swath of rock that was ground down to pebbles by the passage of massive sheets of ice. The slope levels off here, leaving you more exposed to the constant, chilly wind that flows off the icefield. The weather can change very quickly when you're hiking beside a miles-wide block of ice, so be ready for everything from sleet to snow and high winds here, even during summer.

Exactly where the rock gives way to snowpack depends on the year, but somewhere between here and the small, dark emergency shelter at about mile 4.3 (elevation 3500 feet) you'll end up tromping through thick snowfields.

Many would say that the hike ends at the emergency shelter. But weather and trail conditions allowing, I like to keep hiking another 0.25 mile until I reach the "peak" of the mounded rock left behind by the passage of many tons of ice. This viewpoint is the perfect spot for observing the icefield, which spreads to the horizon and miles

beyond, pierced only by the occasional nunatak or "lonely peak."

A few notes on safety: During the winter, this hike becomes a technical mountaineering route that presents serious challenges in routefinding and avalanche hazard evaluation. It poses serious hazards for potential rescuers too. Even in summer, the icefield itself is dangerous; never wander onto it unless you have the right skills and equipment for technical glacier travel. And depending on snow conditions, avalanche hazard can linger into early July on the upper portion of this trail.

78 Mount Marathon

RATING/ DIFFICULTY	ROUNDTRIP	ELEV GAIN/ HIGH POINT	SEASON
****/5	6 miles	2930 feet/ 2840 feet	June–Sept

Map: USGS Seward A7 SW; **Contact:** Seward Chamber of Commerce; **Notes:** Dogs should be on leash. Bear and moose sightings are very common here; **GPS:** 60.10851°, −149.44531°

This is a much more civilized route than the dangerous Mount Marathon runner's trail. Instead of clinging to cliffs by your fingernails, you can relax and enjoy beautiful views over Seward and, depending on how far you go, all the way to the mouth of Resurrection Bay.

GETTING THERE

From downtown Seward, take Third Avenue (which later becomes the New Seward Highway) north to Monroe Street. Turn left onto Monroe Street and look for the small hiker's trailhead, which has a yellow gate with a

"Mount Marathon Hiking Trail" marker on it, to the west side of Monroe and First Avenue (elevation 90 feet). There is very limited parking near the gate, with additional street parking nearby.

ON THE TRAIL

Legend has it that the infamous Mount Marathon Race began as a bar bet between two sourdoughs. It actually began as an organized run in 1915, but that doesn't make the eroded, sometimes near-vertical trail that runners scale every year on July 4 any less dangerous.

The number of warning signs as you approach the running trailhead, which is on Lowell Canyon Road west of First Avenue in Seward, should be an indicator: there are a lot of things here in Alaska that are capable of hurting or killing you but never receive a warning sign. So when we actually bother to put warning signs on something, we mean it! And I'm sure the local SAR groups are tired of putting themselves at risk to rescue hikers who get stuck partway up the runner's trail, unable to continue up or return the way they came.

With that in mind, I've drawn the running trail in as an "other" route, solely for reference. If you feel you really must try it, make friends with a local who can take you up and show you the best ways not to die.

Happily for the rest of us (and I include myself in that), there's a much more civilized route up Mount Marathon: the hiker's trail, which is confusingly also known as the Jeep Trail, the Bench Trail, and the Skyline Trail (not to be confused with Hike 85). It starts at a different trailhead than the runner's trail—see "Getting There"—and follows an old jeep road for almost a mile. That's where the "Jeep Trail" name for this route comes from, although technically it applies only to the first part of the trek.

Although the Jeep Trail rises at a steady incline, it's otherwise a straightforward stroll through the rich, mossy temperate rainforest that is so typical of Alaska's Southcentral coast. Beware devil's club and cow parsnip, which are both plentiful here, although on the flip side you'll also see salmonberries, currants, and blueberries aplenty.

At 0.25 mile (elevation 350 feet) the trail splits; the Jeep Trail levels off and continues left, while pretty little Marathon Waterfall is just a 200-foot side trip to your right. At 0.4 mile you'll reach another signed intersection. Continuing straight keeps you on the Jeep Trail, while turning left puts you on the lower crossover trail, which gives emergency responders quick access to the race trail.

At 0.5 mile (elevation 450 feet) you can turn left for the upper crossover trail—which serves the same purpose as the lower crossover trail—or turn right to stay on the Jeep Trail, which starts getting brushier at 0.75 mile in, as the lush vegetation gives way to thick, brushy plants such as alders and mountain ash.

At about 0.8 mile (elevation 750 feet) the Jeep Trail ends; the next segment is known as the Bench Trail. Skip a tempting left fork, which heads straight uphill and gets you into an uncomfortable rocky scramble, and instead take the right turn that continues more or less level alongside a shallow stream. This part of the trail is very brushy and can be very muddy too. Watch for wildflowers such as wild geranium and chocolate lilies, and remember your best moose and bear manners to avoid surprising wildlife in the bushes.

At 1.7 miles (elevation 1220 feet) the Bench Trail ends in a circular clearing

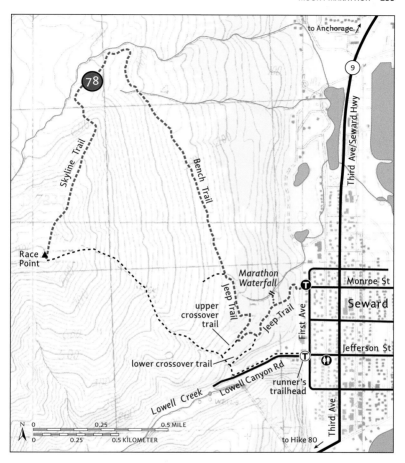

bordered on all sides by brush, with no marker to let you know the jig is up. Most people call it good and turn around here; but if you want to keep going you can follow a poorly defined third segment that some call the Skyline Trail. Continue straight through the clearing on a trail that dips briefly down and to the right before arcing

back up through the bushes and working onto the obvious ridge to your left (west), which you can then follow up to the Race Point.

Make sure you pay close attention to where you will reenter the bushes on your way back, and be warned: if you try to short-cut your way onto the ridge farther to the

Hang in there: you're almost to the end of the Bench Trail portion of Mount Marathon on an early summer day.

south (before going through the aforementioned clearing), you'll be in for an unpleasant scramble on loose ground.

Race Point (3 miles from the trailhead, elevation 2840 feet) isn't the true summit of the mountain but instead a false summit, visible from town, that serves as a turnaround point for Mount Marathon racers. This is where you should turn around too; loose, sketchy footing makes the ascent to the actual peak of the mountain downright dangerous.

79 Alice Ridge

RATING/ DIFFICULTY	ROUNDTRIP	ELEV GAIN/ HIGH POINT	SEASON
*****/4	3.5 miles	2100 feet/ 2110 feet	mid-May– Sept

Maps: USGS Seward A7 SE, USGS Seward A7 NE; **Contact:** Chugach National Forest, Seward Ranger District, Seward; **Notes:** No parking fee, although the proper turnout can be hard to find. Unmarked trailhead. Dogs permitted under direct control. Bear and moose habitat. Upper reaches of Mount Alice are a technical climb; **GPS:** 60.11688°, –149.35884°

A classic Alaska hiking experience on an unmarked trail, this route climbs steeply to alpine slopes with stunning views over Seward and Resurrection Bay. The upper reaches of the mountain are technical; most people turn around at about mile 1.6.

GETTING THERE

From Seward, drive north on the New Seward Highway/Third Avenue for about 3 miles. Turn right (east) onto Nash Road. Watch your odometer and the mile markers: your goal is a pullout on the right, just past mile marker 3, which you can see when going in this direction, and a "ROCKS" sign which you'll see only from the back, as it's on the left side of the road. If you hit mile marker 4 or the point at which Nash Road makes a broad sweep to the left alongside the coast, you've gone too far.

ON THE TRAIL

Directly across the road from the pullout, two unmarked trails descend from the brushy hillside. The leftmost of these trails—lined up with approximately the middle of the pullout—is the most obvious, but starts off with a short, brutally steep scramble up loose dirt. The next trail opening to the right offers a gentler way up, and bends left to join the other trail in less than 0.1 mile.

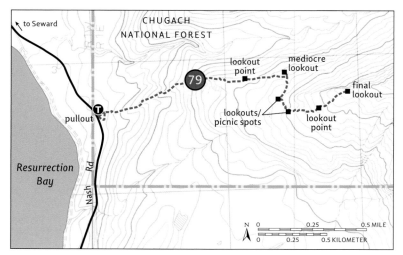

Climbing partway up Alice Ridge offers unparalleled views over Resurrection Bay.

From this point on, you hike more or less straight uphill. The steepness is brutal, but the mossy spruce and hemlock rainforest around you is pleasant, and you can catch peeks at the water of Resurrection Bay through the trees.

The trail occasionally braids and then rejoins itself, or sprouts a side trail into the trees, but it's easy to stick to the most traveled path as you go uphill. At 0.7 mile the vegetation switches abruptly to short, wiry alder trees, with the occasional scrubby hemlock still mixed in.

Just before 1 mile (elevation 1330 feet) you'll find a wonderful lookout point. If you're in a time crunch, you can feel pretty good turning around here. But better views await.

At 1.2 miles (elevation 1530 feet) the trail breaks into a small grassy gully and forks. The impressive peak straight in front of you is the summit of Mount Alice. But if you go straight, the trail quickly peters into

nothing. The left fork does a short, sharp uphill U-turn to a mediocre lookout point; the 1-mile lookout is much better.

If you want to continue onward take the right fork, a rocky, muddy footpath that heads up a small, steep rise. Once past the rise you're in alpine tundra, surrounded by patches of tiny blueberries, crowberries, and alpine flowers, including miniature orchids. The trail fades in and out as it travels past great—and reasonably flat—places to hold a picnic at just past 1.3 miles (elevation 1580 feet) and 1.4 miles (elevation 1620 feet). These are both marked as lookout points on the map.

Most people choose to turn around here. If you want to continue, backtrack less than a hundred feet and look for a trail leading steeply uphill. You'll have to hunt and peck for the trail, which fades in and out and gets increasingly rocky, but there are stunning lookouts over the water at 1.6 miles (elevation 1860 feet) and 1.75 miles (elevation

2120 feet). If you decide to scramble on the rocks at the viewpoints, keep in mind that this type of shale is notoriously loose and crumbly.

From here the trail fades into nothing. Although you can still steer by the obvious ridgeline, it becomes increasingly rocky and exposed, gradually transitioning into a sketchy technical climb along the ridge to the mountain's 5318-foot summit. If you choose to continue upward, make sure you're comfortable coming back down anything you ascend.

80 Caines Head and North Beach

RATING/ DIFFICULTY	ROUNDTRIP	ELEV GAIN/ HIGH POINT	SEASON
*****/3	11.4 miles	2485 feet/ 230 feet	May–Sept

Maps: USGS Seward A7 SW, USGS Seward A7 SE; **Contact:** Alaska State Parks, Kenai/ Prince William Sound office; **Notes:** Alaska State Parks pass or parking fee. Must be timed to low tides of 3 feet or less. Water taxis charge a fee and should be booked in advance. Water taxi service is limited in late fall and winter. Dogs permitted on leash at trailhead, under voice control in backcountry. Bear and moose habitat. Watch for marine wildlife. Can be very slippery; **GPS:** 60.06813°, −149.44258°

This hike has just a little bit of everything Alaska: a forest stroll, beach rambling, old World War II ruins, spectacular views over the sea, and a pretty waterfall that lures you down a side trail. Oh, and fast-moving tides that can leave you trapped if you're not careful.

GETTING THERE

Driving into Seward, continue straight through town on the New Seward Highway, which becomes Third Avenue. Turn right onto Railway Avenue, which travels south out of Seward and becomes Lowell Point Road. After 2 miles, take a left on Border Avenue as if you were heading to Millers Landing, then turn right onto Pinnacle View Road and watch for signs directing you to the upper trailhead.

If the upper trailhead is full, continue straight on Pinnacle View Road and look for the lower trailhead, which will be on your right before Pinnacle View hooks sharply to the left along the coast. You must start the hike from the upper trailhead; a narrow footpath connects the two.

ON THE TRAIL

From the upper trailhead, set out on the obvious gravel road. Make sure that you respect the posted private property on both sides of the road.

At 0.5 mile the road transitions to an old wagon track and takes you up a stiff hill through mixed spruce forest. At 0.8 mile the wide gravel trail crests the hill and begins my favorite part of this forest walk, where the trees are huge, with that old, mossy rainforest feel you don't get from inland portions of the state. You'll see (and hear) plenty of birds here in early summer.

From miles 1.2 to 1.5 you work your way down the far side of the hill on a series of hairpin switchbacks with uneven, rocky footing. Starting at mile 1.7, you'll cross a series of three pretty bridges: first over Tonsina Creek, one of my favorite photo ops; then twice over often-dry arms of the creek. Cross Tonsina Creek on a splendid bridge. Just after that last bridge, the trail

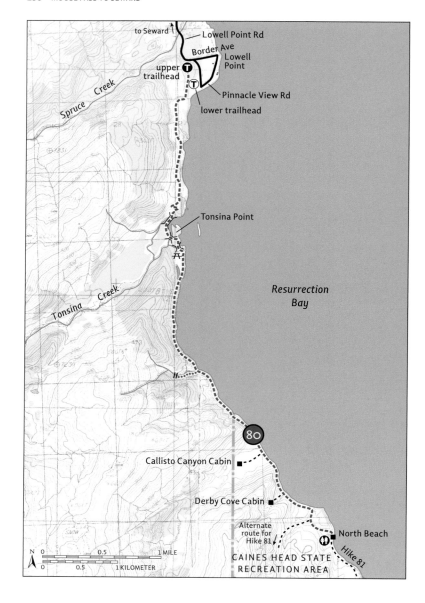

A hiker wanders north, back toward Seward, from the North Beach of Caines Head.

passes through a clump of trees hiding a picnic shelter with a broken-down bearproof locker (the lid won't lock). By 2.2 miles, the trail has deposited you in the open at Tonsina Point—a stark progression of ocean, rocky beach, and thick, tall grass that fades back into the trees, all within the space of a few hundred feet.

Tonsina Point is a pleasant picnicking/day hiking destination in its own right, but it's also the start of the beach walking for anyone going all the way to North Beach. This is where timing matters: you can do the next part of the hike only during low tides of +3 feet or lower (+2 feet or lower during the winter), and should leave Tonsina Point at least two hours before low tide. If you time it wrong, you may find yourself trapped against steep cliffs as fast-moving tides eat the beach out from under you. Also, keep in mind that the tides and wave action can be affected by the wind, and are especially variable during the winter: always apply common sense.

The beach is made of loose shale, and is sometimes strewn with extremely slippery kelp or, in late fall, unexpected rimes of ice. Carry light gloves to protect your hands from the rocks.

Back to the beach: From Tonsina Point, turn right and hike along the shale beach. Keep an eye out for sea otters and other marine wildlife in the water. At 3.3 miles from the trailhead, you'll pass a creek that emerges from a gully to the right. Let the sound of falling water guide you up a faint trail on the left side of the water to a picturesque waterfall—well worth a quick side trip. Strangely, some maps label this as Derby Cove—that is incorrect.

At 4.5 miles you'll pass the cove for the public use Callisto Canyon Cabin. At 5 miles you'll pass the cutoff for another public use cabin, Derby Cove. Both must be prebooked, for a fee, with Reserve America (reserve america.com). At the far end of Derby Cove, the trail cuts up and to the right over a thickly forested bluff, then turns left and downhill at a signed intersection to reach North Beach at 5.7 miles.

The pilings at the beach are the remnants of a World War II–era military dock that survived the 1964 Good Friday Earthquake and the resulting tsunami but was eventually destroyed by wave action. You'll also find a bearproof locker hidden in the trees (look for a reflective sign on the trunk of the biggest spruce, in about the middle of the beach), a seasonally staffed ranger station, a shallow creek for fresh water, the trailhead for a hike to Fort McGilvray (Hike 81), and an outhouse.

You can't hike back until the next low tide, so most people will either camp here or hike one way and take a water taxi the other direction. Cell service on North Beach is sporadic at best, so make your water taxi plans beforehand; find a list of authorized water taxis at the Alaska Department of National Resources website (see Resources). Most carriers will require a minimum of two or three passengers per trip, but during sunny summer weekends it's not hard to combine with other parties.

81 Fort McGilvray

RATING/ DIFFICULTY	ROUNDTRIP	ELEV GAIN/ HIGH POINT	SEASON
****/2	4 miles	1300 feet/ 540 feet	May–Sept

Maps: USGS Seward A7 SE, USGS Blying Sound D7 NE, USGS Blying Sound D7 NW; **Contact:** Alaska State Parks, Kenai/ Prince William Sound office; **Notes:** Alaska State Parks pass or parking fee if you park at Lowell Point and walk the beach to get here. Water taxi availability is limited in winter. Dogs permitted under direct control if a water taxi will transport them but best to leave them at home: the hike in can be hard on their paws. Bear habitat. Watch for marine wildlife, including seals, otters, whales, and sea lions. You might have sporadic cell service at the trailhead; **GPS:** 60.00663°, –149.40492°

Enjoy a walk on old roadbed to World War II–era Fort McGilvray, which is still open for you to explore. You'll have great views from the fort's 650-foot rocky cliffs, but the old fort and the remains of two six-inch gun emplacements are the real treasures here.

GETTING THERE

From Seward, take a water taxi to the Caines Head/North Beach landing, which as the name suggests, is right at sea level. You can also sea kayak from Seward to Caines Head/North Beach, or time the 5.7-mile hike from Seward to North Beach (see Hike 80) with the tide, then take a water taxi back. Water taxi pickups must be arranged in advance (see Alaska Department of Natural Resources listing in Resources).

ON THE TRAIL

North Beach—what most people mean when they say "Caines Head"—is a wide, shallow beach of shale cobbles, backed by large spruce trees. This is a great place to hang out for a day or to camp, although it can get crowded (by Alaska standards) on sunny summer weekends. There is a bearproof locker hidden in the trees—look for a reflective sign on the trunk of the largest spruce tree, near the middle of the beach.

As you face the spruce trees on the beach, look for a triangular trailhead marker at the

A World War II pillbox atop Fort McGilvray

far (south) end of the beach. The trail to Fort McGilvray starts here, winding into the trees past an outhouse and briefly away from the water. The trail is actually an old roadbed, so the walking is generally easy, except in spots where the shale that covers the trail gets so deep it feels like walking on sand.

At 0.1 mile the trail zags back out toward the water, and you pass a monument placard that honors the soldiers who served here as part of the 250th and 267th coastal artillery. Then at 0.3 mile (elevation 100 feet) the trail heads slightly inland. Most of the walk takes place under tree cover, but at 0.7 mile (elevation 240 feet) you'll briefly pass through an open bog meadow. In early summer, look for a scattering of salmonberries beside the trail; by late summer, plentiful tall-bush blueberries take their place.

Just before 1.1 miles (elevation 390 feet) you reach a signed intersection. Continue left to reach Fort McGilvray.

At about 1.6 miles (elevation 530 feet) you'll pass a pedestal that holds a copy of the touching "Pilgrim's Poem." From here the trail descends through the remains of the garrison that supported the fort. Just before 2 miles (elevation 330 feet) you'll reach the fort itself, which is set into the side of the hill. Bring a flashlight or headlamp to explore the dark side rooms, and watch your step.

The interior is shaped roughly like a T, and at each end of the T's crossbars you'll find an old six-inch gun emplacement that once guarded the approach to the Fort of Seward, a vital link in the supply chain for Alaska's air bases. All told, some two thousand troops were housed in Caines Head garrisons for the two years this site was active (1941–1943). When the war conflict moved away from Alaska, the site was stripped and left to nature.

For most people, the hike ends here. But if you were to take the right-hand fork at the intersection before the fort, you'd walk another 1.5 miles on old roadbed until you reached the wild, remote-feeling South

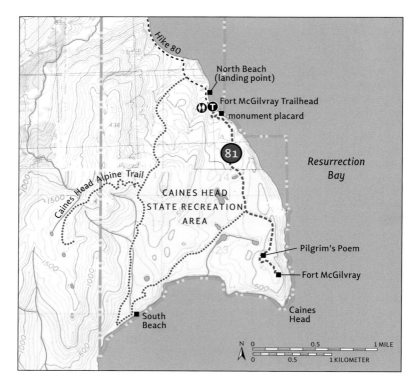

Beach at 3.5 miles from the trailhead. If you're feeling especially plucky you can then turn north, starting on a loop that will lead you back to North Beach.

At 5 miles from the trailhead, you'll pass a turnoff for what's known as the Caines Head Alpine Trail, a narrow, heavily overgrown footpath that climbs some 1200 feet in 1.4 miles, ushering you into breathtaking alpine tundra that includes views of Fort McGilvray from far above.

Continue north on the main loop trail and at 5.6 miles from the trailhead, you'll reach a signed intersection. Turn right here to return to North Beach, another 0.5 mile; or, if you'd planned to hike back to Seward and haven't left anything at North Beach, you can save yourself a mile of walking by turning left here. Make sure you read the details of Hike 80 before doing this. If you don't time your hike properly to the tides, you could be trapped by rising water.

Opposite: The scenery in Alaska is never boring, but the lake-studded tundra around Cooper Landing packs an extra colorful punch in summer and fall (Hike 82).

cooper landing area

Once a mining town, Cooper Landing (population about 290) is now best known for the spectacular fishing in the nearby Kenai and Russian rivers and as a base for exploring up and down the Kenai Peninsula. That makes it the perfect launching point for this cluster of nearby hikes that showcase the mighty rivers, lakes, and alpine beauty of this part of the Kenai Peninsula.

82 Summit Creek

RATING/ DIFFICULTY	ROUNDTRIP	ELEV GAIN/ HIGH POINT	SEASON
*****/4	18 miles	4695 feet/ 3390 feet	June–Oct

Maps: USGS Seward C7, USGS Seward C8, National Geographic Kenai National Wildlife Refuge; **Contact:** Chugach National Forest, Seward Ranger District; **Notes:** Unmarked trailhead. Dogs permitted on leash at trailhead, under direct control on trail. Bear and moose habitat. Requires two fords; **GPS:** 60.61715°, −149.53032°

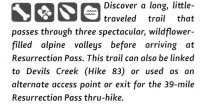 *Discover a long, little-traveled trail that passes through three spectacular, wildflower-filled alpine valleys before arriving at Resurrection Pass. This trail can also be linked to Devils Creek (Hike 83) or used as an alternate access point or exit for the 39-mile Resurrection Pass thru-hike.*

GETTING THERE
From Moose Pass, drive north on the New Seward Highway for about 14 miles. The unmarked trailhead (elevation 1320 feet) is on your right (west) between mile markers 43 and 44, just past Summit Lake.

ON THE TRAIL
This is one of the most pristine hikes close to the road system—so please, if you go, enjoy its lovely alpine valleys and fields of wildflowers responsibly. Nothing would ruin this landscape more than the discarded litter, toilet paper, and food refuse that crop up on heavily traveled trails.

From the unmarked trailhead, you'll cross immediately beneath a set of powerlines and start slogging uphill through ferns, alders, cow parsnip, and false hellebore. By 1.3 miles you're already emerging from treeline at 2300 feet of elevation, although you haven't escaped the burn-inducing cow parsnip that plagues brushy areas just yet.

At 2 miles (elevation 2420 feet) you're firmly out of the treeline, with long views up and down the first of three valleys this trail will traverse. Summit Creek is to your left and a bevy of wildflowers line the dirt footpath, from monkshood and larkspur to gentian, Arctic daisies, wild geraniums, Indian paintbrush, tiny orchids, and glorious stretches of fireweed. Although the trail continues climbing, it's a relatively gentle incline from here on out.

At 2.5 miles the U-shaped, glacier-carved valley is at its widest, with conveniently close access to the creek. Scan the valley walls for the odd, zigzag striping of alders growing in the disturbed ground left from old mining roads. Watch for snow bridges over the creek into summer, marmots in the rocks up and down the valley floor, and bears looking for the plump marmots, which are sometimes jokingly referred to as "bear burritos."

You've been climbing gradually since you entered this valley; by 4 miles (elevation 3390 feet) you'll reach the boulder-studded pass that leads into the next valley. Even

Hiking past a shallow alpine lake in the second of three valleys

if you're out for a day hike it's worth going a little farther, because by about 4.5 miles (elevation 3000 feet) the pass opens up into sweeping views over the next valley and a loose chain of lakes down its center.

If you're game for a few more miles, the trail descends a moderate slope into the valley. Just before 4.6 miles (elevation 2960 feet) you'll cross the first of two notable fords. There's no way to avoid wading, but in normal conditions the stream is no more than knee-deep.

Shortly after, at 4.7 miles, the trail forks. Take the right fork, which soon crosses back over the same stream. Depending on water levels, you might have to wade again. By 5.5 miles (elevation 2500 feet) the trail reaches the bottom of the valley. If ever there were

a place guaranteed to render a wild-minded writer speechless, this is it. As hiking becomes more popular in Southcentral Alaska, there just aren't that many places left where you can access this sort of untouched, lake-studded tundra with so little effort.

By about 6 miles, you'll get good views of a notch in the ridge to the left side of the valley. This is your passage into the third and final valley on this hike. It seems like the trail will continue along the valley floor, but at 6.4 miles (elevation 2650 feet) it zips off to the left and starts a short, steep climb up the valley wall.

Along the way you'll pass the second ford of note, at 7.2 miles. Again, you won't be able to avoid getting your feet wet, but at normal levels there's nothing extraordinary about this crossing. By 7.7 miles (elevation

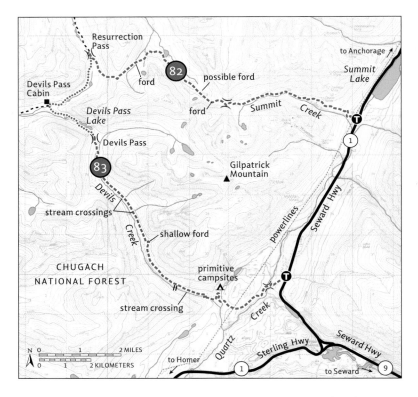

3360 feet) you'll be perched atop the final wildflower-dotted pass, looking down into the third valley of this hike.

For many people, this will be a good turnaround point. But if you want to "tag" Resurrection Pass, you can descend down a fairly steep wall into the third valley. Watch for enormous holes in the trail—easily large enough to put a foot in—that are often obscured by thick grass, false hellebore, and other vegetation.

From here it looks as if the trail should continue straight across the valley floor,

but instead it heads right (north). Continue straight ahead, ignoring periodic turnoffs into the brush, and at 9 miles you'll see the sign for the marvelously open Resurrection Pass, elevation 2600 feet.

If you're the hardcore type and thought to set up a car shuttle for a very long day's thru-hike, you could continue left (south) on the main Resurrection Pass Trail and exit via the mostly downhill Devils Creek Trail (see Hike 83), adding another 12.4 miles to the hike—making the day's distance just short of a full marathon.

I think retracing your steps through the Summit Creek valleys is far prettier, but there's enough up and down on the trail that if you've come this far, it means another 1725 feet of elevation to get back over the passes—whereas the Devils Creek Trail is mostly downhill.

83 Devils Creek

RATING/ DIFFICULTY	ROUNDTRIP	ELEV GAIN/ HIGH POINT	SEASON
****/3	17.2 miles	2450 feet/ 2475 feet	June–Oct

Maps: USGS Seward C7, USGS Seward C8, National Geographic Kenai National Wildlife Refuge; **Contact:** Chugach National Forest, Seward Ranger District, Seward; **Notes:** Open to mountain bikes. Closed to pack/saddle stock April 1–June 30. Open to snowmachines from mile 3 onward (access from Resurrection Pass) December 1 through April 30 in odd-numbered years. Dogs permitted on leash at trailhead, under direct control on trail. Bear and moose habitat. Dolly Varden in Devils Pass Lake. Requires fords. Marked avalanche hazard in winter and spring/early summer; **GPS:** 60.55897°, –149.58214°

 *Once you get past the first three miles of brush-lined trail, the Devils Creek route opens into glacier-sculpted alpine valleys filled with wildflowers and occasional shallow lakes.*

GETTING THERE

From Seward, drive north on the New Seward Highway for about 39 miles. Look for the marked Devils Creek Trailhead, elevation 960 feet, on the left (west) side of the road near mile marker 39.

ON THE TRAIL

Although many hikers refer to this trail as Devils Pass, and it does go through the 2400-foot Devils Pass, its proper name is Devils Creek. It starts off as a wide, packed-dirt trail through tall, slender spruce and birch trees. You'll also see a lot of flowers; look for species such as lupine, wild geranium, and brilliant fireweed.

At 0.6 mile the trail crosses a large footbridge over Quartz Creek. At 1.1 miles, aspens and giant ferns take over the vegetation, giving the trail an almost Jurassic feel. Then, at 1.75 miles, the trail crosses under a set of powerlines.

Next, at just past 2.3 miles, you'll pass a sharp right turn for a set of primitive campsites. Just beyond this the trail jogs sharply to the left and starts a steady climb toward the pass, pushing into an area of stately cottonwood trees and tall grass. At about 3 miles (elevation 1250 feet) the trail goes up a series of sharp switchbacks, breaking abruptly from cottonwood trees and grass to a rocky, brush-lined trail.

From here, the trail follows the contours of the hillside, passing a number of small waterfalls and rivulets that trickle across the trail. Most of them are bridged, but at a minimum you will need to wade a shallow stream at about 3.4 miles, cross the outflow from a small waterfall at 3.8 miles, and wade a shallow ford at 5.3 miles. Water levels in the crossings may vary quite a bit, but generally pose no problem beyond wet feet during the summer.

The next mile of trail is quite grassy, although it's usually pretty well maintained too, and at 6.3 miles you'll have to wade two more shallow streams. Happily, by 7.4 miles (elevation 2200 feet) the grass starts giving way to stretches of rocky ground,

The open tundra around Devils Pass offers a wealth of wildflowers in July.

then open tundra with long views north into Devils Pass.

At 8.6 miles you reach the pass itself (elevation 2400 feet). For most people, this is the ideal turnaround point for a long day's hiking—but it's hard to resist exploring the subalpine tundra and wide landscapes here, and you're within sight of pretty Devils Pass Lake, which offers fishing for Dolly Varden.

If you're really ambitious, you can keep going all the way to 2600-foot Resurrection Pass, the jewel of the 39-mile Resurrection Pass Trail that runs from Hope to Cooper Landing. But first, at mile 10.1 (elevation 2385 feet) you'll pass a turnoff for the Devils Pass Cabin, a six-person public use shelter that must be reserved in advance, for a fee, at recreation.gov.

From there, it's another 2.2 miles northeast to Resurrection Pass. This is also the intersection with Summit Creek (see Hike 82), but there's no sign to point you in the right direction through the brush, so if you want to make a roundtrip of it I recommend starting with Summit Creek and then finishing downhill on the Devils Creek Trail.

A few notes regarding other trail users: Devils Creek and the Resurrection Pass Trail are both extremely popular with mountain bikers. When it comes to hiker-biker encounters, most people are generally considerate. Do your part by staying alert and taking turns giving the right of way.

Regarding winter use: The first 3 miles of the Devils Creek Trail are open only to nonmotorized users (skiers, snowshoers, and hikers). Snowmachines are allowed past mile 3 (accessed via Resurrection Pass) every other year. But winter travel isn't recommended past mile 3 of Devils Creek, because the trail crosses a number of known avalanche paths.

84 Crescent Creek

RATING/ DIFFICULTY	ROUNDTRIP	ELEV GAIN/ HIGH POINT	SEASON
*****/3	12.8 miles	1605 feet/ 1500 feet	May–Oct

Maps: USGS Seward C8 SE, USGS Seward C7 SW, USGS Seward B7 NW (also USGS Seward C7 SW if hiking to Carter Lake Trailhead), National Geographic Kenai National Wildlife Refuge; **Contact:** Chugach National Forest, Seward Ranger District, Seward; **Notes:** Open to mountain bikes. Possible motorized openings after November 30, although not recommended due to narrow sidehills. Open to pack/saddle stock after June 30. Dogs permitted on leash in parking area, under direct control on trail. Bear and moose habitat. Rainbow trout and grayling fishing in the lake and stream; grayling fishing opens July 1. Winter avalanche hazard past mile 3; **GPS:** 60.50259°, –149.67212°

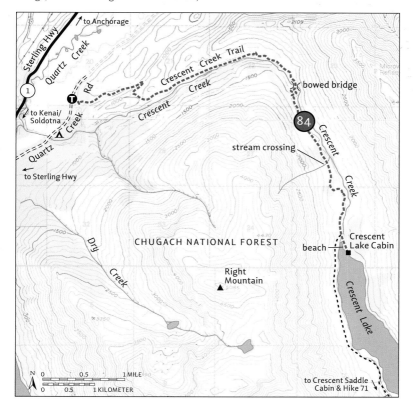

One of the most pleasant trails I've ever hiked, this route starts with lazy switchbacks beneath tall birch trees, then transitions to a sun-dappled walk through spruce forest as you sidehill toward a gravel beach on the shores of Crescent Lake.

GETTING THERE

From Cooper Landing, drive east on the Sterling Highway for about 2.5 miles, to mile 45. Turn right (south) onto Quartz Creek Road, following signs for Quartz Creek and Crescent Creek campgrounds. Drive past both campgrounds on an access road that is sometimes a little rough, but can usually be managed by passenger vehicles. The trailhead (elevation 580 feet) is at mile 3.5 on Quartz Creek Road.

ON THE TRAIL

This trail starts on the east side of the trailhead (the right side as you drive in). The first mile consists of long, lazy switchbacks through mixed birch/spruce forest. At 1 mile, spruce and hemlocks start to take over. After one last switchback the trail levels out (elevation 980 feet) and sidehills along the valley, and at 1.8 miles you'll be able to clearly see Crescent Creek roaring along below you in the canyon to the right, dropping down a series of cascades.

Blazing yellow aspen leaves mark a fall hike alongside Crescent Creek.

From there, the trail narrows. At 2.8 miles you'll be within arm's reach of the creek as it boils along merrily beside the trail. The water cuts quite a picture in fall when it's backed by the vibrant yellow leaves of the trees against a bright blue sky. From here the trail peels away from the water, plugging slowly uphill until it zips back to creekside at mile 3.

This stretch of trail is sometimes muddy, and if you pay attention you can start to feel the swoop and weave of carefully crafted singletrack as the trail runs through the trees—no wonder this is such a popular path for mountain bikers.

At 3.6 miles (elevation 1150 feet) the trail opens back up to valley views, with the creek rushing down below again. You're free of the mud—for a little while—although there can be swampy patches as you cross the creek on a lovely, bowed bridge at just past 3.8 miles.

From here, the trail scales a series of hardened gravel switchbacks before side-hilling again (elevation 1330 feet), passing through patches of grassy hillside, mossy forest, and a number of small streams where in normal water levels you can step across on rocks. However there is one notable crossing at mile 5.25, where your options are to wade or make a big jump across.

By mile 5.8 the valley opens out around you, a hillside of grass and subalpine tundra dotted with sporadic trees; it feels very much like Eagle and Symphony lakes (Hike 36). From here the trail draws closer to Crescent Creek, which is now flat and calm; it's common to see people fishing for grayling along this stretch, although casting can be hard because of the brush right next to the stream.

At 6.4 miles (elevation 1470 feet) you'll reach a signed intersection: turn left and cross a bridge for the Crescent Lake Cabin and the gravel beach; go right for the Crescent Saddle Cabin and the overgrown primitive trail that runs another 11.5 miles to the Carter Lake Trailhead (Hike 71), with one major ford near the end of the trail. These public use cabins must be reserved in advance, for a fee, at recreation.gov.

Assuming you continue on to the left, just before mile 6.4 you'll plow through a meadow of armpit-deep grass and reach a sign for the Crescent Lake Cabin straight ahead. If you haven't reserved the cabin, please respect the privacy of those who have. You'll have a much better time if you turn right instead, reaching what is, except at times of very high water, a wide gravel beach on Crescent Lake.

Two safety notes: One, this is a very popular mountain biking trail, so be alert and take turns yielding the right-of-way. Two, winter travel is not recommended past mile 3 because of avalanche hazard.

85 Skyline Trail

RATING/ DIFFICULTY	ROUNDTRIP	ELEV GAIN/ HIGH POINT	SEASON
*****/5	4.5 miles	2800 feet/ 3240 feet	June–Sept

Maps: USGS Kenai C1 SE (and a tiny corner on USGS Kenai C1 SW), unmarked on National Geographic Kenai National Wildlife Refuge; **Contact:** Kenai National Wildlife Refuge; **Notes:** Dogs permitted on leash in parking area, under direct control in backcountry. Bear and moose habitat. Avalanche hazard in winter; **GPS:** 60.5185°, −150.1881°

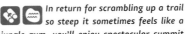 *In return for scrambling up a trail so steep it sometimes feels like a jungle gym, you'll enjoy spectacular summit wildflowers against a pretty background of lowland lakes and the Kenai Mountains, with views all the way to Cook Inlet to the west.*

GETTING THERE

From Cooper Landing, drive west on the Sterling Highway for about 13.5 miles, to milepost 61. The parking area (elevation 480 feet) is on the left (south) side of the road.

ON THE TRAIL

Although the parking for this hike is on the south side of the Sterling Highway, the trail actually begins on the north side, at the west end of the guardrail. Drivers go fast on this narrow stretch of road, so be very careful when you cross the highway.

As is sometimes the case on Kenai Peninsula trails, the one-way distance on the trailhead sign (1 mile) doesn't match up with the 2+ mile distances that hikers, including myself, routinely measure. But don't worry about that too much: right now, your job is to start up the immediate stiff uphill climb through brushy forest full of alder and birch trees, cow parsnip, spiky devil's club, and berry bushes.

By 0.4 mile (elevation 950 feet) the brush has cleared out enough to offer some great lookouts over Jean Lake, the closest lake to the south.

Just before 1 mile (elevation 1700 feet) you'll transition into some of the biggest

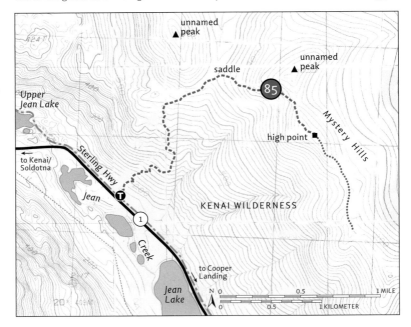

Your reward for the stiff climb up the Skyline trail

alder trees I've seen in Southcentral Alaska. Their roots provide a much-needed lattice-work as you clamber up some of the steepest, loosest sections of this dirt trail.

As you might imagine, that loose dirt makes this trail a miserable, dangerously slippery slog in wet conditions, and it's often wet in the spring. But on a sunny summer day the steepness is so ridiculous that it becomes fun. Just remember to pack plenty of water, a good attitude, and trekking poles to help on the way down—and don't be shy about taking rest stops.

At 1.2 miles (elevation 2020 feet) the trail suddenly flattens out in a saddle between two unnamed peaks, with great views of Jean Lake, Hidden Lake, and Skilak Lake behind you.

I think this is where the trail is supposed to end, but the wildflowers from here on out are spectacular; look for a mix of lupine, wild geranium, wild roses, fireweed, and even chocolate lilies, which look beautiful but smell horrible. And the views are just beginning, so keep going if you can; turn right and follow a braided footpath up the obvious ridge.

By 1.6 miles (2300 feet) the trail is increasingly steep and rocky, but that's compensated for by the ridiculously abundant wildflowers. Look closely for movement on the ridgeline and nearby mountains—you may be able to spot Dall sheep in the distance.

At 1.9 miles (elevation 2750 feet) the trail is particularly steep, with a little sporadic exposure—but you never really have to scramble. There are two high points at miles 2.4 and 2.5; by my measurements, that second point is higher by about 25 feet. Make sure you bring an extra layer, because the weather at the high point is often colder and windier than down below, and you should stay a while to enjoy the views you worked so hard to earn.

86 Slaughter Gulch

RATING/ DIFFICULTY	ROUNDTRIP	ELEV GAIN/ HIGH POINT	SEASON
*****/5	4.2 miles	2740 feet/ 3216 feet	May–Oct

Maps: USGS Seward B8 NE, USGS Seward C8 SE, USGS Seward C8 SW; **Contact:** Chugach National Forest, Seward Ranger District, Seward; **Notes:** Dogs permitted on leash or "restrained." Bear and moose habitat. Avalanche hazard in winter; **GPS:** 60.4952°, −149.8036°

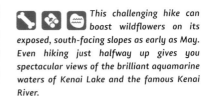

This challenging hike can boast wildflowers on its exposed, south-facing slopes as early as May. Even hiking just halfway up gives you spectacular views of the brilliant aquamarine waters of Kenai Lake and the famous Kenai River.

GETTING THERE

From Anchorage, take the New Seward Highway to the Sterling Highway and into Cooper Landing, about 100 miles. Just before you reach the intersection with Bean Creek Road, turn north onto single-lane Stetson

Don't forget to look behind you for views over Kenai Lake as you climb the ridge.

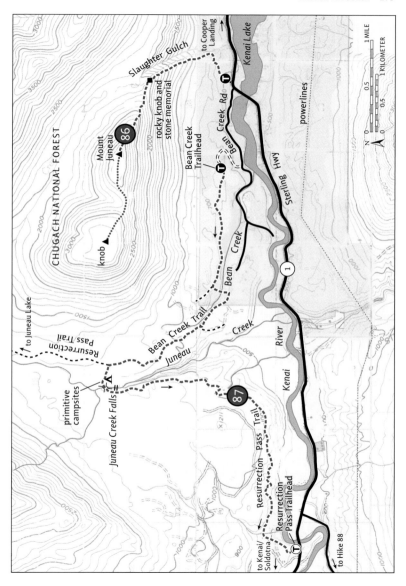

CHUGACH NATIONAL FOREST

Slaughter Gulch

to Cooper Landing

Kenai Lake

rocky knob and stone memorial

Mount Juneau

86

knob

Bean Creek Rd

Bean Creek Trailhead

Sterling Hwy

powerlines

Bean Creek

1

Bean Creek Trail

to Juneau Lake

Juneau Creek

Bean Creek

Resurrection Pass Trail

Kenai River

primitive campsites

Juneau Creek Falls

87

Resurrection Pass Trail

Resurrection Pass Trailhead

to Kenai/ Soldotna

to Hike 88

N

1 MILE

1 KILOMETER

0   0.5   1

0   0.5   1

Road which goes up a short hill and ends in the unofficial, unmarked trailhead for this hike. There's only room for a couple of cars, so park at the high point in the dirt road and look for the obvious trail leading north into the woods.

ON THE TRAIL

Despite the ominous sounding name, Slaughter Gulch is a lovely hike—and if it weren't so steep and the unmarked trailhead so small and hard to find, it would no doubt attract enormous crowds. The hike starts directly from the "pullout" you park in (elevation 500 feet), heading through crunchy fallen leaves beneath a canopy of birch and spindly spruce trees; the understory is filled in largely by berry bushes. Please be considerate of signed private property.

This trail is punishing and steep right from the outset, gaining 1500 feet in the first 1.1 miles with only a few very short switchbacks to ease the way. But that translates to almost immediate rewards, starting with peeks over the treetops at brilliant, aquamarine Kenai Lake as you pause to catch your breath. Look for alpine wildflowers such as lupine, Jacob's ladder, and forget-me-nots on sunny, south-facing slopes; they can emerge as early as May.

By 1.1 miles you'll reach a rocky knob with a small, stone memorial on it. This little bluff offers stunning lookouts over Cooper Landing and Kenai Lake, which now resembles a distant sea against the green mountains. Many people consider this a turnaround point, but I say treat it as a rest stop if you're up to hiking for even better views.

From here the trail heads left (west) onto an increasingly rocky ridgeline that leads to the top of 3216-foot Mount Juneau. The southern exposure means the first part of this trail can be clear of snow by early spring, but you may still encounter icy conditions on this ridge, along with loose rock and some mild exposure on the left (south) side of the trail—so pack ice grippers and a healthy dose of common sense if you're traveling in the spring.

Just before 2.1 miles you'll reach the rounded peak of 3216-foot Mount Juneau, where snowfields can linger well in May. Conditions allowing, you have the option of an off-trail walk another mile farther west, gaining another 600 feet on your way to a high knob, elevation 3285 feet, with steep overlooks of the popular Resurrection Pass Trail to the west. Total one-way hiking distance to this second, optional high point is 3.1 miles and 3300 feet of elevation gain.

87 Juneau Creek Falls

RATING/ DIFFICULTY	ONE-WAY	ELEV GAIN/ HIGH POINT	SEASON
****/2	7.5 miles	1050 feet/ 1190 feet	June–Oct

Maps: USGS Seward B8 NW, USGS Seward C8 SW, National Geographic Kenai National Wildlife Refuge; **Contact:** Chugach National Forest, Seward Ranger District, Seward; **Notes:** Open to mountain bikes. Popular for snowshoeing and cross-country skiing. Closed to pack/saddle stock April 1–June 30. First part of Bean Creek Trail is open to motorized use year-round; watch for dog mushers too. Resurrection Pass Trail is open to snowmachiners during winters in even-numbered years. Dogs permitted on leash at trailhead, under direct control in backcountry. Bear and moose habitat; **GPS:** Resurrection Pass Trailhead: 60.48453°, −149.95315°; Bean Creek Trailhead: 60.49578°, −149.83247°

Juneau Creek Falls, seen from the Resurrection Pass side of the trail

 *Visit one of the few hike-access waterfalls in Alaska that's big enough to make the ground rumble at high flows and throw mist into your face even if you're on the far side of its gorge.*

GETTING THERE

Bean Creek Trailhead: From mile 47.7 of the Sterling Highway in Cooper Landing, turn north onto Bean Creek Road. After 1 mile, turn right onto rough Slaughter Ridge Road; the Bean Creek Trailhead (elevation 600 feet) is at the end of the road.

Resurrection Pass Trailhead: From Cooper Landing, drive west on the Sterling Highway for almost 6 miles. At mile 53.2 of the highway, turn right (north) into the marked Resurrection Pass Trailhead parking area.

ON THE TRAIL

This description is written assuming that you'll do a thru-hike from the Bean Creek Trailhead to the Resurrection Pass Trailhead, although you can also do the hike as an out-and-back from either trailhead. I recommend starting your thru-hike from the Bean Creek Trailhead because the Resurrection Pass end is more heavily traveled, so it makes a better final target.

The first 1.2 miles of the Bean Creek Trail are a fairly unremarkable stroll through dense walls of alders along an old roadbed, climbing at a very gentle grade. At 1.2 miles the road forks; continue straight. Shortly after this, you'll pass a big, looping pullout to the left; again, keep going straight.

At 1.4 miles the road veers off to the right, but you should take the marked ATV trail to the left, which becomes noticeably muddier on wet days. At just past 1.5 miles, stay on the ATV trail as it bends sharply to the right.

At 1.6 miles you'll pass a sign indicating the cutoff point for motorized users, although foot and bike traffic continues on what's now a double-track "road." The trail now starts climbing at a fairly gentle grade, at 2.25 miles (elevation 990 feet).

At 3.25 miles, the Bean Creek Trail intersects the Resurrection Pass Trail. The signage here can be a little confusing, because while you'd think Juneau Creek Falls and Juneau Lake would be in the same direction, they're not. Turn left for Juneau Creek Falls and, at 3.5 miles (elevation 1100 feet) you'll reach a bridge over Juneau Creek (on your right) and a small sign indicating backcountry campsites (straight ahead).

You should be able to hear Juneau Creek Falls from here. Although you can see the falls from either side of the trail, I think the views are much better—and the footing safer—if you cross the bridge and turn left onto the main Resurrection Pass Trail.

At 3.6 miles from the trailhead, look for a clear side trail leading left into the forest for overlooks of the falls. (If you're coming from the Resurrection Pass Trailhead, this will be on your right.) Choose your footing carefully, because in some places the trail that once traced the lip over the overlook now sits on top of crumbling, undercut shelves that I wouldn't want to trust with my weight.

As you continue to the Resurrection Pass Trailhead, the trail stays mostly level—through dense, alder-lined forest that should look very familiar by now—until mile 5.5, at which point it starts to drop gradually into a mixed forest of spruce and birch trees overlooking the Kenai River, then reaches the Resurrection Pass Trailhead at mile 7.5.

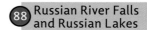
88 Russian River Falls and Russian Lakes

Russian River Falls

RATING/ DIFFICULTY	ROUNDTRIP	ELEV GAIN/ HIGH POINT	SEASON
****/2	4.8 miles	575 feet/ 715 feet	June–Oct

Lower Russian Lake

RATING/ DIFFICULTY	ROUNDTRIP	ELEV GAIN/ HIGH POINT	SEASON
***/2	6.4 miles	215 feet/ 710 feet	June–Oct

Maps: USGS Seward B8 NW (and USGS Kenai B1 NE if you want perspective of what's on the west side of the trail), National Geographic Kenai National Wildlife Refuge; **Contact:** Chugach National Forest, Seward Ranger District, Seward; **Notes:** Closed to motorized vehicles between the Russian River Campground and Upper Russian Lake Cabin; the remainder of the Russian Lakes Trail is closed to motorized vehicles May through November 30. Closed to pack/saddle stock April through June. Dogs must be leashed at trailhead and campground. Keep dogs under direct control in backcountry; keep leashed during salmon season. Bear and moose habitat. Be extremely careful about bears during salmon spawning season. Sockeye fishing downstream of Russian River Falls; rainbow trout fishing in Upper and Lower Russian lakes. Avalanche hazard in winter; **GPS:** 60.47831°, –149.96262°

The Russian River begins its long tumble in a series of cascading waterfalls.

 *Bears and human fishermen alike flock to the Russian River to catch their share of its rich summer salmon runs. Be extremely mindful of your "bear manners" here and on the mellow woodland walk to Lower Russian Lake.*

GETTING THERE

From Cooper Landing, drive west on the Sterling Highway for about 5 miles. At mile 52.6, turn left (south) into the enormous Russian River Campground. Drive another 1 mile to the marked trailhead parking area for the Lower Russian Lakes Trailhead (elevation 490 feet, still inside the campground). For winter use, park at the gate near the campground entrance station and hike the extra mile in. The gate is usually closed sometime in October.

ON THE TRAIL

The stroll to Russian River Falls is the epitome of Alaska easy: the trail is so well-built that it's practically paved, wide enough for two people to walk abreast easily, and always kept clear, despite the surrounding spruce, birch, and alder trees, with the occasional cottonwood mixed in.

That said, the river's rich salmon runs, which start with sockeye runs in mid-June and mid-July and end with a silver salmon run that extends into September, are a powerful attractant for bears. So it's not a question of if you'll meet them on the trail, but when, and whether you'll be using the sort of "good bear manners" that help avoid dangerous surprise encounters. See "Wildlife" in the introduction for important reminders about wildlife safety in Alaska.

Start practicing those good bear manners straight out of the trailhead, as the trail crosses under a set of powerlines and parallels the river at a short distance. At 1.2 miles you'll pass an access trail that leads to the river; but before you whip that fishing pole out, make sure you check the Alaska Department of Fish and Game's regulations for where you can and cannot go sportfishing on the Russian.

Just before 1.7 miles (elevation 700 feet) the trail hits an important junction: continue straight for Russian River Falls, or cross a bridge and veer left to reach Lower Russian Lake. If you continue straight, you'll reach a pair of viewing decks over the falls at 2.4 miles (elevation 510 feet). Get your camera out—if you're very lucky, you might see bears fishing in the falls.

Simply walking out to the falls and back makes for an extremely popular day hike of 4.8 miles roundtrip. But if you'd like a longer walk or a different destination, you can turn left at that intersection that's 1.7 miles from the trailhead.

Once you make that turn the trail narrows a little, and as you head away from the water you'll find yourself looking at mountains over the treetops. The spruce trees that you see sporting dry, orange-red needles have been killed by the spruce bark beetle, but by 2.4 miles (elevation 680 feet) these have mostly given way to slender aspen and willow trees.

At about 2.5 miles you catch your first glimpse of Lower Russian Lake in front of you, and at 2.7 miles (elevation 580 feet) you'll hit another trail intersection. The right fork leads through tall grass to roughly parallel the shore of the lake until 3.2 miles, at which point it heads slightly inland before hooking back to end at Barber Cabin on the shores of the lake. This public use cabin must be reserved in advance at recreation .gov. A fee applies, so if you haven't rented

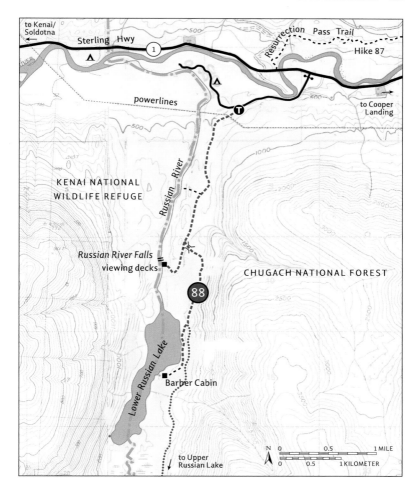

the cabin, the lakeshore is a good place to stop or turn around.

If you're feeling especially ambitious, you can instead take the left fork and hike as far as you like on the 21-mile (one way) Russian Lakes Trail, which swoops to the east, past Upper Russian Lake, before ending near the shores of Cooper Lake. (That trailhead is reached via Snug Harbor Road/Cooper Lake Road, just out of Cooper Landing.)

You'll also find good rainbow trout fishing in Lower Russian Lake, Upper Russian Lake, and the waters in between, and you might be lucky enough to see Dall sheep or mountain goats in the rocky mountains to your east.

One heads up: although this area is in many ways excellent for cross-country skiing, if you come here in the winter, the mountains to the left (east) as you start the hike present serious avalanche danger.

89 Fuller Lakes

RATING/ DIFFICULTY	ROUNDTRIP	ELEV GAIN/ HIGH POINT	SEASON
***/3	7.4 miles	1750 feet/ 1750 feet	May–Oct

Maps: USGS Kenai B1 USGS Kenai NE, USGS Kenai C1 SE, National Geographic Kenai National Wildlife Refuge; **Contact:** Kenai National Wildlife Refuge; **Notes:** Popular for skiing, snowshoeing, and snowmachining during winter. Dogs permitted on leash in parking areas, under direct control in backcountry. Bear and moose habitat. Good birding. Fish for grayling in Lower Fuller Lake, Dolly Varden in Upper Fuller Lake; **GPS:** 60.48515°, −150.07571°

 *This brushy and sometimes wet walk joins an old mining road around two lakes, emerging into subalpine tundra at the second. It's a great birding destination in early summer, with fishing in both lakes and five-hundred-year-old mountain hemlocks.*

GETTING THERE
From Cooper Landing, drive southwest on the Sterling Highway for just under 10 miles, to mile 57. The Fuller Lake Trailhead will be on the right (north) side of the road. If

you reach the intersection with Skilak Lake Road, you've gone too far.

ON THE TRAIL
This well-maintained trail starts by bounding up a fairly steep staircase, but by 0.1 mile it subsides to a lovely, wide footpath through stands of birch trees, mixed spruce, and occasional mountain hemlock. Watch for roots underfoot and occasional mud, although there are boardwalks over the wettest spots.

You'll get most of your elevation gain out of the way early: by about 1.2 miles (elevation 1050 feet) you'll get your first glimpses of the glacier-carved subalpine valley you're about to enter, and the trail becomes a little boggy. Look and listen for birds in early summer, including the calls of the varied, Swainson's, and hermit thrushes.

By 1.6 miles (elevation 1300 feet) you've transitioned from forest to a riot of devil's club, ferns, grass, wild roses, and cow parsnip; wear long sleeves and pants to protect against photosensitivity from the sap of the latter invasive plant.

At 1.9 miles (elevation 1550 feet) the trail pushes through stands of head-high alders and levels off in thick stands of mountain hemlock. Lower Fuller Lake is just around the corner; look for the V-shaped wakes of beavers at work as you cross a bridge over the lake's outflow and skirt its left (west) side. You might also see grayling rising to feed.

At 2.4 miles the trail starts winding away from the lake. Expect sporadic wet, muddy footing between here and Upper Fuller Lake. You're still traveling through a mix of brush and grass, but visibility isn't too bad.

At 2.6 miles you'll pass to the right of another small lake—I call it "Bonus Lake"

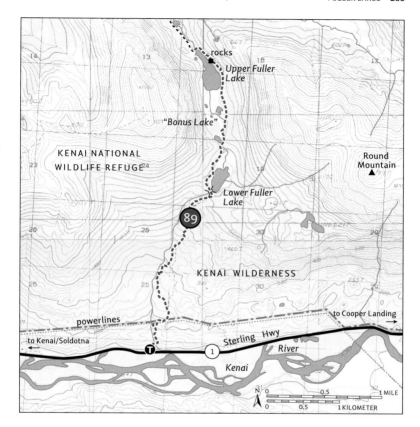

because to the best of my knowledge it doesn't have a name—and by 3.1 miles you can catch a glimpse of Upper Fuller Lake ahead of you.

At 3.2 miles you'll pick your way through a slippery mix of muddy trail, rocks, and grass, then forge into dense, shoulder-high willow thickets as you start passing along the right-hand (east) shore of Upper Fuller Lake. Although the valley is mostly open tundra at

this point, stands of mountain hemlock and dwarf willow cluster close to the lake. You can fish for Dolly Varden here.

At 3.5 miles there are a couple of big rocks on the lakeshore that make for great lookouts over the water. For many this will be the ideal stopping point, but you can continue another 0.2 mile and rock-hop across a few small streams to another, marshier lookout on the far end of the lake and the true end

Along the grassy shores of Upper Fuller Lake

of the trail. Watch for willow ptarmigan and American pipits nesting in the rocky tundra, and look for white dots moving in the rocky bluffs—Dall sheep.

The berry picking is great here during the fall and, as a point of curiosity, core samples taken by federal biologists have shown that some of the twisted little hemlocks near treeline at Upper Fuller Lake sprouted in the 1500s.

Although there is no established trail, the ridge to the left (west) of Upper Fuller Lake connects to the aptly named Skyline Trail (Hike 85). If you choose to make this linkup you'll need routefinding, map-reading, and scrambling skills, and a willingness to travel off-trail (which is relatively easy in this valley). Neither end of the linkup is signed or marked in any way, so it helps to be familiar with the trail you're heading toward.

Opposite: *The trails around Skilak Lake are short but gorgeous, and placid Engineer Lake makes the perfect trailside companion (Hike 96).*

skilak lake area

At a whopping 15 miles long, Skilak Lake is a landmark and a destination all its own. It's also a stunning centerpiece for most of these hikes, which range from distant, panoramic overlooks to close-up wanders on the lake's pebbly shore. The trails around Skilak Lake tend to be relatively flat and easy by Alaska standards, but they're never boring. All are accessed from the unpaved 18-mile-long Skilak Lake Road, which arcs down from the Sterling Highway to roughly parallel Skilak Lake's northern shore.

90 Skilak Hideout

RATING/ DIFFICULTY	ROUNDTRIP	ELEV GAIN/ HIGH POINT	SEASON
***/3	2.2 miles	925 feet/ 1550 feet	May–Oct

Maps: USGS Kenai B1 NE, National Geographic Kenai National Wildlife Refuge;

Contact: Kenai National Wildlife Refuge; **Notes:** Skilak Lake Road may not be plowed during winter. Dogs permitted on leash at trailhead, under direct control at all times. Bear and moose habitat; **GPS:** 60.47183°, –150.15437°

Skilak Hideout (sometimes just called the Hideout Trail) hopscotches through a relatively open hillside from one rocky viewpoint to another, giving you lookouts over serpentine, blue-green Kenai River and Skilak Lake in the distance.

GETTING THERE
From Cooper Landing, take the Sterling Highway west for about 10 miles to its first juncture with Skilak Lake Road at mile 58. Turn left onto barely maintained Skilak Lake Road, which is sometimes extremely rough with deep, muddy ruts. At mile 1.8 of Skilak

Skilak Hideout Trail puts the gorgeous landscape around Skilak Lake into full perspective.

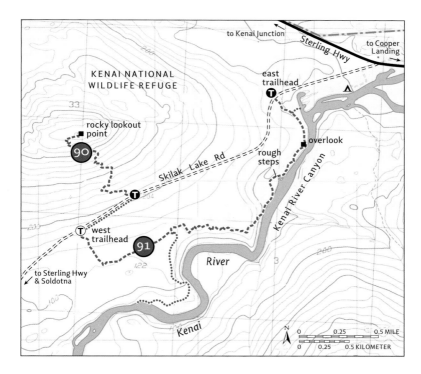

Lake Road, park in a lot on the left side of the road. Look for the trail sign (elevation 675 feet) on the other side of the road.

ON THE TRAIL

Some maps incorrectly label this hike as being on the south side of the road; that is actually part of the Kenai River Trail (see Hike 91). Instead, the Skilak Hideout Trail starts on the north side of the road, opposite the parking area, trending west on a constant but moderate grade on a forest trail lined with fireweed, ferns, devil's club, and cow parsnip.

Because it's set so far back from Skilak Lake, the Hideout Trail lacks the high-humidity, rainforesty feel of trails closer to the water. Instead you find yourself walking through a mix of birch and spruce trees, patches of straight young aspens, and the occasional old-growth cottonwood among them; the overall effect is much more open than other trails in the area.

At 0.2 mile (elevation 800 feet) you'll start to catch sight of distant Skilak Lake to your left. You lose those views when the trail bends inland, but a lookout at 0.3 mile (elevation 880 feet) gives you a better vantage point. Although you'll continue to see brush at either side of the trail, the views here are remarkably open, and by about 0.6 mile (elevation 1180 feet) you start to catch sight of the Kenai River as it ties into Skilak Lake.

At 0.8 mile (elevation 1350 feet) you can see your final destination, a rocky lookout point uphill to your right. The trail continues straight ahead, winding up a couple of rough switchbacks before cutting back across the hilltop to that lookout point at 1.1 miles (elevation 1550 feet).

91 Kenai River Trail

RATING/ DIFFICULTY	ROUNDTRIP	ELEV GAIN/ HIGH POINT	SEASON
***/2	5.6 miles	760 feet/ 580 feet	Year-round, best May–Oct

Maps: USGS Kenai B1 NE, National Geographic Kenai National Wildlife Refuge; **Contact:** Kenai National Wildlife Refuge; **Notes:** Access road may not be plowed during the winter. Dogs permitted on leash in parking area, under direct control on trails. Bear and moose habitat. Bear encounters are extremely common here, especially during salmon runs; **GPS:** Upper Kenai River Trailhead: 60.48142°, –150.12887°; Lower Kenai River Trailhead: 60.46867°, –150.16448°

 *Sometimes called the Upper or Lower Kenai River Trail, this easy walk tours through views of the rock-walled Kenai River Canyon, young aspen trees overtaking the stumps left behind by old burns, and the glittering blue-green Kenai River. There's just one catch: bear encounters are extremely common here.*

GETTING THERE

From Cooper Landing, drive west on the Sterling Highway for about 10 miles. At mile marker 58, turn south onto unpaved Skilak Lake Road, which sometimes has soft mud and terrible ruts. At times passenger vehicles can navigate this road easily; other times they can't. The east trailhead (elevation 360 feet) will be on your left after 0.7 mile. There is a second trailhead, which I call the west trailhead (elevation 580 feet), at 2.3 miles from the turn onto Skilak Lake Road.

ON THE TRAIL

Although this hike has two trailheads, I prefer the views starting from the east trailhead, which some refer to as the Upper Kenai River Trailhead. Please note: bear encounters are so common here, there is a permanent "bears in the area" warning sign at the trailhead. This is not the place for a DIY bear-viewing expedition. Instead, be respectful of the bears' presence and practice your best "bear aware" tactics to avoid a conflict. That includes making plenty of noise so the bears can hear you coming; see "Wildlife" in the introduction for more information on hiking in bear country.

Now, the trail. Starting from the east trailhead, after just 0.2 mile you'll reach a fork. To the left, a 0.1-mile side trail delivers you straight to the side of the river, a marvel of milky blue-green water when seen up close.

The main trail continues to the right, where just past 0.4 mile the trees open up for a stunning overlook from atop the steep rock walls of the Kenai River Canyon. It's not that you've climbed far above the river, but instead the river drops in steps through the canyon, with the water turning a brighter blue-green when seen from a distance. Be

There's no mistaking the brilliant aquamarine waters of the famed Kenai River.

very careful about approaching the edges of the cliffs, which are made of notoriously crumbly, unstable rock.

The trail leaves the canyon lip at 0.75 mile, curving inland and dropping down a series of rough, rock-slab steps. From here, it winds along the contours of the brushy, forested hillside as if it were tracing one of the lines on a topo map. The river's gem-like water snakes away from you in the near distance, on its way to a rendezvous with enormous Skilak Lake.

This portion of the trail received a major reworking by Kenai Wildlife Refuge trail crews in 2013 to guide it away from per-sistently swampy areas. The mature for-est is also interrupted by the relics of two forest fires, which are most obvious at an intersection just under 2 miles from the east trailhead. Here the alders, willow, and spruce, with their understory of lupine and wild roses, give way to straight young aspen trees, some of the first colonizers that come in after a fire.

Turn right at the junction, and the trail gradually climbs uphill to the west trailhead (elevation 580 feet), snagging a few more views of the distant river along the way. Part of this stretch of trail was reworked in 2014 to avoid boggy areas, with the help of high school students on a Student Conservation Association crew.

This little thru-hike from east trailhead to west trailhead is 2.8 miles one way. If you haven't parked a second car at the west trailhead you can either retrace your steps to the east trailhead, enjoying pretty views of the Kenai Mountains on the horizon, or turn right from the west trailhead and take the shorter, 1.6-mile walk along Skilak Lake Road back to the east trailhead.

Your other option is to bear left at the fork, at which point the trail drops down a strange grassy ridgeline in the forest, losing 300 feet of elevation on the way to the river's edge at 2.9 miles from the east trailhead. As soon as you hit the water you'll find a tiny but obvious black sand beach, which I consider to be the end of this trail. Technically it continues along the riverbank, but that grassy, overgrown slog is best left to determined fishermen and bears.

Remember: bear encounters can happen anywhere in Alaska, but they're especially likely near active salmon streams such as this one, particularly when the salmon runs are at their peak (typically July and August,

although the timing can vary and runs extend into the fall). Stay well away from the river when the fish are running.

92 Hidden Creek

RATING/ DIFFICULTY	LOOP	ELEV GAIN/ HIGH POINT	SEASON
****/2	3.2 miles	260 feet/ 460 feet	Year-round

Maps: USGS Kenai B1 NW, National Geographic Kenai National Wildlife Refuge; **Contact:** Kenai National Wildlife Refuge; **Notes:** Access road may not be plowed during the winter. Dogs permitted on leash at the trailhead, under direct control at all times. Bear and moose habitat; **GPS:** 60.45411°, –150.21849°

The breezy, wave-washed shore of Skilak Lake

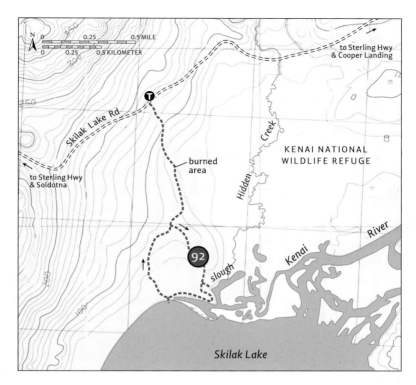

    *A charming and easy hike travels through lowland spruce forest to the shores of enormous Skilak Lake, where a windswept day can generate waves worthy of an ocean shore. Watch for bears near the creek; they're drawn by rainbow trout, lake trout, and Dolly Varden.*

GETTING THERE

From Cooper Landing, drive west on the Sterling Highway for about 10 miles. At mile marker 58, turn south onto unpaved Skilak Lake Road, which sometimes has terrible ruts and spots of soft mud; proceed with caution. The Hidden Creek parking area (elevation 470 feet) will be on your right after 4.6 miles; the trail starts on the opposite side of the road.

ON THE TRAIL

The trail starts on the far side of Skilak Lake Road from the parking area. You can't miss the wide dirt trail that descends gently through birch and spruce forest. Just past 0.5 mile (elevation 280 feet) you'll pass through the tall, slim alders and bare, burned logs that mark the remains of a long-ago forest fire, the 5200-acre Hidden Creek Fire in 1996.

Just past 0.8 mile the trail reaches a signed fork. Either fork will take you to the shore of Skilak Lake, and in fact you can use them to walk a loop in either direction. But turning left here also takes you close to a picturesque slough formed by Hidden Creek. At 1.3 miles you'll see the slough on your left; bear encounters are especially common here, thanks to the rainbow trout, lake trout, and Dolly Varden you'll find in the creek. If you're here to fish as well, make sure you read up on the latest area regulations, as they're subject to change.

At 1.5 miles you'll make a quick left turn and emerge on the lakeshore. This is a wonderful place for a picnic, skipping stones, or just exploring with the whole family—but sometimes it's surprising just how windy this area can be, once you pop out of the protecting trees. Pay attention to where you emerge from the woods, because there is no marker. If you look to your right, the prominent overlook point atop the distant but obvious finger of land that protrudes into the lake is the end of the Skilak Lookout Trail (see Hike 93).

When you're ready, head back into the woods and continue walking your loop. Just after 2.2 miles you'll hit a nice stand of aspens, a sign that you're reentering the old burn area. (Aspens are often the first tree species to colonize after a burn.) You'll also find a lot of bog cranberries, yarrow, fireweed, and, one of my favorite plants, the astringent-smelling Labrador tea.

Just before 2.4 miles you'll get back to that signed intersection on the main trail. From here, it's a straight, 0.8-mile shot back to the trailhead, completing a lollipop-shaped loop hike.

93 Skilak Lookout

RATING/ DIFFICULTY	ROUNDTRIP	ELEV GAIN/ HIGH POINT	SEASON
****/3	4.5 miles	975 feet/ 1450 feet	Year-round

Maps: USGS Kenai B1, National Geographic Kenai National Wildlife Refuge; **Contact:** Kenai National Wildlife Refuge; **Notes:** Good snowshoeing in winter; dogs permitted on leash at trailhead, under direct control in backcountry. Moose and bear habitat. Good birding in summer; **GPS:** 60.44976°, −150.23752°

 *What more could a hiker want? This family-friendly trail through a grassy, wildflower-strewn forest ends in a rocky promontory offering panoramic views of 15-mile-long Skilak Lake, the Kenai Mountains, and the lower stretch of the Kenai River.*

GETTING THERE
From Cooper Landing, take the Sterling Highway southwest for about 10 miles to its first juncture with Skilak Lake Road, at mile 58. Turn left onto barely maintained Skilak Lake Road, which is sometimes extremely rough with deep, muddy ruts. The Skilak Lookout parking area (elevation 700 feet) is on the right at mile 5.4; the trail begins on the opposite side of the road.

ON THE TRAIL
The first part of this trail showcases the aftereffects of a forest fire: around 0.2 mile, see if you can spot the conspicuously younger trees—mostly alders and aspens—clustered in the forest. Along with understory species such as devil's club, cow parsnip, wild roses,

The "peak" of the lookout offers expansive views over massive Skilak Lake.

fiddlehead ferns, and assorted berries, these young trees are recolonizing ground that was scorched by the 5200-acre 1996 Hidden Creek Fire.

Just past 0.3 mile you'll get the first real glimpse of Skilak Lake's jewel-blue water in the distance. At just past 0.5 mile there's another lookout—this one's even better—and then yet another at just past 0.6 mile. Watch for blackened logs—more relics of the 1996 burn—and bountiful wildflowers tucked into the vibrant young forest, which also has good birding in the early summer. Keep one eye on your footing too: although this trail is easy, there are a lot of muddy spots, rocks, and small rivulets to navigate past.

The trail is mostly flat until this point, but at 0.8 mile the trail crests a short hill, and at just past 1 mile (elevation 800 feet) it starts

a moderate, sustained climb that continues all the way to the final lookout. That modest elevation gain means better and better lookouts every time you crest a hill, with a particularly nice viewpoint at mile 1.4 (elevation 980 feet).

At 1.8 miles (elevation 1220 feet) the trail works up a series of grassy switchbacks, ascending the rocky knob that holds your final lookout point. At 2.1 miles the real panoramic views start, giving you a feel for just how wide and far Skilak Lake stretches. It feels expansive enough to be an ocean, with boats reduced to tiny dots in the water, but this is really only half of it. The other half is hidden around a bend to your right.

At 2.2 miles follow a footpath that veers up and to the right, through patches of scrubby trees. After less than 0.1 mile the path ends on the exposed face of the rocky

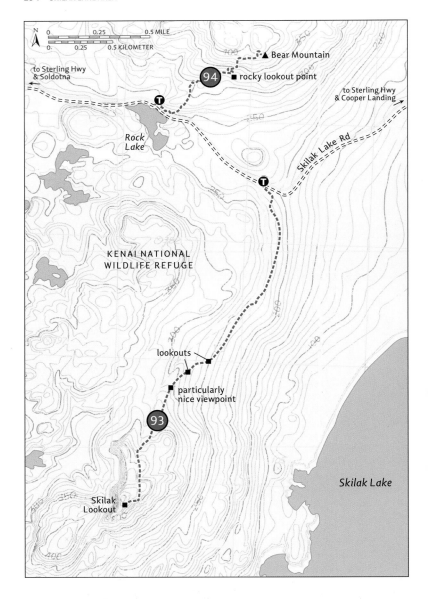

knob overlooking Skilak Lake—the true Skilak Lookout. You might be surprised by just how windy it can get up here; bring a jacket and, if necessary, retreat to a more sheltered spot in the trees.

94 Bear Mountain (Skilak version)

RATING/ DIFFICULTY	ROUNDTRIP	ELEV GAIN/ HIGH POINT	SEASON
***/3	1.8 miles	615 feet/ 1320 feet	May–Oct

Maps: USGS Kenai B1 NW, National Geographic Kenai National Wildlife Refuge; **Contact:** Kenai National Wildlife Refuge; **Notes:** Skilak Lake Road may not be plowed during winter. Dogs permitted on leash at trailhead, under direct control at all times. Bear and moose habitat; **GPS:** 60.45542°, –150.25241°

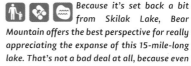 *Because it's set back a bit from Skilak Lake, Bear Mountain offers the best perspective for really appreciating the expanse of this 15-mile-long lake. That's not a bad deal at all, because even if the hike itself isn't so sweet, it's short—and the views more than make up for the brushy climb.*

GETTING THERE

From Cooper Landing, take the Sterling Highway west for about 10 miles to its first juncture with Skilak Lake Road, at mile 58. Turn left onto barely maintained Skilak Lake Road, which is sometimes extremely rough with deep, muddy ruts. At mile 6 of Skilak Lake Road, turn right into the Bear Mountain parking area (elevation 875 feet).

ON THE TRAIL

The entirety of this trail passes through a seemingly schizophrenic forest that just

Bear Mountain offers a more removed, panoramic vista over Skilak Lake.

can't decide if it's a mossy rainforest, dense alders, or the standard boreal mix of birch and spindly spruce. So you get a little of each as you first sidehill for about 0.1 mile, overlooking Rock Lake to your right, then start climbing straight up the mountainside.

Like many classic Alaska trails, switchbacks are nothing but a dream on Bear Mountain. But the grade, though sustained, is never more than moderate. At just past 0.2 mile you'll pass a rocky area that seems like it should be a lookout point . . . but you can't see much from here. Keep going.

At 0.3 mile (elevation 1000 feet) you'll cross a short boardwalk—the only real sign of trail improvement here, not that it needs much—and at 0.6 mile (elevation 1150 feet) you'll reach a really nice lookout to the right (south) side of the trail.

Although it looks like the trail continues straight ahead and down the far side of this lookout, it actually turns sharply left and uphill instead. Remember this point because on the way down, it'll be tempting to take that wrong turn to the left.

At 0.75 mile (elevation 1300 feet) the trail levels out on a grassy shelf, then cuts to the right. It's easy walking from here, and the end of the trail—and its phenomenal, near-distance views of Skilak Lake—comes up surprisingly fast, at just 0.9 mile (elevation 1320 feet).

95 Vista Trail

RATING/ DIFFICULTY	ROUNDTRIP	ELEV GAIN/ HIGH POINT	SEASON
****/3	3.4 miles	1295 feet/ 1350 feet	May–Oct

Map: USGS Kenai B1 NW; **Contact:** Kenai National Wildlife Refuge; **Notes:** Skilak Lake Road may not be plowed during winter. Dogs permitted on leash at trailhead, under direct control at all times. Bear and moose habitat; **GPS:** 60.43838°, –150.31981°

The fog parts for a glimpse of Skilak Lake from the Vista Trail.

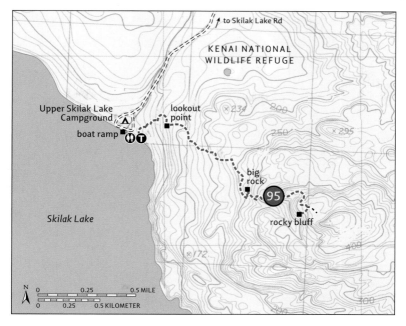

By late summer, this is truly a candidate for "brushiest trail." But on clear days it lives up to its name by offering some of the prettiest vistas you could hope for, over not only Skilak Lake itself but also the remarkable lake-pocked landscape just to the north.

GETTING THERE

From Cooper Landing, take the Sterling Highway about 10 miles west to its first juncture with Skilak Lake Road, at mile 58. Turn left onto barely maintained Skilak Lake Road, which is sometimes extremely rough with deep, muddy ruts. At mile 8.5 of Skilak Lake Road, turn left onto the access road to the Upper Skilak Lake Campground.

Park in the upper lot designated for day users, then walk down toward the boat ramp, keeping an eye out for a pedestrian bridge on the left within view of the water. Cross this bridge then turn right onto the campground road, which immediately forks. Take the left fork, then look for the trail sign on your left (elevation 200 feet), directly opposite the pit toilets.

ON THE TRAIL

Most of the time when I use the term "brushy" to describe a trail, I'm referring to alders or scrubby willows that crowd in close to the trail. But in this case, it's mostly fireweed and grass that crowd the trail by the time late summer rolls around, with just a few patches of alders and the occasional upright birch.

If you don't mind diving into the undergrowth—and sometimes it does feel like you're submerged in a sea of blazing pink fireweed—you'll get great views across massive Skilak Lake after you crest a set of stairs at 0.2 mile (elevation 350 feet). The lake is so large that it often feels like you're overlooking an inlet instead of a landlocked body of water.

At 0.3 mile you can take a short rightward spur for a nice lookout point over the lake, or stay left to continue on the main trail.

At about 0.6 mile (elevation 690 feet) the thick growth around the trail starts to open up, but the hillside can't make up its mind: the grassy patches are interspersed with stretches of quiet woodland path, with slim birch trees standing sentinel and the start of a mossy understory.

At 1.1 mile (elevation 900 feet) the trail starts to climb sharply through a few switchbacks; a big rock at one apex makes a great lookout point over the water. Just past 1.5 miles (elevation 1270 feet) you'll scale a set of log stairs—the wood can be slippery when wet—and at 1.7 miles you reach a relatively flat shelf and a small fork that marks the end of the trail. The left fork peters off into nothing in the bushes, while another short spur to the right leads to a rocky bluff that showcases not only the great expanse of Skilak Lake but also Ohmer Lake and a profusion of small, unnamed lakes to the north.

On the way back downhill, take a minute to appreciate just how overgrown this trail really gets; at some points in late summer, it looks like any hikers in front of you are swimming through the bushes.

96 Seven Lakes

RATING/ DIFFICULTY	ONE-WAY	ELEV GAIN/ HIGH POINT	SEASON
***/2	5.5 miles	150 feet/ 440 feet	Year-round

Maps: USGS Kenai B1, USGS Kenai C1, National Geographic Kenai National Wildlife Refuge; **Contact:** Kenai National Wildlife Refuge; **Notes:** Dogs permitted on leash at trailhead, under direct control in backcountry. Moose and bear habitat. Fishing for rainbow trout in Kelly Lake, rainbow trout and land-locked silver salmon in Engineer Lake; **GPS:** Engineer Lake Trailhead: 60.4738°, –150.3278°; Kelly Lake Trailhead: 60.5209°, –150.3889°

Leading to a clever staircase after you pass Engineer Lake on the Seven Lakes Trail

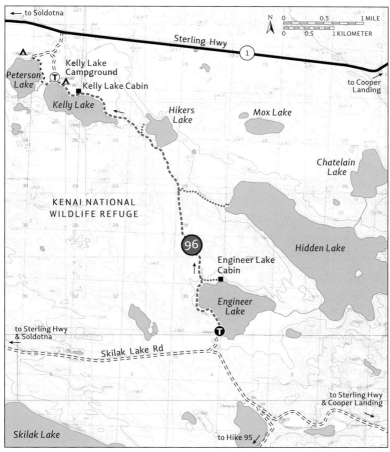

Despite the name, you get views of "only" four lake on this easy ramble through spruce forest. Look and listen for migratory songbirds in May, June, and July, and come back in winter for excellent snowshoeing and ungroomed cross-country skiing.

GETTING THERE

Engineer Lake Trailhead: From Cooper Landing, take the Sterling Highway west for about 10 miles to its first juncture with Skilak Lake Road, at mile 58. Turn left (south) onto barely maintained Skilak Lake Road, which is sometimes extremely rough with deep, muddy ruts. The Engineer Lake Trailhead (elevation 290 feet) is at mile 9.5 of Skilak Lake Road and, unless they improve the trailhead sign, you can see it only when coming from this direction.

Kelly Lake Trailhead: From Cooper Landing, take the Sterling Highway west for about 20 miles. At mile 68.8, follow signs for the Kelly Lake Campground, which will be on the left (south) side of the highway.

ON THE TRAIL

This trail can be done as a thru-hike or as an out-and-back. If you're doing the latter, I recommend starting from Kelly Lake to maximize your time near the lakes. If you're doing a thru-hike, start at Engineer Lake, which is how this description is written.

From the Engineer Lake Trailhead, the first mile of trail is an easy stroll along the lakeshore; there is fair to good fishing here for rainbow trout and landlocked silver salmon. At 1 mile, the trail forks. The main trail continues left into the forest, heading up a beautiful, shallow staircase framed with logs. The right fork is a 0.2-mile side trail that takes you to the Engineer Lake public use cabin. This cabin must be reserved in advance, for a fee, at Recreation.gov. If you haven't reserved the cabin, please respect the privacy of those who have.

Except for the staircase just mentioned, the rest of the trail is a relatively unremarkable—though lovely—stroll on very gently rolling terrain through thick stands of black spruce trees, which look for all the world like fuzzy green pipe cleaners stuck in the soil. In places the passage of many feet has worn the trail into a shallow trench, and you may see the forest floor flex and heave nearby in response to your footsteps.

At 2.6 miles, a signed, 0.6-mile side trail forks off to the right, giving you access to the shores of Hidden Lake. At about 3.3 miles, you'll see the pretty but marshy Hikers Lake just off the trail to the right, and at 3.6 miles, there's a marked turnoff to access the lake.

Mosquitoes like marshy lakes too, so unless you're hiking on a breezy day, come prepared with plenty of insect repellent. Just before 4 miles you'll catch sight of the much more photogenic Kelly Lake, which has fair to good fishing for rainbow trout. The trail quickly dips down to the lakeshore.

Just before 5 miles the trail cuts right past Kelly Lake Cabin, which, like the Engineer Lake Cabin, must be reserved in advance, for a fee, at Recreation.gov. The rowboat you see on the shore at each cabin is reserved for the renters. At 5.5 miles, the trail ends in the Kelly Lake Campground.

Opposite: *Observation platforms like this are a great vantage point for surveying the "flaming" fields of fireweed that carpet the hillsides around Homer in late summer (Hike 99).*

homer and kachemak bay

The popular art, foodie, and fishing town of Homer (population 5600) is the literal end of the road; you can't drive any farther because you're surrounded on three sides by water. But all that water makes for some gorgeous backdrops to local trails that look out from both sides of Kachemak Bay, framed by meadows of fireweed, miles of beaches, and a glacier-backed lake.

97 Diamond Gulch

RATING/ DIFFICULTY	ROUNDTRIP	ELEV GAIN/ HIGH POINT	SEASON
****/2	1.2 miles	365 feet/ 265 feet	Year-round

Map: USGS Seldovia C5 NW; **Contact:** Alaska State Parks, Kenai/Prince William Sound Region; **Notes:** No parking fee. Unmarked trailhead. Dogs permitted on leash on trailhead, under direct control on trail. Bear and moose habitat. Be aware of the tide. Stay off the dangerous mudflats; **GPS:** 59.6730°,–151.6999°

 Although it's easy and short, this trail packs big rewards—and some unusual scenery for Southcentral Alaska—as it leads you down to Diamond Beach where, tides allowing, you can walk and beachcomb for miles.

GETTING THERE
From Homer, drive north (out of town) on the Sterling Highway. At the intersection with Diamond Ridge Road, just on the outskirts of town, turn left onto an unpaved road. The only giveaway marking is a tiny brown State Parks sign on the gate. If the gate is closed for winter, you'll have to park here. If it's open, continue driving for 0.9 mile on the rough but usually passable gravel road until it ends at the unmarked trailhead (elevation 265 feet). If you're concerned for your car, there is a small turnaround/unmarked parking area at 0.1 mile in.

ON THE TRAIL
The trail down to the beach starts as a packed dirt track on the southeast side of

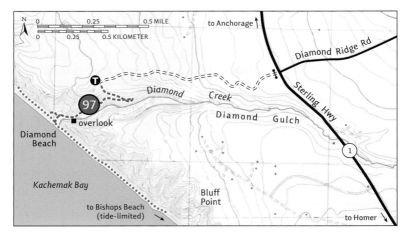

The lush growth of this short trail opens onto a pleasant, sandy beach.

the parking area (to driver's left as you're coming in). It dives straight into what can only be described as "Jurassic Park" vegetation: a lush pile of alders, berry bushes, and cow parsnip that cluster so thickly over one side of the trail, the trees on the other side have to lean away just to get some sun.

At 0.2 mile (elevation 190 feet) the trail makes a sharp right and runs parallel to Diamond Gulch. Kids (and adults!) are naturally fascinated by the sedimentary layers on display in the gulch's steep, exposed walls, but make sure everyone stays on the trail—there are a couple of precipitous drop-offs hidden in the bushes.

At 0.5 mile (elevation 50 feet) you get one of the best overlooks into the gorge, which isn't at all what you might expect in Alaska: in fact, the sandy bluffs and overall feel remind me strongly of summers spent hiking near my grandmother's farm in New Mexico.

Just before 0.6 mile (elevation a whopping 15 feet) the trail forks; take the more-traveled left fork. The trail then delivers you through a patch of grass onto the beach, a world of swooshing waves, kelp-strewn sand, tiny crabs, and tumbled stones. There is no marker; take special note of where the trail meets the beach so you can find it on your way back.

Many Alaska beaches are covered with gravel, so finding this kind of sand beach in Southcentral is a real treat. However, this region has one of the world's most extreme tidal fluctuations. The tides come in much faster than you might expect, and the strip of beach right in front of Diamond Gulch can all but disappear in a high tide. Always keep an eye on the water.

That said, when tides are low, you have enough open beach to walk the sand southeast until you reach Bishops Beach in Homer—6 miles one way. You can either drop off a car shuttle beforehand (take the Sterling Highway to Main Street to East Bunnell Avenue to Beluga Place, which ends in the beach parking area) or catch a taxi back to your car at the Diamond Gulch Trailhead.

Again, keep the tides in mind if you do the walk to Bishops Beach. Always start your walk on an outgoing tide, and be realistic about your walking speed so you'll have plenty of time to make it to Bishops Beach.

Last but not least, pay close attention to where you're walking. Low tides expose stretches of dangerous glacier silt mudflats, which feel like firm land when the water is out but quickly turn to gooey quicksand as the water table rises beneath you. People have died when the mud trapped them and the tide came roaring in—so make sure you stay on the sandy part of the beach.

98 Homestead Trail

Homestead Loop plus viewpoints

RATING/ DIFFICULTY	LOOP	ELEV GAIN/ HIGH POINT	SEASON
***/2	4.5 miles	660 feet/ 1130 feet	Year-round

Homestead Loop

RATING/ DIFFICULTY	LOOP	ELEV GAIN/ HIGH POINT	SEASON
**/2	3.2 miles	430 feet/ 970 feet	Year-round

Maps: USGS Seldovia C5 NE, National Geographic Kachemak Bay State Park; **Contact:** Kachemak Nordic Ski Club; **Notes:** Popular for cross-country skiing and snowshoeing in winter. Dogs permitted on leash. Bear and moose habitat. Can be quite muddy in spots; **GPS:** 59.65971°, −151.62874°

On its surface, this is an unassuming walk through the woods near town. But if your eyes are properly calibrated

you'll also see tiny boats in the water far below, brilliant meadows of pink fireweed, and tall, stately spruce trees with skirts of grass, all painted against a bright blue sky.

GETTING THERE

From downtown Homer, drive west on the Sterling Highway toward Baycrest Hill (this big hill on the outskirts of town has a wonderful viewpoint overlooking Homer, the Homer Spit, and Kachemak Bay). Shortly before you top the hill, turn right onto Rogers Loop Road. Park in a vestigial pullout to the right (really more of a wide spot in the road) just before Rogers Loop Road hooks sharply to the left. The wide, obvious trail (starting elevation 800 feet) begins in a dip to the right side of the road.

ON THE TRAIL

In winter, these trails are maintained by the Kachemak Nordic Ski Club, so if you're thinking of snowshoeing, make sure you stay out of the groomed tracks. But by summer the trails are open to hikers. Make sure you take a picture of one of the maps posted at intervals along the trail, and consider using a GPS mapping app to compare your route to what the map shows. Otherwise, it's fairly easy to get disoriented your first few times through.

The trailhead isn't immediately obvious from the road, but if you see a wooden sign declaring "Kachemak Heritage Land Trust Trail Parking," you're in the right place. Shortly down the very wide, obvious footpath, you'll find a wooden kiosk advertising the Rogers Loop Trailhead—that's your true starting spot.

At less than 0.1 mile, the trail forks; you can go around the loop in either direction. Turn to the right, and at 0.1 mile you'll see

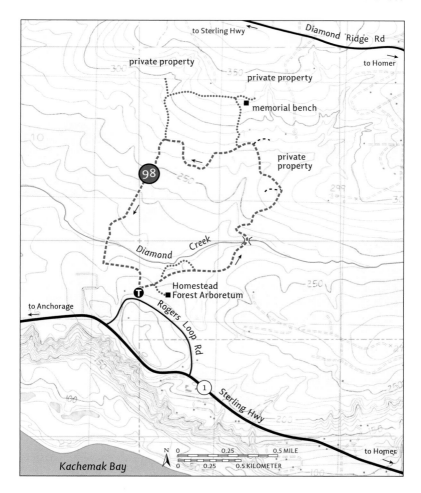

a marked side trail to the quarter-acre Homestead Forest Arboretum, where you're encouraged to tour the collection of native and nonnative trees.

If you continue straight, at 0.2 mile you'll see a boardwalk trail that branches off to the left. It crosses a muskeg meadow, briefly paralleling Diamond Creek before arcing back to rejoin the main trail at about 0.3 mile. Follow the trail markers for "Homestead Trail" until at 0.75 mile the trail crosses a rough wooden bridge over Diamond Creek

Wide-open vistas from the upper reaches of the Homestead Trail loop

and gets a little drier; up until this point, it's prone to mud and, in the late fall, ice.

At 1 mile, just after cresting a short, steep hill, you'll see some trampled-down trails going off through the grass on the right. Stay on the most heavily traveled trail—in fact, this should be your mantra for the rest of the outing. Just past 1.1 miles, turn around to look back over extensive fields of blazing pink fireweed and, in the distance, the mountains that rule the far side of Kachemak Bay.

Just before 1.2 miles the trail hooks to the left, but don't go down the brutally steep hill; instead, follow the relatively level, grass-lined trail as it leads into the trees and *up* a small hill. By 1.5 miles you've hit the initial loop's highest point (970 feet) and a marked right fork to the Rucksack Trailhead, which is blocked by no trespassing signs.

There's a side trail here that's well worth exploring. Just before 1.6 miles from the trailhead, look for an unmarked trail leading uphill to the right. Despite the tall grass and lack of markings, the trail is impossible to miss, and you can see the signpost it heads for, a short distance uphill. Once you crest the hill—actually a small ridge—that trail ends in a T intersection.

Diamond Ridge Road is just a short distance up ahead of you, but to reach it you'd have to cross private property. So instead, turn right and visit an enormous, rough-hewn wooden bench placed here as a memorial to Reuben Call. On clear days, it's the perfect outsize perch for taking in views of the bay below you.

When you go back to the T intersection, continue straight to explore the left arm of the T. After 0.2 mile, you'll reach an intersection with spectacular views across the bay and the bright pink fireweed meadows that cover the hillside. The right fork leads to private property, and the left fork takes a long, swooping loop down to rejoin the main Homestead Trail. Or you can retrace your steps back to the T where you departed from the main trail, and continue the loop from there. No matter which option you take, the loop distance is still about 4.5 miles.

Assuming you take the latter option, it's pretty straightforward to turn right (if you're coming downhill) or continue straight (if you never explored that side trail) and follow the obvious best-traveled trail as it completes the rest of the 3.2-mile loop back to the trailhead. You'll pass through muskeg meadows, corridors of spruce and hemlock trees, and more meadows of blazing fireweed. Just be aware that when you pass an intersection at mile 2.6, with a trail map but no markers to indicate which trail is which, you should continue straight to stay on the main trail.

99 Wynn Nature Center

RATING/ DIFFICULTY	LOOP	ELEV GAIN/ HIGH POINT	SEASON
***/2	2 miles	85 feet/ 1325 feet	Year-round

Map: USGS Seldovia C4 NW; **Contact:** Center for Alaskan Coastal Studies; **Notes:**

Entrance fee; free for members of Center for Alaskan Coastal Studies. Nature center is open daily 10:00 AM–6:00 PM from mid-June to Labor Day. Parking lot is plowed during off-season; trails are open but not maintained. Eight-hundred-foot boardwalk leading to nature center is wheelchair accessible, but the other trails are not. Dogs permitted on leash. Bear and moose habitat; **GPS:** 59.68466°, –151.47376°

Stroll on gentle woodland trails overlooking vivid wildflower-filled muskeg meadows and blazing pink stands of fireweed.

GETTING THERE
As you drive the Sterling Highway into Homer, turn left onto Pioneer Avenue and continue straight through the three-way

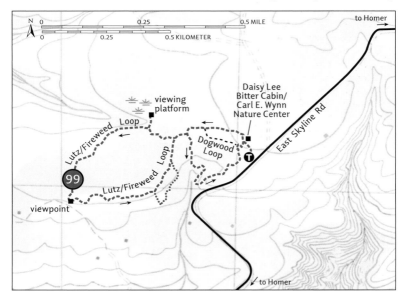

intersection with Lake Street/East End Road. About 1 mile past that intersection, turn left onto East Hill Road. Continue up a series of switchbacks until East Hill Road becomes East Skyline Road. After another 1.5 miles, the parking lot of the Carl E. Wynn Nature Center will be on your left.

ON THE TRAIL

For kids and families in search of a friendly, nature-rich environment, look no further than the Carl E. Wynn Nature Center, which is run by the Center for Alaskan Coastal Studies. If you're walking here in early or midsummer, make sure you bring your flower- and bird-identification books, or join naturalists for guided, educational hikes through the boreal forest during the open season.

There are essentially two loops here. Starting behind the nature center (which is marked on maps as the Daisy Lee Bitter Cabin), the Dogwood Loop includes four benches, perfect for anyone who wants

to rest or take in the views. Start on the right-hand trail as you walk past the cabin, and walk west on the easy, level trail. Walk through the intersection for the Audrey Clauson Trail and turn left at the next intersection, just after 0.2 mile. The loop measures about 0.6 mile in total.

If you were to turn right at that last intersection, you'd walk a 200-foot connector trail to the Lutz/Fireweed Loop, a pleasant forest stroll interspersed with occasional flower-filled muskeg meadows. At about 0.3 mile a short spur trail leads to the right, where you'll find a viewing platform overlooking one of those boggy meadows.

Keep walking around the main loop and at 0.7 mile you'll reach a pretty viewpoint overlooking the tree-filled hillside below you. Although you won't see much of the water, you can see the mountains on the far side of the bay. Keep going and at 1 mile you'll find a spur trail to the right, leading through a patch of what feels like mossy,

The easy trails around the Wynn Nature Center are perfect for spotting birds and flowers.

damp rainforest. That little side spur rejoins the main trail at 1.1 miles, and just past that you'll reach the connector trail that takes you back to the Dogwood Loop for a total loop distance of 2 miles.

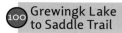

100 Grewingk Lake to Saddle Trail

RATING/ DIFFICULTY	ONE-WAY	ELEV GAIN/ HIGH POINT	SEASON
****/2	4.5 miles	645 feet/ 400 feet	May–Sept

Maps: USGS Seldovia C4 SE, Seldovia C4 NE, National Geographic Kachemak Bay State Park; **Contact:** Alaska State Parks, Kachemak Bay Region; **Notes:** Requires a water taxi (fee varies by provider). Dogs permitted on leash in established areas such as trailheads/campgrounds, under direct control in backcountry. Bear and moose habitat; **GPS:** Glacier Spit Trailhead: 59.62264°, -151.19562°; Saddle Trailhead: 59.60123°, –151.16408°

This short thru-hike is the rarest of treats in Alaska: gentle and nearly flat but not boring, with good signage, switchbacks on the only part that gets a little steep, great glacier views, and—a bonus—two boat rides.

GETTING THERE
Both trailheads can be reached only by water taxi from Homer. Usually you can walk right up and book passage with any water taxi provider along the Homer Spit, but on busy summer days it's best to call and book your seat on the water taxi in advance. This description is written as a thru-hike with a drop-off at the Glacier Spit Trailhead (for the

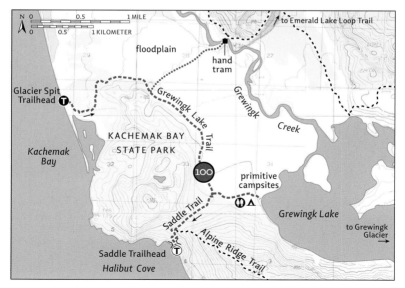

Grewingk Lake Trail; elevation 10 feet) and a pickup at the Saddle Trailhead (elevation 35 feet).

ON THE TRAIL

One of the most popular walks in Kachemak Bay State Park, this is a great introduction to the world of boat-based hiking. It's actually two trails, each of which you could do as an out-and-back. But it's much more interesting to make them into a thru-hike, with the prize—Grewingk Lake and just beyond it, Grewingk Glacier—in the middle.

Be aware, if you start this hike late in the day (or do an out-and-back on the Grewingk Lake Trail), afternoon breezes can make pickup and drop-off problematic at the exposed Glacier Spit Trailhead, where a wooden kiosk and a weathered orange triangular sign mark the start of the Grewingk Lake Trail.

From the Glacier Spit Trailhead, follow trail signs for Grewingk Lake or Grewingk Tram. Trails don't come much gentler than this soft, footpath stretch covered with spruce needles.

Starting at about 0.9 mile the trail borders on the broad floodplain left by the Grewingk Glacier. Here, the trail is made of hardened gravel, and the scattered plants are mostly young willows spiked by occasional cottonwoods.

Just past 1.4 miles (elevation 160 feet) you'll reach a major intersection. The main trail continues straight to Grewingk Lake, while a 1-mile spur trail cuts off to the left to the hand tram across Grewingk Creek, which then hooks into the often-overgrown Emerald Lake Loop Trail. If you want to take the tram across the creek and back again, you usually need two people—one to pull from inside the tram and another to help pull

from the shore—and gloves to protect your hands.

Assuming you continue on the main trail you'll walk a clear, easy path along the glacier floodplain, with almost no change in elevation, until you hit the next major intersection just before 3 miles. This is where the Grewingk Lake and Saddle trails meet, but of course you have to see the glacier before continuing on to the other trailhead.

So, turn left for the 0.5-mile walk to the broad, open shores of Grewingk Lake, where you'll find a number of great picnic spots, primitive campsites along the beach, dramatic views of the glacier across the water, and, charmingly, an outhouse hidden in the trees. Bring your own toilet paper.

When you're ready, retrace your steps back to the main trail; there's an enormous cairn to help you find your way back onto the trail from the beach. When you reach the intersection with the Saddle Trail, turn left. The Saddle Trail makes a gradual ascent, gaining 180 feet of elevation in just over 0.5 mile, reaching the modest high point of 400 feet. The vegetation is more lush here, with a bounty of wildflowers, including the exotic-looking foxglove.

At that high point, you might see a faint trail leading left into the brush. This is part of what's marked on maps as the Alpine Ridge Trail, but it's usually so overgrown that you can't even see your feet, and there is likely to be at least one hornet nest buried in the ground. So, unless/until trail crews are able to clear the Alpine Ridge Trail, stick to the Saddle Trail as it switchbacks down the steepest slope you'll find in this hike, losing 360 feet in 0.5 mile.

Just before reaching the Saddle Trailhead you'll cross a clever wooden bridge across a gully, then descend one of the steepest

Hikers settle down for a picnic lunch at Grewingk Lake.

sets of wooden stairs I've ever seen to the rocky beach below, which looks out on a mist-shrouded Halibut Cove (the cove itself, not the town of the same name). For all intents and purposes, the stairs serve as the trailhead.

Depending on tide levels, you might be able to hop boulders and explore small sandy coves to your south, but be conscious of the fast-moving tide and incoming boats so you don't get trapped or miss your water taxi out. Although the water taxis can be likened to a bus service, you do have to book (and pay for) your passage in advance, so make sure you don't hop on the wrong boat.

As of late 2018, rangers with Kachemak Bay State Park have plotted out a fairly major reroute of the Saddle Trail, which will offer better vantages for a peek over the glacier and its floodplain but still follow the same general terrain—so you shouldn't have trouble finding your way on this well-traveled trail, even after the reroute.

Most likely the reroute will be done while this edition of the book is still in use, but it's hard to say for sure because the state is enduring a real budget crunch, and the budget for public lands projects like trail maintenance and building is extremely low as a result. If you've ever considered supporting your public lands, whether through monetary donations or by lending your muscle as a trail volunteer, now's a great time to pitch in. To volunteer, just contact the state park or your favorite public lands agency—they'll be happy to put you to work.

acknowledgments

Thank you to everyone who hiked the trails in this book with me, but especially Eric, My, Suu, Lina, and Kelly, who powered me through more trails than I ever thought could be squeezed into a set of summers. Your presence made the journey a grand adventure. Also special thanks to Eric for donating some of his wonderful hiking photos, and an enormous thank you to Kate Rogers, editor-in-chief at Mountaineers Books, for her patience as I got my act together.

1% for trails–outdoor nonprofits in partnership

Where would we be without trails? Not very far into the wilderness.

That's why Mountaineers Books designates 1 percent of the sales of select guidebooks in our *Day Hiking* series toward volunteer trail maintenance. Since launching this program, we've contributed more than $22,000 toward improving trails.

For this book, our 1 percent of sales is going to **Alaska Trails**, a nonprofit dedicated to building and maintaining Alaska's world-class trails. Their program, Alaska Trail Stewards, connects land managers with volunteers to help them better maintain trails. It also offers people a chance to give back to the trails they love.

Mountaineers Books donates many books to nonprofit recreation and conservation organizations. Our 1% for Trails campaign is one more way we can help fellow nonprofit organizations as we work together to get more people outside, to both enjoy and protect our wild public lands.

If you'd like to support Mountaineers Books and our nonprofit partnership programs, please visit our website to learn more or email mbooks@mountaineersbooks.org.

resources

LAND MANAGEMENT AGENCIES
NATIONAL FORESTS
Chugach National Forest
(See "contact information" on the Chugach
National Forest website for websites of indi-
vidual districts.)
161 East 1st Avenue, Door 8
Anchorage, AK 99501
(907) 743-9500
www.fs.usda.gov/chugach

Glacier Ranger District
PO Box 129
145 Forest Station Road
Girdwood, AK 99587
(907) 783-3242

Seward Ranger District
33599 Ranger Station Spur
    (mile marker 23.5)
Seward, AK 99664
(907) 288-3178

NATIONAL PARKS
Kenai Fjords National Park
PO Box 1727
Seward, AK 99664
(907) 422-0500
www.nps.gov/kefj

STATE PARKS
Alaska State Parks
550 W. 7th Avenue, Suite 1360
Anchorage, AK 99501
 (907) 269-8400
http://dnr.alaska.gov/parks/

Kenai Area Office
PO Box 1247
Soldotna, AK 99669
(907) 262-5581

Mat-Su Region
7278 East Bogard Road
Wasilla, AK 99654
(907) 745-3975
http://dnr.alaska.gov/parks/units/index
    .htm#matsu

Chugach State Park
18620 Seward Highway
Anchorage, Alaska 99516
(907) 345-5014
http://dnr.alaska.gov/parks/units/chugach/

Kachemak Bay State Park and
State Wilderness Park
Homer Ranger Station
Homer, AK
(907) 235-7024
http://dnr.alaska.gov/parks/units/kbay
    /kbayl.htm

OTHER LAND MANAGEMENT
CONTACTS
Alaska Department of
Natural Resources
http://dnr.alaska.gov/

Alaska Department of Transportation
and Public Facilities
http://dot.alaska.gov/creg/whittiertunnel
    /index.shtml

Alyeska Resort
1000 Arlberg Avenue
Girdwood, AK 99587
(907) 754-7669
http://alyeskaresort.com/

Arctic Valley Ski Area
PO Box 200546
Anchorage, AK 99520
(907) 428-1208 (ski hotline)
(907) 428-1269 (lodge information)
http://arcticvalley.org

Center for Alaskan Coastal Studies
708 Smokey Bay Way
Homer, AK 99603
(907) 235-6667
https://akcoastalstudies.org

Eagle River Nature Center
32750 Eagle River Road
Eagle River, AK 99577
(907) 694-2108
http://ernc.org

iSportsman, Joint Base Elmendorf-Richardson
(907) 552-8609
http://jber.isportsman.net

Kachemak Nordic Ski Club
PO Box 44
Homer, AK 99603
http://kachemaknordicskiclub.org

Kenai National Wildlife Refuge
PO Box 2139
Soldotna, AK 99669
(877) 285-5628
(907) 262-7021
http://fws.gov/refuge/Kenai/

Matanuska Greenbelt Trails
http://matanuska-greenbelt.org

Matanuska-Susitna Borough
350 East Dahlia Avenue
Palmer, AK 99645
(907) 861-7801
www.matsugov.us/

City of Whittier
PO Box 608
Whittier, AK 99693
(907) 336-1490
www.whiittieralaska.gov

AVALANCHE INFORMATION
Alaska Avalanche Information Center
http://alaskasnow.org

Anchorage Backcountry Center
http://anchorageavalanchecenter.org

Avalanche.org (Nationwide Avalanche Education)
http://avalanche.org

Chugach National Forest Avalanche Information Center
http://cnfaic.org

OTHER INFORMATION
Alaska Railroad
(800) 544-0552
(907) 265-2300
http://alaskarailroad.com

Alaska State Parks Pass
http://dnr.alaska.gov/parks/asp
    /passes.htm

Friends of Nike Site Summit
PO Box 102205
Anchorage, AK 99510
http://nikesitesummit.net

Learn to Return
5761 Silverado Way, Unit Q
Anchorage, AK 99518
(907) 563-4463
http://survivaltraining.com

Lifetime Adventures
PO Box 1205
Palmer, AK 99645
(907) 746-4644
http://lifetimeadventure.net

Mountaineering Club of Alaska
PO Box 243561
Anchorage, AK 99524
http://mtnclubak.org

Portage Glacier Cruises
(800) 544-2206
(907) 783-2687
http://portageglaciercruises.com

Recreation.gov
(877) 444-6777
(518) 885-3639 (international calls)
http://recreation.gov

Reindeer Farm
http://reindeerfarm.com

Reserve America
www.reserveamerica.com

Seward Chamber of Commerce & CVB
PO Box 749
Seward, AK 99664
(907) 224-8051
www.seward.com

Tippecanoe Rentals in Willow
(907) 355-6687

**CONSERVATION AND TRAIL
ORGANIZATIONS**
Alaska Native Plant Society
PO Box 141613
Anchorage, AK 99514
http://aknps.org

Alaska Trails
PO Box 100627
Anchorage, AK 99510
(907) 334-8049
www.alaska-trails.org

Audubon Alaska
431 West 7th Ave
Suite 101
Anchorage, AK 99501
(907) 276-7034
http://ak.audubon.org

Great Land Trust
PO Box 101272
Anchorage, AK 99510
(907) 278-4998
http://greatlandtrust.org

Leave No Trace
http://lnt.org

index

about the author

Lisa Maloney has lived in Alaska for more than thirty years. A former outdoors columnist for the *Anchorage Press*, she also covered a nationwide hiking and backpacking beat for About.com, served as senior editor at *Alaska* magazine, authored the award-winning travel guidebook *Moon Alaska*, and contributes outdoors and travel articles to a number of publications. Find her at www.maloneywrites.com, or follow her hiking adventures at www.hikingalaska.net and on Facebook, Instagram, and Twitter @HikingAlaska.

Twenty to

Crocheted
Purses

Anna Nikipirowicz

Search Press

First published in 2015

Search Press Limited
Wellwood, North Farm Road,
Tunbridge Wells, Kent TN2 3DR

Text copyright © Anna Nikipirowicz 2015

Photographs by Fiona Murray

Photographs and design copyright
© Search Press Ltd 2015

Print ISBN: 978-1-78221-194-5
ebook ISBN: 978-1-78126-252-8

Suppliers
If you have difficulty in obtaining any of the
materials and equipment mentioned in this book,
then please visit the Search Press website for
details of suppliers: www.searchpress.com

Printed in China

Dedication
*I would like to thank my partner David
for his constant love and support,
and Angela for everything.*

Contents

Introduction

Crocheting and accessorising are my passions and I am delighted to introduce my book, which combines both. From a delicate, lacy pouch to a sweet keyring purse, I have designed projects to suit many tastes, and I am sure that you will find plenty of lovely projects to get your hook stuck in to.

The emphasis in this book is on stunning design coupled with simplicity. I have kept the patterns fairly basic so that they are all relatively easy to make, creating designs to appeal to both beginners and more advanced crocheters. The variety in the designs is created by simple shaping rather than using difficult stitches. Some of the projects in this book are super quick – you can make them in just a few hours.

Yarn is such an amazing medium to work with – there are so many shades and textures available that we are truly spoiled for choice. In this book you will find plenty of yarn variety, with purses worked in silk, linen, pure wool and many exciting fibre mixes. Some of the projects are embellished with flowers and corsages, such as the Isabel purse. As an alternative, you can add a brooch back to the corsage and use it to add some 'oomph' to your favourite outfit.

Whether you make them for yourself or as gifts for family and friends, I hope you have as much fun crocheting the purses as I had designing them.

Crochet know-how

US and UK crochet terminology

The names for basic crochet stitches differ in the UK and the US. In all patterns, US terms are given first (see opposite), followed by the UK terms in brackets – for example, US single crochet is written as sc (UKdc), and US double crochet as dc (UKtr).

Yarn

Most yarns on the market today come ready wound in balls, but some come in hanks which need to be wound into balls beforehand to stop them from knotting. All yarns come in different weights and thicknesses.

I have used a variety of yarns for the purses which can be substituted, but it is important to check the weight and length of yarn you choose against the ones used in this book to ensure you have enough yarn to finish your projects. Synthetic yarns might be easier to wash, but natural fibres keep their shape a lot better for many years and are a lot nicer to work with.

Lace yarn (1–3-ply) is a very fine yarn, used mostly for delicate openwork. Some of the projects in this book use the yarn doubled to add thickness (this is noted in the pattern).

4-ply yarn (fingering) is a superfine yarn, used for most work producing lightweight fabric; 4-ply mercerised cotton is fantastic for crocheting as it does not split, defines each stitch beautifully and produces a durable fabric with amazing drape.

DK yarn (8-ply) is a medium weight yarn, and is the most commonly used. It can be used for most types of crocheting, from plain, lace and textured, producing medium weight garments.

Worsted/aran yarns (10-ply) are both slightly thicker than DK yarn. Worsted yarn is slightly lighter than aran, but both weights of yarn can be used on any of the purses that call for medium weight yarn. Worsted/aran yarn produces medium weight fabrics that are suitable for many crochet projects.

Tension

I have not given a specific tension for any of the projects, but the approximate completed size. It is not essential to achieve any particular tension on any of the items as they are accessories, so if they turn out a bit bigger or smaller it will not make much difference. However, the finished guide should provide a basic idea of what size the completed purse should be if you use yarn of a similar weight.

Crochet hooks

It is essential to work with a hook that is easy on your hands. Crochet hooks are made from aluminium, steel, plastic, bamboo and wood. I have always found wooden hooks wonderful to work with; however, it is best to experiment with different types to find one that suits you and offers comfort and control.

Other materials

I have used a range of clasps for the purses. They are produced by Prym and are widely available online. You will also need scraps of fabric for purse linings; a good pair of scissors for cutting fabric and ends of yarn; a tapestry needle for weaving in ends of yarn and sewing motifs on top of purses; and a standard household needle and thread for attaching the lining fabric to the insides of the purses. It may also be useful to have some iron-on medium-weight interfacing. You simply iron this on to the back of the fabric to stiffen it, and it will help your purse keep its shape.

Mattress stitch

Mattress stitch is very useful, as it makes a practically invisible and nicely flexible seam for joining pieces of crocheted fabric together.

1 With RS of work facing, insert a tapestry needle through a stitch in the bottom right corner, then across to the bottom left corner, then through both pieces again to secure firmly.

2 Take your needle back to the right edge and insert it a little further up, then across to catch a stitch on the left side.

3 Repeat step 2 to continue.

4 After every few stitches, gently pull the long end of the yarn to draw the stitches together so that the seam yarn disappears and is not visible on the right side of the crochet.

5 Fasten off yarn securely at the other end.

Yarns used for the purses

Lace (2-ply)

Rowan Fine Lace – 80% baby Suri alpaca, 20% merino wool fine.

Yardage: 50g ball/400m/437yd.

Rowan Kidsilk Haze – 70% mohair, 30% silk.

Yardage: 25g ball/210m/229yd.

4-ply yarn

Rowan Wool/Cotton 4-ply – 50% cotton, 50% merino wool.

Yardage: 50g/180m/197yd.

Rowan Cotton glace – 100% mercerised cotton.

Yardage: 50g/115m/125yd.

Double knitting (8-ply)

Rowan Felted Tweed DK – 50% merino wool, 25% alpaca, 25% viscose.

Yardage: 50g/175m/191yd.

Rowan Wool Cotton – 50% cotton, 50% merino wool.

Yardage: 50g/113m/123yd.

Rowan Pure Wool DK – 100% superwash wool.

Yardage: 50g/130m/142yd.

Rowan Pure Linen – 100% linen.

Yardage: 50g/130m/142yd.

Worsted/aran (10-ply)

Rowan Pure Wool worsted – 100% superwash wool.

Yardage: 100g/200m/219yd.

Rowan Creative Focus Worsted – 75% wool, 25% alpaca.

Yardage: 100g/200m/219yd.

Rowan Creative Linen – 50% linen, 50% cotton.

Yardage: 100g/200m/219yd.

Rowan Kid Classic – 70% lambswool, 22% kid mohair, 8% polyamide.

Yardage: 50g/140m/153yd.

Rowan Softknit Cotton – 92% cotton, 8% polyamide.

Yardage: 50g/105m/115yd.

Crochet Abbreviations

The abbreviations listed below are the most frequently used terms in the book. Any special abbreviations in a crochet pattern are explained on the relevant project page.

US	UK
sl st (slip stitch)	sl st (slip stitch)
ch st (chain stitch)	ch st (chain stitch)
ch sp (chain space)	ch sp (chain space)
sc (single crochet)	dc (double crochet)
hdc (half double crochet)	htr (half treble crochet)
dc (double crochet)	tr (treble crochet)
tr (treble crochet)	dtr (double treble crochet)
dtr (double treble crochet)	trtr (triple treble crochet)
skip	miss
yrh (yarn round hook)	yrh (yarn round hook)
beg (beginning)	beg (beginning)
rep (repeat)	rep (repeat)
sp/s (space(s))	sp/s (space(s))

Olivia

Materials:

4 x 50g balls of 4-ply mercerised cotton yarn –
 1 x light grey (A), 1 x heather (B), 1 x rose (C),
 1 x garnet (D), each 125yd/115m

Hook:

3.5mm (US E/4, UK 9) crochet hook

Notions:

Approx. 144 x small beads

Finished size:

Approx. 6in (15cm) wide and 3½in (9cm) high

Instructions:

Work beads into each sc (*UKdc*) on second row of colour A; beads are worked on WS of work.

With yarn A and 3.5mm (US E/4, UK 9) crochet hook, make 45 ch.

Row 1 (RS): 2 sc (*UKdc*) in second ch from hook, [1 sc (*UKdc*) in next 4 ch, skip 2 ch, 1 sc (*UKdc*) in next 4 ch, 3 sc (*UKdc*) in next ch] three times, 1 sc (*UKdc*) in next 4 ch, skip 2 ch, 1 sc (*UKdc*) in next 4 ch, 2 sc (*UKdc*) in last ch.

Row 2: 1 ch, 2 sc (*UKdc*) in base of ch, [1 sc (*UKdc*) in next 4 sts, skip 2 sts, 1 sc (*UKdc*) in next 4 sts, 3 sc (*UKdc*) in next st] three times, 1 sc (*UKdc*) in next 4 sts, skip 2 sts, 1 sc (*UKdc*) in next 4 sts, 2 sc (*UKdc*) in last st.

Row 2 forms the pattern.

Work in pattern following the stripe sequence as follows:

Rows 3 and 4: yarn B.

Rows 5 and 6: yarn C.

Rows 7 and 8: yarn D.

Rows 9 and 10 (beaded): yarn A.

Repeat stripe sequence four more times, ending with row 2 of yarn A repeat (beaded).

Making up

Fold work in three parts and secure sides by working a row of sc (*UKdc*) in yarn B, then continue with sc (*UKdc*) along top of inner edge of purse.

Watermelon

Materials:

4 x 100g balls of worsted yarn
(UK light aran) – 1 x deep
rose (A), 1 x white (B), 1 x
green (C), each 220yd/200m

Hook:

4.5mm (US 7, UK 7)
crochet hook

Notions:

Approx. 111 x small
black beads

1 x 6¾in (17cm) zip

Finished size:

Approx. 3½in (9cm) end to
end and 7½in (19cm) at the
widest point

Instructions:

Thread all the beads onto yarn A and with
4.5mm (US 7, UK 7) crochet hook make 6 hdc
(*UKhtr*) in adjustable ring. Join with a sl st to
first st.

Work a bead into every other hdc (*UKhtr*) on
rounds: 1, 3, 5, 7 and 9 only.

Round 1: 2 ch (count as 1 hdc (*UKhtr*)), 1 hdc
(*UKhtr*) into base of 2 ch, *2 hdc (*UKhtr*) in next
st, rep from * to end, sl st into second ch at beg
of round (12 sts).

Round 2: 2 ch (count as 1 hdc (*UKhtr*)), 1 hdc
(*UKhtr*) into base of 2 ch, *1 hdc (*UKhtr*) in next
st, 2 hdc (*UKhtr*) in next st, rep from * to last st,
1 hdc (*UKhtr*) into last st, sl st into second ch at
beg of round (18 sts).

Round 3: 2 ch (count as 1 hdc (*UKhtr*)), 1 hdc
(*UKhtr*) in next st, 2 hdc (*UKhtr*) in next st, *1
hdc (*UKhtr*) in next 2 sts, 2 hdc (*UKhtr*) in next
st, rep from * to end, sl st into second ch at beg
of round (24 sts).

Round 4: 2 ch (count as 1 hdc (*UKhtr*)), 1 hdc
(*UKhtr*) in next 2 sts, 2 hdc (*UKhtr*) in next st, *1
hdc (*UKhtr*) in next 3 sts, 2 hdc (*UKhtr*) in next
st, rep from * to end, sl st into second ch at beg
of round (30 sts).

Round 5: 2 ch (count as 1 hdc (*UKhtr*)), 1 hdc
(*UKhtr*) in next 2 sts, 2 hdc (*UKhtr*) in next st, *1
hdc (*UKhtr*) in next 3 sts, 2 hdc (*UKhtr*) in next st,
rep from * to last 2 sts, 1 hdc (*UKhtr*) in next 2
sts, sl st into second ch at beg of round (37 sts).

Round 6: 2 ch (count as 1 hdc (*UKhtr*)), 1 hdc
(*UKhtr*) in next 2 sts, 2 hdc (*UKhtr*) in next st, *1

hdc (*UKhtr*) in next 3 sts, 2 hdc (*UKhtr*) in next
st, rep from * to last st, 1 hdc (*UKhtr*), sl st into
second ch at beg of round (46 sts).

Round 7: 2 ch (count as 1 hdc (*UKhtr*)), 1 hdc
(*UKhtr*) in next 2 sts, 2 hdc (*UKhtr*) in next st, *1
hdc (*UKhtr*) in next 3 sts, 2 hdc (*UKhtr*) in next st,
rep from * to last 2 sts, 1 hdc (*UKhtr*) in next 2
sts, sl st into second ch at beg of round (57 sts).

Round 8: 2 ch (count as 1 hdc (*UKhtr*)), 1 hdc
(*UKhtr*) in next 2 sts, 2 hdc (*UKhtr*) in next st, *1
hdc (*UKhtr*) in next 3 sts, 2 hdc (*UKhtr*) in next
st, rep from * to last st, 1 hdc (*UKhtr*), sl st into
second ch at beg of round (71 sts).

Round 9: 2 ch (count as 1 hdc (*UKhtr*)), 1 hdc
(*UKhtr*) in next 2 sts, 2 hdc (*UKhtr*) in next st, *1
hdc (*UKhtr*) in next 3 sts, 2 hdc (*UKhtr*) in next st,
rep from * to last 3 sts, 1 hdc (*UKhtr*) in next 3
sts, sl st into second ch at beg of round (88 sts).

Round 10: 2 ch (count as 1 hdc (*UKhtr*)), 1 hdc
(*UKhtr*) in every st to end, sl st into second ch at
beg of round. Change to yarn B.

Round 11: 2 ch (count as 1 hdc (*UKhtr*)), 1 hdc
(*UKhtr*) in every st to end, sl st into second ch at
beg of round. Change to yarn C.

Round 12: 2 ch (count as 1 hdc (*UKhtr*)), 1 hdc
(*UKhtr*) in every st to end, sl st into second ch at
beg of round.

Fasten off yarn.

Making up

Weave in ends. Fold purse in half and stitch for
2in (5cm) up each side. Insert zip.

Karen

Materials:
1 x 50g ball of worsted (UK light aran) yarn in burgundy, 153yd/140m

8¼ x 13in (21 x 33cm) piece of lining fabric

Hook:
4.5mm (US 7, UK 7) crochet hook

Notions:
1 x 6¾in (17cm) zip

Finished size:
Approx. 6¼ x 8in (16 x 20cm)

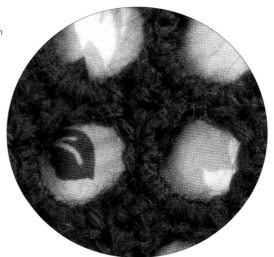

Instructions (make 2):
With 4.5mm (US 7, UK 7) crochet hook make 32 ch.

Row 1: 1 sc (*UKdc*) into second ch from hook, 1 sc (*UKdc*) into every ch to end (31 sts).

Row 2: 1 ch, 1 sc (*UKdc*) in next 2 sts, [5 ch, skip 2 sts, 1 sc (*UKdc*) in next 3 sts] five times, 5 ch, skip 2 sts, 1 sc (*UKdc*) in last 2 sts.

Row 3: 1 ch, 1 sc (*UKdc*) in next st, skip 1 st, [5 sc (*UKdc*) in next ch sp, skip 1 st, 1 sc (*UKdc*) in next st, skip 1 st] five times, 5 sc (*UKdc*) in next ch sp, skip 1 st, 1 sc (*UKdc*) in last st.

Row 4: 6 ch (counts as 1 tr (*UKdtr*) and 2 ch), skip first 2 sts, 1 sc (*UKdc*) in next 3 sts, [5 ch, skip 3 sts, 1 sc (*UKdc*) in next 3 sts] five times, 2 ch, 1 tr (*UKdtr*) in last st.

Row 5: 1 ch, 1 sc (*UKdc*) in first tr (*UKdtr*), 2 sc (*UKdc*) in next 2-ch sp, skip 1 st, 1 sc (*UKdc*) in next st, [5 sc (*UKdc*) in next 5-ch sp, skip 1 st, 1 sc (*UKdc*) in next st, skip 1 st] five times, 2 sc (*UKdc*) in last ch sp, 1 sc (*UKdc*) in fourth ch of 6-ch at beg of previous round.

Row 6: 1 ch, 1 sc (*UKdc*) in next 2 sts, skip 1 st, [5 ch, skip next 3 sts, 1 sc (*UKdc*) in next 3 sts] five times, 5 ch, skip next 3 sts, 1 sc (*UKdc*) in next 2 sts.

Rep rows 3 to 6 twice more, then rows 3 to 5 once.

Next row: 1 ch, 1 sc (*UKdc*) in next 3 sts, skip 1 st, *5 sc (*UKdc*) in next 5 sts, skip 1 st, rep from * to last 3 sts, 1 sc (*UKdc*) in next 3 sts.

Fasten off yarn.

Strap
With 4.5mm (US 7, UK 7) crochet hook, make 44 ch.

Row 1: 1 sc (*UKdc*) in second ch from hook, 1 sc (*UKdc*) in each st to end (43 sts).

Row 2: 1 ch, 1 sc (*UKdc*) in every st to end.

Rep row 2 once more.

Fasten off yarn.

Making up
With WS facing, pin the strap into position at the right side of the purse and, using mattress stitch, join the back and front pieces together along three sides, trapping the strap in the seam. Insert the zip into the top of the purse and sew in the lining.

Aria

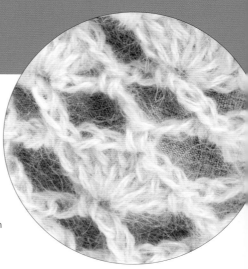

Materials:

- 1 x 25g ball of mohair and silk lace/2-ply yarn in white (A), 229yd/210m
- 1 x 50g ball of alpaca and merino lace/2-ply yarn in white (B), 437yd/400m
- 1 x round piece of lining fabric 5½in (14cm) in diameter and 1 x rectangular piece 6 x 12¼in (15 x 31cm)

Hook:

4mm (US G/6, UK 8) crochet hook

Notions:

2 x large beads

Finished size:

Approx. 5¼in (13cm) in diameter and 7½in (19cm) high

Pattern note: Use one strand of A and one of B held together throughout.

Instructions:

With yarn A and B held together and 4mm (US G/6, UK 8) crochet hook make 6 ch, join with sl st to first ch to form a ring.

Round 1: 1 ch, work 12 sc (UKdc) into ring, sl st to first st (12 sts).

Round 2: 1 ch, 2 sc (UKdc) in every st to end, sl st to first st (24 sts).

Round 3: 1 ch, *1 sc (UKdc) in next st, 2 sc (UKdc) in next st, rep from * to end, sl st to first st (36 sts).

Round 4 and 5: 1 ch, 1 sc (UKdc) in every st to end, sl st to first st.

Round 6: 1 ch, *1 sc (UKdc) in next 2 sts, 2 sc (UKdc) in next st, rep from * to end, sl st to first st (48 sts).

Round 7: 1 ch, 1 sc (UKdc) in every st to end, sl st to first st.

Round 8: 1 ch, *1 sc (UKdc) in next 3 sts, 2 sc (UKdc) in next st, rep from * to end, sl st to first st (60 sts).

Round 9: As round 7.

Round 10: 1 ch, *1 sc (UKdc) in next 4 sts, 2 sc (UKdc) in next st, rep from * to end, sl st to first st (72 sts).

Round 11: As round 7.

Round 12: 1 ch, *1 sc (UKdc) in next 5 sts, 2 sc (UKdc) in next st, rep from * to end, sl st to first st (84 sts).

Round 13: As round 7.

Start of lace pattern

Round 1: 3 ch, (counts as 1 dc (UKtr)), 2 dc (UKtr) in st at the base of 3 ch, skip 2 sts, 1 sc (UKdc) in next st, 5 ch, skip 5 sts, 1 sc (UKdc) in next st, *skip 2 sts, 5 dc (UKtr) in next st, skip 2 sts, 1 sc (UKdc) in next st, 5 ch, skip 5 sts, 1 sc (UKdc) in next st, rep from * to last 2 sts, skip 2 sts, 2 dc (UKtr) in st at base of beg 3 ch, sl st to third ch at beg of round.

Round 2: 1 ch, 1 sc (UKdc) in first dc (UKtr), *5 ch, 1 sc (UKdc) in next ch sp, 5 ch, 1 sc (UKdc) in third of next 5 dc (UKtr), rep from * five times more, 5 ch, 1 sc (UKdc) in next ch sp, 5 ch, sl st to first sc (UKdc).

Round 3: *5 ch, 1 sc (UKdc) in next ch sp, 5 dc (UKtr) in next dc, 1 sc (UKdc) in next ch sp, rep from * six times more, 3 ch, sl st to third ch at beg of round.

Round 4: 1 ch, 1 sc (UKdc) in base of 1 ch, *5 ch, 1 sc (UKdc) in third of next 5 dc (UKtr), 5 ch, 1 sc (UKdc) in next ch sp, rep from * five times more, 5 ch, 1 sc (UKdc) in third of next 5 dc (UKtr), 5 ch, sl st to first sc (UKdc).

Round 5: 3 ch (counts as 1 dc (UKtr)), 2 dc (UKtr) in sc (UKdc) at base of ch, 1 sc (UKdc) in next ch sp, ch 5, 1 sc (UKdc) in next ch sp, *5 dc (UKtr) in next sc (UKdc), 1 sc (UKdc) in next ch sp, 5 ch, 1 sc (UKdc) in next ch sp, rep from * five times more, 2 dc (UKtr) in st at base of 3 ch, sl st to third ch at beg of round.

Rep rounds 2–5 three more times, then rounds 2 and 3 once. Fasten off yarn.

Ties (make 2)

With yarn A and B held together and 4mm (US G/6, UK 8) crochet hook, make 60 ch.

Fasten off yarn.

Making up

Weave in all loose ends and sew the lining in place, leaving a 1cm (½in) seam allowance. Thread ties (from opposite directions) into round 6 of the pattern from the top, bring each pair of ends out (again at opposite sides), thread the beads on and tie a knot in each end.

Music b

Freya

Materials:

1 x 50g ball of DK yarn in purple (A), 142yd/130m

1 x 25g ball of lace/2-ply yarn in light purple (B), 229yd/210m

Hook:

4mm (US G/6, UK 8) crochet hook

Notions:

1 x large button

1 x 7in (18cm) zip

Finished size:

Approx. 5½in (14cm) in diameter

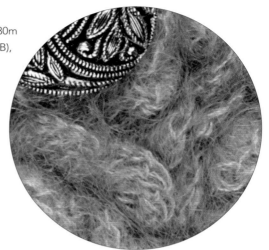

Instructions (make 2):

With yarn A and 4mm (US G/6, UK 8) crochet hook, make an adjustable ring and work 10 dc (*UKtr*) into ring, join with sl st to first st (10 sts).

Round 1: 3 ch (counts as 1 dc (*UKtr*)), *2 dc (*UKtr*) in next st, rep from * to end, 1 dc (*UKtr*) in base of beg ch, sl st to third of 3-ch at beg of round (20 sts).

Round 2: As round 1 (40 sts).

Round 3: 3 ch (counts as 1 dc (*UKtr*)), [2 dc (*UKtr*) in next st, 1 dc (*UKtr*) in next st] eight times, [1 dc (*UKtr*) in next st, 2 dc (*UKtr*) in next st, 1 dc (*UKtr*) in next st] four times, [2 dc (*UKtr*) in next st, 1 dc (*UKtr*) in next st] five times, 2 dc (*UKtr*) in next st, sl st to third of ch-3 at beg of round (58 sts).

Round 4: 3 ch (counts as 1 dc (*UKtr*)), *1 dc (*UKtr*) in next 2 sts, 2 dc (*UKtr*) in next st, rep from * to last st, 1 dc (*UKtr*) in last st, sl st to third of 3-ch at beg of round (77 sts).

Round 5: 3 ch (counts as 1 dc (*UKtr*)), 1 dc (*UKtr*) in each st to end, sl st to third of ch-3 at beg of round.

Flower

With yarn B and 4mm (US G/6, UK 8) crochet hook, make 162 ch.

Row 1: Skip 7 ch (counts as 1 dc (*UKtr*) and 4 ch), 1 dc (*UKtr*) in next ch, *ch 4, 1 dc (*UKtr*) in next ch, rep from * to end.

Row 2: *[1 dc, 4 dc (*UKtr*)] into next 4-ch sp, rep from * until all spaces have been worked.

Fasten off yarn.

Making up

Press front and back pieces lightly with an iron. Wind the flower in a spiral, securing it to the front of the purse as you wind. Attach the button to the centre of the flower. Join the front and back pieces together leaving a 7in (18cm) gap. Weave in all loose ends and then sew the zip into the gap.

Tate

Materials:
4 x 50g balls of DK yarn – 1 x ginger (A), 1 x avocado (B), 1 x yellow (C), 1 x light brown (D), each 191yd/175m

Hook:
3.75mm (US F/5) crochet hook

Notions:
1 x magnetic flex frame kiss clasp, approx. 4¾in (12cm)

Finished size:
Approx. 3½ x 5¼in (9 x 13.5cm)

Instructions:
With yarn A and 3.75mm (US F/5) crochet hook, make 64 ch.

Row 1: Skip 3 ch (counts as 1 dc (*UKtr*)), 2 dc (*UKtr*) in next ch, *skip 3 ch, 1 sc (*UKdc*) in next ch, 3 ch, 1 dc (*UKtr*) in next 3 ch, rep from * to last 4 ch, skip 3 ch, 1 sc (*UKdc*) in last ch. Change to yarn B.

Row 2: 3 ch (counts as 1 dc (*UKtr*)), 2 dc (*UKtr*) in first sc (*UKdc*), *skip 3 dc (*UKtr*), 1 sc (*UKdc*) in first of 3-ch, 3 ch, 3 dc (*UKtr*) in next 2-ch sp, rep from * to last 2 dc (*UKtr*), skip 2 dc (*UKtr*), 1 sc (*UKdc*) in top chain of previous round.

Rep row 2 eleven more times, changing colour on every row to yarn C and D then A, B, C and D again, ending last row with colour A.

Fasten off yarn.

Making up
With WS facing, fold the work in half and turn it around, so that the sides are now at the top. Stitch the magnetic flex frame into place by turning a hem over it at the purse opening, and then sew up the sides. You may wish to line the inside of the purse with a piece of felt.

Birdie

Materials:

3 x 100g balls of worsted weight yarn (UK light aran) – 1 x white (A), 1 x green (B), 1 x teal (C), each 220yd/200m

3 x skeins of tapestry wool – 1 x brown (D), 1 x turquoise (E), 1 x yellow (F)

Hooks:

4.5mm (US 7, UK 7) crochet hook

4mm (US G/6, UK 8) crochet hook

Notions:

1 x 7in (18cm) zip

Finished size:

Approx. 4½ x 7½in (11.5 x 19cm)

Instructions (make 2):

With yarn A and 4.5mm (US 7, UK 7) crochet hook, make 35 ch.

Row 1: 2 sc (*UKdc*) into third ch from hook (first 2 ch count as 1 sc (*UKdc*), *skip 1 ch, 2 sc (*UKdc*) in next ch, rep from * to end.

Row 2: 2 ch (count as 1 sc (*UKdc*)), *skip next st, 2 sc (*UKdc*) in next st, rep from * to end.

Repeat row 2 twenty-one more times, work should measure 4½in (11.5cm).

Fasten off yarn.

Bird

With yarn C and 4mm (US G/6, UK 8) crochet hook, work 6 sc (*UKdc*) into adjustable ring, join with sl st to first sc (*UKdc*).

Round 1: 1 ch, 1 sc (*UKdc*) in base of ch, *2 sc (*UKdc*) in next st, rep from * to end, join with sl st to first st (11 sts).

Round 2: 1 ch, 1 sc (*UKdc*) in base of ch, 1 sc (*UKdc*) in next 3 sts, 2 hdc (*UKhtr*) in next st, [1 hdc (*UKhtr*), 1 dc (*UKtr*)] in next st, 2 dc (*UKtr*) in next st, 3 ch, sl st in the base of last dc (*UKtr*), 1 sc (*UKdc*) into next 2 sts, [2 hdc (*UKhtr*) into next st] twice, join with sl st to first st.

Wing

With yarn E and 4mm (US G/6, UK 8) crochet hook, make 7 ch.

Row 1: 1 dc (*UKtr*) into fourth ch from hook, 1 dc (*UKtr*) in next ch, 1 hdc (*UKhtr*) in next ch, 1 sc (*UKdc*) in next ch.

Fasten off yarn.

Beak

With yarn F and 4mm (US G/6, UK 8) crochet hook, make 2 sc (*UKdc*) in 2 sts on the curved head side of bird.

Fasten off yarn.

Leaf (make 6)

With yarn B and 4mm (US G/6, UK 8) crochet hook, make 7 ch.

Row 1: 1 sc (*UKdc*) into second ch from hook, 1 hdc (*UKhtr*) in next ch, 1 dc (*UKtr*) in next ch, 1 hdc (*UKhtr*) in next ch, 1 dc (*UKtr*) in next ch, 1 sc (*UKdc*) in next ch.

Fasten off yarn.

Making up

With WS together and using mattress stitch, sew three sides of the back and front together. Using yarn D and the photograph as a guide, embroider on RS of work a curling branch stretching to the back of the purse. Sew the leaves onto the branch (three at the front, two at the back).

Attach the wing to the bird and embroider an eye using yarn A. Sew the bird into place on the branch. Insert the zip into the top of the purse and attach a leaf to the zip loop by making 8 ch.

Cherry

Materials:

3 x 50g balls of worsted yarn (UK light aran) – 1 x smoke (A), 1 x cherry red (B), 1 x green (C), each 153yd/140m

Hook:

4mm (US G/6, UK 8) crochet hook

Notions:

1 x snap fastener

Small amount of toy stuffing

Finished size:

Approx. 4in (10cm) high and 6in (15cm) at the widest point

Instructions:

With yarn A and 4mm (US G/6, UK 8) crochet hook, make 18 ch.

Round 1: 2 sc (*UKdc*) in second ch from hook, 1 sc (*UKdc*) in next 15 ch, 4 sc (*UKdc*) in next ch, working on the other side of ch, 1 sc (*UKdc*) in next 15 ch, 2 sc (*UKdc*) in last ch, sl st to first st (38 sts).

Round 2: 1 ch, 2 sc (*UKdc*) in next 2 sts, 1 sc (*UKdc*) in next 15 sts, 2 sc (*UKdc*) in next 4 sts, 1 sc (*UKdc*) in next 15 sts, 2 sc (*UKdc*) in next 2 sts, sl st to first st (46 sts).

Round 3: 1 ch, [1 sc (*UKdc*) in next st, 2 sc (*UKdc*) in next st] twice, 1 sc (*UKdc*) in next 15 sts, [2 sc (*UKdc*) in next st, 1 sc (*UKdc*) in next st] four times, 1 sc (*UKdc*) in next 15 sts, [2 sc (*UKdc*) in next st, 1 sc (*UKdc*) in next st] twice, sl st to first st (54 sts).

Round 4: 1 ch, [1 sc (*UKdc*) in next st, 2 sc (*UKdc*) in next st] three times, 1 sc (*UKdc*) in next 15 sts, [2 sc (*UKdc*) in next st, 1 sc (*UKdc*) in next st] six times, 1 sc (*UKdc*) in next 15 sts, [2 sc (*UKdc*) in next st, 1 sc (*UKdc*) in next st] three times, sl st to first st (66 sts).

Round 5: 1 ch, sc2tog (*UKdc2tog*), 1 sc (*UKdc*) in every st to end, sl st to first st (65 sts).

Rounds 6–8: 1 ch, 1 sc (*UKdc*) in every st to end, sl st to first st.

Round 9: 1 ch, *1 sc (*UKdc*) in next 5 sts, sc2tog (*UKdc2tog*), rep from * to last 2 sts, 1 sc (*UKdc*) in next 2 sts, sl st to first st (56 sts).

Rounds 10–13: 1 ch, 1 sc (*UKdc*) in every st to end, sl st to first st.

Round 14: 1 ch, *1 sc (*UKdc*) in next 4 sts, sc2tog (*UKdc2tog*), rep from * to last 2 sts, 1 sc (*UKdc*) in next 2 sts, sl st to first st (47 sts).

Rounds 15–18: 1 ch, 1 sc (*UKdc*) in every st to end, sl st to first st.

Round 19: 1 ch, sc2tog (*UKdc2tog*), 1 sc (*UKdc*) in next 3 sts, sc2tog (*UKdc2tog*), 1 sc (*UKdc*) in next 11 sts, sc2tog (*UKdc2tog*), [1 sc (*UKdc*) in next 3 sts, sc2tog (*UKdc2tog*)] twice, 1 sc (*UKdc*) in next 11 sts, sc2tog (*UKdc2tog*), 1 sc (*UKdc*) in next 4 sts, sl st to first st (41 sts).

Rounds 20–29: 1 ch, 1 sc (*UKdc*) in every st to end, sl st to first st.

Fasten off yarn.

Cherries (make 2)

With yarn B and 4mm (US G/6, UK 8) crochet hook, make 4 ch, sl st to first ch to form a ring.

Round 1: 1 ch, 6 sc (*UKdc*) into ring, sl st to first st (6 sts).

Round 2: 1 ch, 2 sc (*UKdc*) in every st to end, sl st to first st (12 sts).

Rounds 3 and 4: 1 ch, 1 sc (*UKdc*) in every st to end, sl st to first st.

Round 5: 1 ch, *sc2tog (*UKdc2tog*), rep from * to end, sl st to first st (6 sts).

Fill cherry with toy stuffing.

Round 6: 1 ch, *sc2tog (*UKdc2tog*), rep from * to end, sl st to first st (3 sts).

Fasten off yarn.

Leaf (make 2)

With yarn C and 4mm (US G/6, UK 8) crochet hook, make 8 ch.

Row 1: 1 sc (*UKdc*) into second ch from hook, 1 hdc (*UKhtr*) in next ch, 1 dc (*UKtr*) in next ch, 1 tr (*UKdtr*) in next ch, 1 dc (*UKtr*) in next ch, 1 hdc (*UKhtr*) in next ch, 1 sc (*UKdc*) in next ch.

Fasten off.

Stem (make 2)

With yarn C held double and 4mm (US G/6, UK 8) crochet hook, make 5 ch, fasten off yarn.

Attach the stems to the cherries and leaves.

Making up

Weave in all loose ends. Fold the top of the purse over (around 1in (2.5cm)) to create a cuff.

Attach the leaves to the cuff, using the photograph as a guide. Sew the snap fastener to the inside of the purse at the centre top.

Lottie

Materials:

1 x 50g ball of 4-ply yarn in red, 197yd/180m

2 x pieces of fabric for lining, approx. 4in (10cm) in diameter (optional)

Hook:

3.5mm (US E/4, UK 9) crochet hook

Notions:

1 x rounded purse clasp approx. 3¼in (8cm) wide

Finished size:

Approx. 4¾in (12cm) at the widest point and 4in (10cm) in height

Instructions (make 2):

With 3.5mm (US E/4, UK 9) crochet hook make 5 ch, join with sl st to first ch to form a ring.

Round 1: 3 ch (counts as 1 dc (UKtr)), 1 dc (UKtr) into ring, *1 ch, 2 dc (UKtr) into ring, rep from * four more times, 1 ch, sl st in top of 3 ch.

Round 2: sl st to first dc (UKtr) and ch sp, 3 ch (counts as 1 dc (UKtr)), [1 dc (UKtr), 1 ch, 2 dc (UKtr)] into same sp, 1 ch, *[2dc (UKtr), 1 ch, 2 dc (UKtr)] into next ch sp, 1 ch, rep from * four more times, sl st in top of 3 ch.

Round 3: sl st to first dc (UKtr) and ch sp, 3 ch (counts as 1 dc (UKtr)), 2 dc (UKtr) into same ch sp, 1 ch, *3 dc (UKtr) into next ch sp, 1 ch, rep from * to end, sl st in top of 3 ch.

Round 4: sl st to next 2 dc (UKtr) and ch sp, 3 ch (counts as 1 dc (UKtr)), 2 dc (UKtr) into same ch sp, 1 ch, *3 dc (UKtr) into next ch sp, 1 ch, rep from * to end, sl st in top of 3 ch.

Round 5: sl st to next 2 dc (UKtr) and ch sp, 3 ch (counts as 1 dc (UKtr)), 1 dc (UKtr) into same ch sp, 1 ch, *[2dc (UKtr), 1 ch, 2 dc (UKtr)] into next ch sp, 1 ch, rep from * five more times, 2 dc (UKtr) into next ch sp.

Fasten off yarn.

Shell edge

With RS facing, attach yarn to top of 3 ch at beg of last round, 1 ch, *6 dc (UKtr) into next ch sp, 1 sc (UKdc) into next ch sp, rep from * five more times, 6 dc (UKtr) into next ch sp, 1 sc (UKdc) to top of last dc (UKtr) from previous round.

Making up

Weave in all loose ends. Attach the narrower parts of the circle to the purse clasp and sew together around the shell edging. Sew the lining to the inside of the purse, leaving a ½in (1cm) seam allowance.

Bobbles

Materials:

1 x 100g ball of worsted yarn (UK light aran) in gold, 219yd/200m

Hook:

4mm (US G/6, UK 8) crochet hook

Notions:

1 x rounded purse clasp approx. 3¼in (8½cm) wide

Finished size:

Approx. 5in (13cm) wide and 6in (15cm) high

Special abbreviations:

Tr5tog (UKdtr5tog) cluster: [yrh twice and insert into st, yrh and draw a loop through, yrh and draw through first 2 loops on hook, yrh and draw through next 2 loops on hook] rep four times all in the same st, yrh and draw a loop through all 6 loops on hook.

Tr6tog (UKdtr6tog) cluster: [yrh twice and insert into st, yrh and draw a loop through, yrh and draw through first 2 loops on hook, yrh and draw through next 2 loops on hook] rep five times all in the same st, yrh and draw a loop through all 7 loops on hook.

Instructions (make 2):

With 4mm (US G/6, UK 8) crochet hook make 20 ch.

Row 1: Tr5tog (UKdtr5tog) in fourth ch from hook, *2 ch, skip 1 ch, 1 sc (UKdc) in next ch, *2 ch, skip 1 ch, tr6tog (UKdtr6tog) in next ch, rep from * to end.

Row 2: 2 ch, 1 sc (UKdc) in base of ch, 2 ch, tr5tog (UKdtr5tog) in next sc (UKdc), 2 ch, 1 sc (UKdc) in top of next cluster, *2 ch, tr6tog (UKdtr6tog) in next sc (UKdc), 2 ch, 1 sc (UKdc) in top of next cluster, rep from * to end.

Row 3: 3 ch, tr6tog (UKdtr6tog) in base of 3-ch, *2 ch, 1 sc (UKdc) in top of next cluster, 2 ch, tr6tog (UKdtr6tog) in next sc (UKdc), rep from * to end.

Repeat rows 2 and 3 twice more, then row 2 once.

Start of top shaping

Row 1: 1 ch, *2 sc (UKdc) in 2-ch sp, 1 sc (UKdc) in top of next cluster, skip 2 ch and 1 sc (UKdc), rep from * to end (12 sts).

Row 2: 1 ch, 1 sc (UKdc) in each st to end.

Rep row 2 twice more.

Row 5: 1 ch, sc2tog (UKdc2tog), 1 sc (UKdc) in each st to last 2 sts, sc2tog (UKdc2tog) (10 sts).

Rep row 2 once more.

Rep row 5 (8 sts).

Rep row 2.

Fasten off yarn.

Making up

Using mattress stitch and with WS together, sew the front and back pieces together along the two sides and the bottom of the purse. Turn it through, then attach the clasp to the top. Attach a lining to the inside of the purse if desired.

Katie

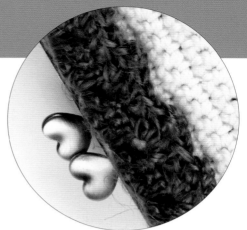

Materials:

1 x 50g ball of DK yarn in white (A), 123yd/113m
1 x 50g ball of DK yarn in green (B), 142yd/130m/

Hook:

3.5mm (US E/4, UK 9) crochet hook

Notions:

1 x purse frame approx. 6in (15cm)

Finished size:

Approx. 6½in (17cm) wide x 3in (8cm) high x 2in (5cm) deep

Instructions:

With yarn A and 3.5mm (US E/4, UK 9) crochet hook, make 41 ch.

Row 1: 1 sc (*UKdc*) into second ch from hook, 1 sc (*UKdc*) into every ch to end (40 sts).

Row 2: 1 ch, 1 sc (*UKdc*) in every st to end.

Rep row 2 five more times.

Row 8: 1 ch, sc2tog (*UKdc2tog*), 1 sc (*UKdc*) in every st to last 2 sts, sc2tog (*UKdc2tog*) (38 sts).

Rows 9–11: As row 8 (32 sts).

Row 12: 1 ch, 1 sc (*UKdc*) in every st to end.

Rep row 12 seventeen more times.

Row 30: 1 ch, 2 sc (*UKdc*) in next st, 1 sc (*UKdc*) in every st to last st, 2 sc (*UKdc*) in last st (34 sts).

Rows 31–33: As row 30 (40 sts).

Row 34: 1 ch, 1 sc (*UKdc*) in every st to end.

Rep row 34 six more times.

Fasten off yarn.

Sides (make 2)

With yarn A and 3.5mm (US E/4, UK 9) crochet hook, make 11 ch.

Row 1: 1 sc (*UKdc*) into second ch from hook, 1 sc (*UKdc*) in every st to end (10 sts).

Row 2: 1 ch, 1 sc (*UKdc*) in every st to end.

Rep row 2 once more.

Row 4: 1 ch, sc2tog (*UKdc2tog*), 1 sc (*UKdc*) in every st to last 2 sts, sc2tog (*UKdc2tog*) (8 sts).

Rep row 4 three more times (2 sts).

Fasten off yarn.

Edging (make 2)

With yarn B and 3.5mm (US E/4, UK 9) crochet hook, make 31 ch.

Row 1: 1 dc (*UKtr*) into fourth ch from hook, *2 ch, skip 2 ch, 2 dc (*UKtr*) into next ch, rep from * to end.

Row 2: *[2 dc (*UKtr*), 2 ch, 2 dc (*UKtr*)] all into next 2-ch sp, rep from * until every 2-ch sp has been worked, sl st to last st at beg of previous round.

Row 3: As row 2.

Fasten off yarn.

Making up

With RS facing, fold the main body of the purse in half and, using mattress stitch, sew the side pieces into the lower side opening on both sides of the purse, then continue up the sides to the top. Turn through. Block the edging by pressing it gently with an iron, and sew it to the top of the purse. Stitch the purse frame to the purse. If desired, you can line the front and back of the purse, leaving the sides free.

Evie

Materials:

1 x 50g ball of worsted yarn (UK light aran) in walnut (A), 115yd/105m

1 x 25g ball of mohair and silk lace/2-ply yarn in white (B), 229yd/210m

1 x 50g ball of alpaca and merino lace/2-ply yarn in white (C), 437yd/400m

Hook:

4mm (US G/6, UK 8) crochet hook

Notions:

5 x large assorted beads

1 x 6¾in (17cm) purse clasp

Finished size:

Approx. 4 x 6¾in (10 x 17cm)

Instructions:

With yarn A and 4mm (US G/6, UK 8) crochet hook, make 30 ch.

Row 1: 1 hdc (*UKhtr*) in third ch from hook, 1 hdc (*UKhtr*) in every ch to end. (28 sts).

Row 2: 2 ch, 1 hdc (*UKhtr*) in every st to end.

Repeat row 2 until work measures 8in (20cm).

Fasten off yarn.

Flowers (make 5)

With yarns B and C held together and 4mm (US G/6, UK 8) crochet hook, make 5 ch, join with sl st to first ch to form a ring.

Round 1: 5 ch (counts as 1 dc (*UKtr*) and 2 ch), 1 dc (*UKtr*) into ring, [2 ch, 1 dc (*UKtr*) into ring] 5 times, 2 ch, sl st to third ch of 5-ch at beg of round.

Round 2: [1 hdc (*UKhtr*), 2 dc (*UKtr*), 1 hdc (*UKhtr*), sl st to next dc (*UKtr*)] into every 2-ch space.

Fasten off yarn.

Making up

Press the main piece of the purse gently with an iron, then fold it in half so the RS is facing you. Using the photograph as a guide, sew the flowers to the right side of the purse and sew the beads to the flower centres. Then attach the clasp to the purse. Using mattress stitch, join together the side openings below the clasp on both sides. Attach a lining to the inside if desired.

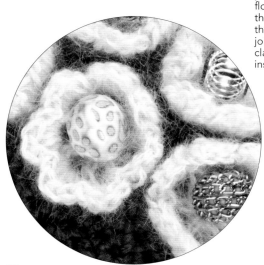

Anna

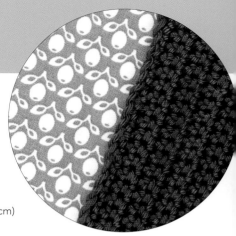

Materials:

1 x 50g ball of mercerised cotton in blackcurrant (A), 125yd/115m

Oddments of mercerised cotton for cross stitch –

1 x lavender (B), 1 x garnet (C), 1 x rose (D), 1 x white (E), 1 x light green (F), 1 x ivy (G)

1 x 7½in x 12¼in (19cm x 31cm) fabric for lining (optional)

Hook:

3.5mm (US E/4, UK 9) crochet hook

Notions:

2 x snap fasteners

Finished size:

Approx. 4 x 7in (10 x 18cm)

Instructions:

With yarn A and 3.5mm (US E/4, UK 9) crochet hook, make 38 ch.

Row 1: 1 sc (*UKdc*) into second ch from hook, 1 sc (*UKdc*) into every ch to end (37 sts).

Row 2: 1 ch, 1 sc (*UKdc*) in every st to end.

Rep row 2 until work measures 11¾in (30cm).

Fasten off yarn.

Weave in all loose ends. Press work lightly with an iron, fold 4in (10cm) of the lower part up with RS facing, and stitch the sides together using mattress stitch.

Now start working the design from the chart below on the 4in (10cm) purse flap. Starting on the second row and 24th stitch from the bottom right corner, start cross stitching the design on row 1 of the chart (bottom of leaf).

Making up

When the cross stitch design is completed, turn the purse inside out and sew in the lining, leaving a 1cm (½in) seam allowance. Turn through and attach the snap fasteners to either corner of the flap.

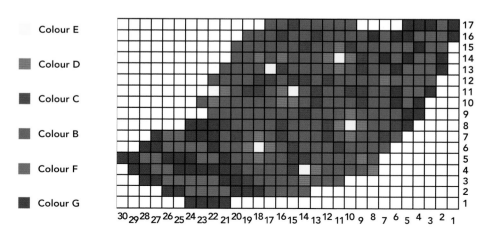

Colour E

Colour D

Colour C

Colour B

Colour F

Colour G

Apple

Materials:

2 x 100g balls of worsted yarn (UK light aran) –
  1 x burgundy (A), 1 x white (B), each 220yd/200m
Oddments of tapestry wool – green (C), brown (D)

Hook:

4mm (US G/6, UK 8) crochet hook

Notions:

4 x small black beads

1 x snap hook

1 x snap fastener

Finished size:

Approx. 3in x 3½in (8¼ x 9cm)

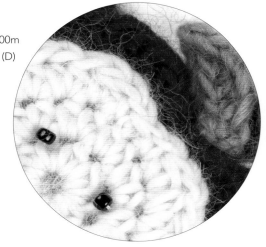

Instructions (make 2):

With yarn A and 4mm (US G/6, UK 8) crochet
hook, make 5 ch, join with sl st to first st to form
a ring.

Round 1: 2 ch (counts as 1 hdc (*UKhtr*)), 9 hdc
(*UKhtr*) into ring, sl st to top of 2 ch (10 sts).

Round 2: 2 ch (counts as 1 hdc (*UKhtr*)), 1 hdc
(*UKhtr*) in base of 2 ch, *2 hdc (*UKhtr*) in next st,
rep from * to end, sl st to first st (20 sts).**

Round 3: 2 ch (counts as 1 hdc (*UKhtr*)), 2 hdc
(*UKhtr*) in next st, *1 hdc (*UKhtr*) in next st, 2 hdc
(*UKhtr*) in next st, rep from * to end, sl st to first
st (30 sts).

Round 4: sl st in next st, 1 sc (*UKdc*) in next st,
[2 hdc (*UKhtr*) in next st] 11 times, 1 sc (*UKdc*) in
next st, sl st in next 2 sts, 1 sc (*UKdc*) in next st,
[2 hdc (*UKhtr*) in next st] 11 times, 1 sc (*UKdc*) in
next st, sl st in next st.

Fasten off.

Apple centre

With yarn B and 4mm (US G/6, UK 8) crochet
hook work to ** of back.

Next round: sl st to first st, 1 sc (*UKdc*) in next
st, [2 hdc (*UKhtr*) in next st] 7 times, 1 sc (*UKdc*)
in next st, sl st in next st, 1 sc (*UKdc*) in next st,
[2 hdc (*UKhtr*) in next st] 7 times, 1 sc (*UKdc*) in
next st.

Fasten off yarn.

Leaf

With yarn C and 4mm (US G/6, UK 8) crochet
hook, make 8 ch.

Row 1: 1 sc (*UKdc*) into second ch from hook,
1 hdc (*UKhtr*) in next st, 1 dc (*UKtr*) in next st, 1
tr (*UKdtr*) in next st, 1 dc (*UKtr*) in next st, 1 hdc
(*UKhtr*) in next st, 1 sc (*UKdc*) in next st.

Stalk and snap hook loop (make 1 of each)

With yarn A or D and 4mm (US G/6, UK 8)
crochet hook, make 7 ch.

Row 1: 1 sc (*UKdc*) in second ch from hook, 1 sc
(*UKdc*) in every ch to end.

Fasten off yarn.

Making up

Sew the beads to the white centre of the apple,
then attach the apple centre to the front. Sew
the leaf and stalk to the top curve of the apple.
Feed the snap hook through the loop and sew
the loop onto the side of the purse. With RS
together and using mattress stitch, sew the
back and front pieces of the apple together
leaving a 1½in (4cm) opening on the left side.
Turn through and sew the snap fastener to the
inside edges of the opening.

Ava

Materials:

1 x 100g hand of worsted yarn (UK light aran) in turquoise, 219yd/200m

Fabric for lining (optional)

Stiff iron-on interfacing (optional)

Hook:

4mm (US G/6, UK 8) crochet hook

Notions:

1 x large snap fastener

Finished size:

Each hexagon measures approx. 4in (10cm) wide

Instructions:

Hexagons (make 8)

With 4mm (US G/6, UK 8) crochet hook make 5 ch, join with sl st to form a ring.

Round 1: 4 ch (counts as 1 dc (*UKtr*) and 1 ch), [1 dc (*UKtr*) in ring, 1 ch] eleven times, join with sl st to third ch of 4-ch at beg of round.

Round 2: 3 ch (counts as 1 dc (*UKtr*)), 2 dc (*UKtr*) in next 1-ch sp, 1 dc (*UKtr*) in next dc (*UKtr*), 2 ch, [1 dc (*UKtr*), in next dc (*UKtr*), 2 dc (*UKtr*) in next 1-ch sp, 1 dc (*UKtr*) in next dc (*UKtr*), ch 2] five times, join with sl st to top of beg 3-ch.

Round 3: 3 ch (counts as 1 dc (*UKtr*)), 1 dc (*UKtr*) in base of 3-ch, 1 dc (*UKtr*) in each of next 2 dc (*UKtr*), 2 dc (*UKtr*) in next dc (*UKtr*), 2 ch, [2 dc (*UKtr*) in next dc (*UKtr*), 1 dc (*UKtr*) in each of next 2 dc (*UKtr*), 2 dc (*UKtr*) in next dc (*UKtr*), ch 2] five times, join with sl st to top of beg 3-ch.

Fasten off yarn.

Making up

Press each hexagon gently with an iron and weave in all loose ends. Using the diagram (right) as a guide, join the hexagons together using sc (*UKdc*) on the right side of the work.

Hexagons A form the sides; join to one side of hexagons B and C. Join each A, B and C on one side to the centre hexagon. Join D to each B on one side. Cut approximately 7½ x 13in (19 x 33cm) of fabric and interfacing, leaving ¼in (5mm) for the seam allowance, cut to shape and sew to the inside of the purse.

Sew a snap fastener to the underside of hexagon D and in the middle of the two C hexagons to finish.

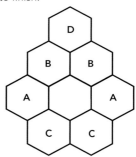

Isla

Materials:
1 x 50g ball of DK yarn in sage, 123yd/113m

Hook:
4mm (US G/6, UK 8) crochet hook

Notions:
64 x small beads

1 x snap fastener or magnetic snap

Finished size
Approx. 4¾ x 6in (12 x 15cm)

Special abbreviation:
Bsc (UKBdc) – beaded sc (h): insert hook into stitch, yrh, pull loop through, slide bead up close to work, yrh (catching yarn beyond bead), pull through both loops.

Instructions:
Front
With 4mm (US G/6, UK 8) crochet hook make 21 ch.

Row 1: 1 sc (UKdc) in second ch from hook, 1 sc (UKdc) in every ch to end (20 sts).

Row 2: 1 ch, 2 sc (UKdc) in next st, 1 sc (UKdc) in every st to last one, 2 sc (UKdc) in last st (22 sts).

Row 3: 1 ch, 1 sc (UKdc) in every st to end.

Rep rows 2 and 3 twice more (26 sts).**

Row 8: 1 ch, 1 sc (UKdc) in every st to end.

Repeat last row sixteen more times.

Fasten off yarn.

Back and flap (made in one piece)
Work as for front to **.

Next row: 1 ch, 1 sc (UKdc) in every st to end.

Repeat last row thirty-two more times.

Start of front decrease.

Row 1: 1 ch, sc2tog (UKdc2tog) over next 2 sts, 1 sc (UKdc) in every st to last 2 sts, sc2tog (UKdc2tog) over last 2 sts (24 sts).

Row 2: 1 ch, 1 sc (UKdc) in every st to end.

Repeat rows 1 and 2 once more, then row 1 once (20 sts).

Fasten off yarn.

Bow
Before starting to crochet, thread all beads onto yarn.

With 4mm (US G/6, UK 8) crochet hook make 16 ch.

Row 1: 1 sc (UKdc) in second ch from hook, *1 Bsc (UKBdc) in next ch, 1 sc (UKdc) in next 2 ch, rep from * to last 2 ch, 1 Bsc (UKBdc) in next ch, 1 sc (UKdc) in last ch (15 sts).

Row 2: 1 ch, 1 sc (UKdc) in every st to end.

Row 3: 1 ch, *1 sc (UKdc) in next 2 sts, 1 Bsc (UKBdc) in next st, rep from * to last 3 sts, 1 sc (UKdc) in next 3 sts.

Row 4: 1 ch, 1 sc (UKdc) in every st to end.

Row 5: 1 ch, 1 sc (UKdc) in next st, 1 Bsc (UKBdc) in next st, *1 sc (UKdc) in next 2 sts, 1 Bsc (UKBdc) in next st, rep from * to last st, 1 sc (UKdc) in last st.

Rep rows 2 to 5 twice more.

Row 14: 1 ch, 1 sc (UKdc) in every st to end.

Rep row 14 four more times.

Row 19: 1 ch, 1 sc (UKdc) in next st, 1 Bsc (UKBdc) in next st, *1 sc (UKdc) in next 2 sts, 1 Bsc (UKBdc) in next st, rep from * to last st, 1 sc (UKdc) in last st.

Row 20: 1 ch, 1 sc (UKdc) in every st to end.

Row 21: 1 ch, *1 sc (UKdc) in next 2 sts, 1 Bsc (UKBdc) in next st, rep from * to last 3 sts, 1 sc (UKdc) in next 3 sts.

Row 22: 1 ch, 1 sc (UKdc) in every st to end.

Rep rows 19 to 22 twice more.

Row 31: 1 ch, 1 sc (*UKdc*) in next st, 1 Bsc (*UKBdc*) in next st, *1 sc (*UKdc*) in next 2 sts, 1 Bsc (*UKBdc*) in next st, rep from * to last st, 1 sc (*UKdc*) in last st.

Do not fasten off yarn.

Edging

With RS facing, work a row of sc (*UKdc*) all along the edges of bow.

Fasten off yarn.

Making up

With WS facing and using mattress stitch, join the front piece to the lower part of the back piece. Work 1 row of sc (*UKdc*) all along the flap. Tighten the bow in the middle by winding yarn around it, then sew the bow onto the front flap of the purse. Sew lining to the inside of the purse if desired. Attach snap fasteners or a magnetic snap to the flap and front.

Ruby

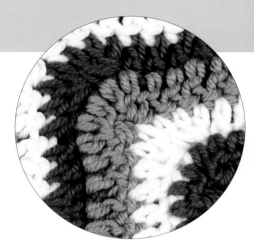

Materials:
3 x 50g balls of DK yarn –
  1 x bilberry (A), 1 x sage (B),
  1 x cream (C), 123yd/113m

Hook:
4mm (US G/6, UK 8)
  crochet hook

Notions:
1 x 6in (15cm) zip

Small amount of
  toy stuffing

Finished size:
Approx. 5½ x 8in
  (14 x 20cm)

Instructions:
Work in pattern following the stripe sequence as follows:

Row 1: yarn A.

Row 2: yarn B.

Row 3: yarn C.

With yarn A and 4mm (US G/6, UK 8) crochet hook, make 45 ch.

Row 1: Skip 3 ch (counts as 1 dc (*UKtr*)), 2 dc (*UKtr*) in next ch, 1 dc (*UKtr*) in next 3 ch, [dc3tog (*UKtr3tog*) over next 3 ch] twice, *1 dc (*UKtr*) in next 3 ch, [3 dc (*UKtr*) in next ch] twice, 1 dc (*UKtr*) in next 3 ch, [dc3tog (*UKtr3tog*) over next 3 ch] twice, rep from * once, 1 dc (*UKtr*) in next 3 ch, 3 dc (*UKtr*) in last ch.

Row 2: Following stripe sequence, change to yarn B, 3 ch (counts as 1 dc (*UKtr*)), 2 dc (*UKtr*) in base of ch, *1 dc (*UKtr*) in next 3 sts, [dc3tog (*UKtr3tog*)] twice, 1 dc (*UKtr*) in next 3 sts, [3 dc (*UKtr*) in next st] twice, rep from * once, 1 dc (*UKtr*) in next 3 sts, [dc3tog (*UKtr3tog*)] twice, 1 dc (*UKtr*) in next 3 sts, 3 dc (*UKtr*) in last st.

Working in stripe sequence, rep row 2 seventeen more times, ending last row with yarn A.

Fasten off yarn.

Edging
With RS facing, attach yarn B to the right corner of work at the last row and continue as follows:

Row 1: 1 ch, 1 sc (*UKdc*) in next 2 sts, 1 hdc (*UKhtr*) in next 3 sts, 1 dc (*UKtr*) in next 2 sts, *1 hdc (*UKhtr*) in next 3 sts, 1 sc (*UKdc*) in next 6 sts, 1 hdc (*UKhtr*) in next 3 sts, 1 dc (*UKtr*) in next 2 sts, rep from * once, 1 hdc (*UKhtr*) in next 3 sts, 1 sc (*UKdc*) in last 3 sts.

With RS facing, attach yarn B to the right corner of work at beg of first row and continue as follows:

Row 1: 3 ch (counts as 1 dc (*UKtr*)), 1 hdc (*UKhtr*) in next 3 sts, *1 sc (*UKdc*) in next 6 sts, 1 hdc (*UKhtr*) in next 3 sts, 1 dc (*UKtr*) in next 2 sts, 1 hdc (*UKhtr*) in next 3 sts, rep from * once, 1 sc (*UKdc*) in next 6 sts, 1 hdc (*UKhtr*) in next 3 sts, 1 dc (*UKtr*) in last st.

Fasten off yarn.

Charm
With yarn A and 4mm (US G/6, UK 8) crochet hook make 4 ch, sl st to first ch to form a ring.

Round 1: 1 ch, 6 sc (*UKdc*) into ring, sl st to first st (6 sts).

Round 2: 1 ch, 2 sc (*UKdc*) into every st to end, sl st to first st (12 sts).

Rounds 3 and 4: 1 ch, 1 sc (*UKdc*) in every st to end, sl st to first st.

Round 5: 1 ch, *dc2tog (*UKtr2tog*), rep from * to end, sl st to first st (6 sts).

Fill charm with toy stuffing.

Round 6: 1 ch, *dc2tog (*UKtr2tog*), rep from * to end, sl st to first st (3 sts).

Fasten off yarn.

Making up
Fold the work in half with RS together and join the sides using mattress stitch. Turn through and insert the zip. Attach the charm to the zip pull by making 8 ch and attaching the other end to the charm.

Myrtle

Materials:
1 x 50g ball of DK yarn in black, 142yd/130m

2 x oval pieces of 6¼ x 6½in (15 x 16cm) lining fabric

Hook:
3.75mm (US F/5) crochet hook

Notions:
1 x rounded purse clasp approx.
   4¾in (12cm) wide

Finished size:
Approx. 6in (15cm) wide and 5½in (14cm) high

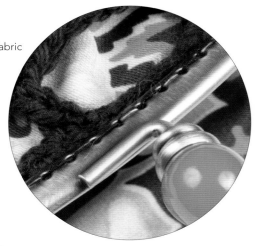

Special abbreviations:
**dc3tog (UKtr3tog) – dc (UKtr) 3 together
cluster:** [yrh and insert into st, yrh and draw a
loop through, yrh and draw through first 2 loops
on hook], rep twice more all in the same st, yrh
and draw a loop through all 4 loops on hook.

**dc4tog (UKtr4tog) – dc (UKtr) 4 together
cluster:** [yrh and insert into st, yrh and draw a
loop through, yrh and draw through first 2
loops on hook], rep three times more all in
the same st, yrh and draw a loop through all 5
loops on hook.

Instructions (make 2):
With 3.75mm (US F/5) crochet hook make 6 ch,
sl st to first ch to form a ring.

Round 1: 1 ch, work 11 sc (UKdc) into ring, sl st
to first st.

Round 2: 6 ch (counts as 1 dc (UKtr) and 3 ch),
*1 dc (UKtr) in next st, 3 ch, rep from * to end, sl
st to top of 3-ch at beg of round (11 dc (UKtr)).

Round 3: 3 ch (counts as 1 dc (UKtr)), dc3tog
(UKtr3tog) in next 3-ch sp, 4 ch, *dc4tog
(UKtr4tog) in next 3-ch sp, 4 ch, rep from * until
all spaces have been worked, sl st to first 3-dc
(UKtr) cluster (11 clusters).

Round 4: 1 ch, *5 sc (UKdc) in next 4-ch sp, 1 sc
(UKdc) in top of next cluster, rep from * until all
spaces have been worked, sl st to first st.

Round 5: 1 ch, sl st into next 2 sts, 3 ch (counts
as 1 dc (UKtr)), *7 ch, skip next 5 sts, 1 dc (UKtr)
in next st, rep from * ten times more, sl st to
first st.

Round 6: 1 ch, *8 sc (UKdc) in next 7-ch sp, 1 sc
(UKdc) in top of 1 dc (UKtr), rep from * to end.

Round 7: 1 ch, 1 sc (UKdc) in every st to end, sl
st to first st, turn.

Row 8: 1 ch, 1 sc (UKdc) in next 63 sts.

Fasten off yarn.

Making up
With RS facing and using mattress stitch, join
the front and back together by sewing all along
the raised part. Turn through. This leaves a gap
of approximately 6¾in (17cm) to attach to the
clasp. Sew in the lining, leaving a ¼in (1cm)
seam allowance.

Lucy

Materials:
4 x 25g balls of lace/2-ply
  yarn – 1 x light brown (A),
  1 x brown (B), 1 x yellow
  (C), 1 x green (D), each
  229yd/210m

Hook:
4mm (US G/6, UK 8)
  crochet hook

Notions:
1 x purse clasp approx.
  9in (23cm) wide

Finished size:
Approx. 11¾in
  (30cm) at the
  widest point and
  6in (15cm) high

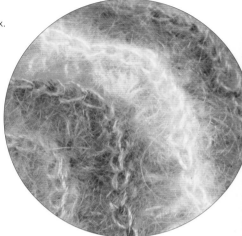

Special abbreviation:
Fpsc (*UKfpdc*) – front post sc (*UKdc*): insert
hook from the front to the back around the post
of the sc (*UKdc*) on the previous row. Complete
as for regular sc (*UKdc*).

Instructions (make 2):
Work in pattern following the stripe sequence
as follows:

Rows 7 and 8: yarn A.

Rows 9 and 10: yarn B.

Rows 11 and 12: yarn C.

Rows 13 and 14: yarn D.

With yarn A and 4mm (US G/6, UK 8) crochet
hook, make 45 ch.

Row 1: 1 sc (*UKdc*) into second ch from hook, 1
sc (*UKdc*) in every ch to end (44 sts).

Row 2: 1 ch, 1 sc (*UKdc*) in every st to end.

Rep row 2 four more times.

Row 7: 3 ch (counts as 1 dc (*UKtr*)), 1 dc (*UKtr*)
in next 4 sts, *[5 dc (*UKtr*) in next st] twice, 1 dc
(*UKtr*) in next 6 sts, rep from * three times, [5 dc
(*UKtr*) in next st] twice, 1 dc (*UKtr*) in next 5 sts.

Row 8: 1 ch, 1 fpsc (*UKfpdc*) in each st to end.

Row 9: Change to colour B, 3 ch (counts as 1
dc (*UKtr*)), working in tops of fpsc (*UKfpdc*) row,
[1 dc (*UKtr*) in next st, skip next st] four times,
[5 dc (*UKtr*) in next st] twice, *skip 2 sts, [1 dc
(*UKtr*) in next st, skip 1 st] twice, 1 dc (*UKtr*) in
next st, [1 dc (*UKtr*) in next st, skip 1 st] twice, 1
dc (*UKtr*) in next st, skip 2 sts, [5 dc (*UKtr*) in next
st] twice, rep from * three more times, skip 1 st,
[1 dc (*UKtr*) in next st, skip 1 st] three times, 1 dc
(*UKtr*) in each of last 2 sts.

Row 10: As row 8.

Rows 9 and 10 form the pattern, rep the pattern
twice more, following the colour sequence.

Row 15: Change to colour A, 3 ch (counts as
1 dc (*UKtr*)), working in tops of fpsc (*UKfpdc*)
row, 2 dc (*UKtr*) in st at base of ch, [1 dc (*UKtr*)
in next st, skip next st] four times, [5 dc (*UKtr*) in
next st] twice, *skip 2 sts, [1 dc (*UKtr*) in next st,
skip 1 st] twice, 1 dc (*UKtr*) in next st, [1 dc (*UKtr*)
in next st, skip 1 st] twice, 1 dc (*UKtr*) in next st,
skip 2 sts, [5 dc (*UKtr*) in next st] twice, rep from
* three more times, skip 1 st, [1 dc (*UKtr*) in next
st, skip 1 st] three times, 1 dc (*UKtr*) in next st, 3
dc (*UKtr*) in last st (48 sts).

Row 16: As row 8.

Row 17: Change to colour B, 3 ch (counts as
1 dc (*UKtr*)), working in tops of fpsc (*UKfpdc*)
row, 1 dc (*UKtr*) in st at base of ch, [1 dc (*UKtr*)
in next st, skip next st] five times, [5 dc (*UKtr*) in
next st] twice, *skip 2 sts, [1 dc (*UKtr*) in next st,
skip 1 st] twice, 1 dc (*UKtr*) in next st, [1 dc (*UKtr*)
in next st, skip 1 st] twice, 1 dc (*UKtr*) in next st,
skip 2 sts, [5 dc (*UKtr*) in next st] twice, rep from
* three more times, skip 1 st, [1 dc (*UKtr*) in next
st, skip 1 st] four times, 1 dc (*UKtr*) in next st, 2
dc (*UKtr*) in last st.

Row 18: As row 8.

Rows 17 to 18 form the pattern; rep the pattern six more times, following the colour sequence as set, ending last row on row 18 of pattern in colour D.

Fasten off yarn.

Making up

Do not press. Weave in all loose ends. Using mattress stitch and with RS together, join the back and front pieces along the lower edge and 3¼in (8cm) up both sides. Turn through, line the purse if desired, then attach the clasp.

Isabel

Materials:
1 x 100g ball of worsted yarn (UK light aran) in lilac (A), 219yd/200m

1 x 25g ball of lace/2-ply yarn in light pink (B), 229yd/210m

Oddments of worsted yarn (UK light aran) in green (C)

Hook:
4mm (US G/6, UK 8) crochet hook

Notions:
1 x purse clasp approx. 3½in (9cm) wide

Approx. 102 x small beads

Finished size:
Approx. 3¾ x 4¼in (9.5 x 10.75cm)

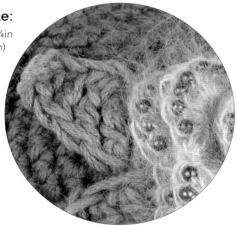

Instructions (make 2):
With yarn A and 4mm (US G/6, UK 8) crochet hook, make 4 ch and join with sl st to form a ring.

Round 1: 1 ch, 8 sc (UKdc) into ring, sl st to first sc (UKdc) (8 sts).

Round 2: 1 ch, work 2 sc (UKdc) into every sc (UKdc), sl st to first sc (UKdc) (16 sts).

Round 3: 1 ch, *1 sc (UKdc) into next sc (UKdc), 2 sc (UKdc) into next sc (UKdc), rep from * to end, sl st to first sc (UKdc) (24 sts).

Round 4: 1 ch, * 1 sc (UKdc) into each of next 2 sc (UKdc), 2 sc (UKdc) into next sc (UKdc), rep from * to end, sl st to first sc (UKdc) (32 sts).

Round 5: 1 ch, * 1 sc (UKdc) into next 3 sc (UKdc), 2 sc (UKdc) into next sc (UKdc), rep from * to end, sl st to first sc (UKdc) (40 sts).

Rounds 6 and 7: 1 ch, 1 sc (UKdc) into every sc (UKdc) to end, sl st to first sc (UKdc), turn after round 7.

Row 8: 1 ch, 1 sc (UKdc) into base of ch, 1 sc (UKdc) into next 22 sc (UKdc), turn.

Rows 9 and 10: 1 ch, 1 sc (UKdc) into base of ch, 1 sc (UKdc) into next 22 sc (UKdc), 1 sc (UKdc) into ch made on previous round, turn.

Fasten off yarn.

Rose
Thread 102 beads onto yarn B.

With 4mm (US G/6, UK 8) crochet hook and yarn B, make 57 ch.

Row 1: (dc (UKtr), ch 2, dc (UKtr)) in sixth ch from hook (5 skipped chs count as first dc (UKtr) plus 2 ch), *ch 2, skip next 2 chs, (dc (UKtr), ch 2, dc (UKtr)) in next ch; rep from * across (36 sps).

Row 2: 3 ch (counts as first dc (UKtr)), working one bead into each dc (UKtr) continue as follows: 5 dc (UKtr) in next 2-ch sp, sc (UKdc) in next 2-ch sp, *6 dc (UKtr) in next 2-ch sp, sc (UKdc) in next 2-ch sp, rep from * to end.

Fasten off leaving a long piece of yarn for sewing the rose together.

With RS facing and beg with last petal made, roll petals to form rose; sew to secure as you roll with the length of yarn left.

Leaf (make 2)
With 4mm (US G/6, UK 8) crochet hook and yarn C, make 10 ch.

Round 1: 1 sc (UKdc) into second ch from hook, 1 hdc (UKhtr) in next ch, 1 dc (UKtr) in next ch, 1 tr (UKdtr) in next 3 ch, 1 dc (UKtr) in next ch, 1 hdc (UKhtr) in next ch, 1 sc (UKdc) in next ch.

Fasten off yarn.

Making up
With WS together, join the two larger sides of the purse together with a row of sc (UKdc). Attach the purse clasp and sew the rose and leaves to the front of the purse. Attach a lining if desired.

Acknowledgements

I would like to say a big thank you to Rowan Yarns for providing all the yarn, The Creative Sanctuary for providing all the lovely purse clasps and fabrics, and the team at Search Press for doing such an amazing job on this book.